Developing
Number
Knowledge

Education at SAGE

SAGE is a leading international publisher of journals, books, and electronic media for academic, educational, and professional markets.

Our education publishing includes:

- accessible and comprehensive texts for aspiring education professionals and practitioners looking to further their careers through continuing professional development

- inspirational advice and guidance for the classroom

- authoritative state of the art reference from the leading authors in the field

Find out more at: **www.sagepub.co.uk/education**

Developing Number Knowledge

Assessment, Teaching & Intervention with 7–11-Year-olds

Robert J. Wright

David Ellemor-Collins

Pamela D. Tabor

Los Angeles | London | New Delhi
Singapore | Washington DC

First published 2012. Reprinted 2012

SAGE Publications Ltd
1 Oliver's Yard
55 City Road
London EC1Y 1SP

SAGE Publications Inc.
2455 Teller Road
Thousand Oaks, California 91320

SAGE Publications India Pvt Ltd
B 1/I 1 Mohan Cooperative Industrial Area
Mathura Road
New Delhi 110 044

SAGE Publications Asia-Pacific Pte Ltd
3 Church Street
#10-04 Samsung Hub
Singapore 049483

Library of Congress Control Number: 2011922541

British Library Cataloguing in Publication data

A catalogue record for this book is available from the British Library

ISBN 978-0-85702-060-4
ISBN 978-0-85702-061-1 (pbk)

Typeset by C&M Digitals (P) Ltd, Chennai, India
Printed in Great Britain by the MPG Books Group
Printed on paper from sustainable resources

To Patrick, Henry and Finn
Heather, Miriam and Jeremy
Ron, Jeremy and Zack

Brief Contents

Contents

List of Boxes

List of Tables

List of Figures

List of Photographs

Contents of Resource CD

The files have been formatted into two styles: 8½ x 11 inch USA format and spellings; A4 International format and spellings. Each file is available in three file formats: MS Word, PDF and XPS.

Also included on the CD is each Instructional Activity in the book.

Acknowledgements

The three authors of this book share a consuming interest in advancing what is known about the teaching of number to children. Our collaborative work over the last eight years related to assessment and instruction in number, provides an appropriate back-drop for the writing of this book. In addition, the book is a major outcome of a multi-year research project for which the first and second authors were the lead and associate researchers respectively. The goal of this project was to develop pedagogical tools for intervention in the number learning of low-attaining 8–10-year-olds. During the course of the project, the research team worked with a teacher from each of 25 schools and a total of 200 low-attaining students.

The authors wish to express their gratitude and appreciation to the joint funders of this project – the Australian Research Council via the Linkage Grants Program under grant LP0348932, the Catholic Education Office Melbourne, and the Victorian Catholic Education Commission – in whose schools the project was conducted.

The authors also express their sincere gratitude and appreciation to the 25 schools involved in the project and to the participating students. We particularly wish to thank the 25 teachers, each of whom worked diligently over the course of a school year, to assess students, provide intensive instruction and actively participate in our on-going project workshops. Their hard work and collaboration in the development of new approaches to assessment and instruction have contributed significantly to the achievements and outcomes of the project.

We wish to acknowledge and give thanks to Andrea Dineen, Ann Stafford, Debra Meagher, Jackie Amato, Jeanna Gentile, Johti Kidd, Martin Gill, Rebecca Stewart and Ron Stump for contributions to the photographs, and Jeremy Tabor for contributions to the illustrations.

Our final thanks go to Mr Gerard Lewis, Team Leader in Mathematics for the School Services Staff Group of the Catholic Education Office, Melbourne, with whom we have worked closely for the duration of the planning and conducting of the project. We acknowledge and very much value his strong and on-going support, encouragement and affirmation for our endeavours on the project.

About the Authors and Contributor

Authors

Dr Robert J. (Bob) Wright holds Bachelor's and Master's degrees in mathematics from the University of Queensland (Australia) and a doctoral degree in mathematics education from the University of Georgia. His current position is adjunct professor in mathematics education at Southern Cross University in New South Wales. Bob is an internationally recognized leader in understanding and assessing children's numerical knowledge and strategies, publishing many articles and papers in this field. His work over the last 20 years has included the development of the Mathematics Recovery Programme which focuses on providing specialist training for teachers to advance the numeracy levels of young children assessed as low-attainers. In Australia and New Zealand, Ireland, the UK, the USA, Canada, Mexico and elsewhere, this programme has been implemented widely and applied extensively to classroom teaching and to average and able learners as well as low-attainers. He has conducted several research projects funded by the Australian Research Council including the most recent project focusing on assessment and intervention in the number learning of low-attaining 8–10-year-olds.

David Ellemor-Collins holds a Bachelor's degree with honours in mathematics and philosophy from Harvard University, and a Graduate Diploma in Education from the University of Melbourne. For the past seven years, he has worked as a researcher with an Australian Research Council-funded project focusing on assessment and intervention in the number learning of low-attaining 8–10-year-olds. David has worked as a mathematics teacher in primary schools, high schools and universities. He has contributed curriculum development to school mathematics programmes, provided professional development courses for schools, and published articles and papers for both researchers and practitioners in mathematics education.

Dr Pamela Tabor holds a Bachelor's degree in elementary education and Bible from Kentucky Christian University, a Master's degree in elementary education from East Tennessee State University, and a Doctor of Philosophy in mathematics education from Southern Cross University. She is a school-based elementary mathematics specialist and grant project manager with Harford County Public Schools, Harford County, Maryland. She has been a contracted researcher with several bodies researching fidelity of programme implementation, programme evaluation and professional development.

Contributor (Chapters 10 and 11)

Dr Peter Gould holds Bachelor's and Master's degrees in science and mathematics from the University of Sydney (Australia). His doctoral dissertation examined the way that children come to develop a sense of fractions as numbers and the challenges they face along the way. Peter has been the Chief Education Officer in Mathematics with the New South Wales Department of Education and Training in Australia for 16 years. He taught mathematics classes for 13 years in schools serving disadvantaged communities as well as Technical and Further Education courses and University courses. Peter is well known for his work as a Mathematics Consultant and he readily acknowledges that his students and colleagues have taught him many useful things over the years.

Series Preface

If you ask educationalists and teachers whether numeracy intervention deserves equal attention with literacy intervention the overwhelming answer is 'Yes, it should'. If you then ask whether this happens in their experience the answer is a resounding 'No!' What then are the reasons for this discrepancy? Research shows that teachers give more attention to addressing difficulties in literacy than difficulties in early numeracy. Teachers also state that there is a lack of suitable tools for assessing young children's numeracy skills and knowledge, and appropriate programmes available to address the deficits.

The four books in this series make a significant impact to redress the imbalance by providing practical help to enable schools and teachers to give equal status to early numeracy intervention. The books are:

- *Early Numeracy: Assessment for Teaching and Intervention, 2nd edition*, Robert J. Wright, Jim Martland and Ann K. Stafford, 2006
- *Teaching Number: Advancing Children's Skills and Strategies, 2nd edition*, Robert J. Wright, Jim Martland, Ann K. Stafford and Garry Stanger, 2006
- *Teaching Number in the Classroom with 4–8 Year-olds*, Robert J. Wright, Garry Stanger, Ann K. Stafford and Jim Martland, 2006
- *Developing Number Knowledge: Assessment, Teaching and Intervention with 7–11-Year-olds*, Robert J. Wright, David Ellemor-Collins and Pamela Tabor, 2012.

The authors are internationally recognized as leaders in the field of numeracy intervention. They draw on considerable practical experience of delivering training courses and materials on how to assess students' mathematical knowledge, skills and strategies in addition, subtraction, multiplication and division. This is the focus of *Early Numeracy*. The revised edition contains six comprehensive diagnostic assessment tools to identify children's strengths and weaknesses and has a new chapter on how the assessment provides the direction and focus for intervention. *Teaching Number* sets out in detail nine principles which guide the teaching, together with 180 practical, exemplar teaching procedures to advance children to more sophisticated strategies for solving arithmetic problems. The third book, *Teaching Number in the Classroom with 4–8 Year-olds*, extends the work of assessment and intervention with individual and small groups to working with whole classes. In this text the authors have been assisted by expert, primary practitioners from Australia, the USA and the UK who have provided the best available Instructional Activities for each of eight major topics in early number learning. The fourth book, *Developing Number Knowledge: Assessment, Teaching and Intervention with 7–11-Year-olds* extends the focus of the series to include older students and more advanced learning and includes chapters on early algebraic reasoning and fractions.

The four books in this series provide a comprehensive package on:

1. The identification, analysis and reporting of children's arithmetic knowledge, skills and strategies
2. How to design, implement and evaluate a course of intervention
3. How to incorporate both assessment and teaching in the daily numeracy programme in differing class organizations and contexts.

The series is distinct from others in the field because it draws on a substantial body of recent theoretical research supported by international, practical application. Because all the assessment and teaching activities portrayed have been empirically tested, the books have the additional, important distinction that they indicate to the practitioner, ranges of students' responses and patterns of their behaviour.

The book series provides a package for professional growth and development and an invaluable, comprehensive resource for both the experienced teacher concerned with early numeracy intervention and for the primary teacher who has responsibility for teaching numeracy in kindergarten to upper primary levels. Primary numeracy consultants, mathematics advisors, special education teachers, teaching assistants and initial teacher trainees around the world will find much to enable them to put numeracy intervention on an equal standing with literacy. At a wider level the series will reveal many areas of interest to educational psychologists, researchers and academics.

Introduction

This introduction sets out the purpose, background and structure of the book, and also includes a section of important notes for the reader.

The Purpose of the Book

The purpose of this book is to outline an extensive and detailed approach to instruction aimed at developing the number and arithmetic knowledge of 7–11-year-olds. This approach to instruction is constructivist and inquiry-based, and builds on clear understandings of students' current levels of knowledge, the directions towards which their learning should progress, and the means by which students can develop deep, conceptually based arithmetic knowledge. The book complements three earlier books, all of which focus on teaching number in the first three to four years of school. These books are *Early Numeracy: Assessment for Teaching and Intervention (2nd edn); Teaching Number: Advancing Children's Skills and Strategies (2nd edn)* and *Teaching Number in the Classroom with 4–8 Year-olds*. Brief overviews of these books can be found in the Series Preface earlier in this book.

The Background to the Book

The approach and methods presented in this book are a culmination of an extensive and ongoing programme of research and development related to the teaching of number and arithmetic in the primary and elementary grades. In the case of the first author, this programme spans at least 20 years, and includes several multi-year projects funded by the Australian Research Council (ARC) and a range of education departments and jurisdictions. One outcome of this programme is Mathematics Recovery, a programme focusing on intensive intervention for low-attaining students in the early years of school. This programme was developed in New South Wales and has been widely implemented internationally. In addition, the programme has been extensively adapted to classroom teaching for average and able learners and it provided a basis for the three earlier books referred to above.

The collaborative work of the three authors of this book over the last eight years provides a basis for the writing of this book. Since 2004, the first and second authors have collaborated on a project focusing on intervention in the number learning of low-attaining 8–10-year-olds and this project provides the main focus of this book. The project is funded by the ARC and the

Catholic Education Office, Melbourne (CEOM) and extends our earlier work on intensive intervention for younger students. As is the case with all of our research and development work, we have drawn extensively on a range of international research and development related to students' learning of arithmetic. Equally, our ongoing research and development in general, and this book in particular, are outcomes of intensive, long-term collaborations with teachers, schools and school systems. We have drawn extensively on their insights into students' learning and purposeful instruction, as well as their trialling of a range of pedagogical tools that we have developed.

The focus of the book on the teaching of whole number arithmetic is complemented by a detailed overview of assessment and instruction related to students' development of fraction concepts (Chapters 10 and 11). This section is written by Dr Peter Gould and is informed by his extensive research on that topic.

The book should be of interest to all who are concerned with finding new ways to teach number and with advancing the levels of learning in schools. Teachers, advisers, numeracy consultants, mathematics supervisors, curriculum leaders and learning support personnel, as well as teacher educators and researchers whose work relates to this field, will find much of interest from both theoretical and practical perspectives.

The Structure of the Book

The book is organized into three parts. Part I (Chapters 1–2) provides a general orientation to the book; Part II (Chapters 3–8) overviews six domains of instruction in whole number arithmetic; and Part III (Chapters 9–11) addresses the additional topics of early algebraic reasoning and the development of students' fraction concepts.

Part I

Chapter 1 explains the central role of teachers as reflective practitioners and as pedagogical engineers and describes four ways the book can be used: for professional learning, intervention, classroom instruction, and parental involvement.

Chapter 2 provides an account of our general approach to instruction in number and arithmetic, at three levels. At the first level, we describe a broad developmental progression of mental and written computation, and explain the use of domains to structure instruction, which is central to the organization of this book. At the second level, we characterize the directionality of instruction in terms of the *progressive mathematization* of students' knowledge, including eight themes: structuring numbers; extending the range of numbers; decimalizing; unitizing; distancing the setting; notating; formalizing; and generalizing. The third section summarizes key elements of an inquiry-based approach to day-to-day assessment and teaching, including: assessment to inform instruction; teaching just beyond the cutting edge; solving genuine problems; reflecting on problem solving; emphasizing mathematical thinking; using settings; inquiry mode and rehearsal mode.

Part II

In Part II (Chapters 3–8), instruction is organized into six domains, each of which is the focus of a chapter. These topics range over: learning about number words and numerals; structuring numbers in the ranges 1 to 10 and 1 to 20; conceptual place value; strategies for adding and subtracting two 2-digit numbers; multiplication and division; and written computation. Each of the chapters in Part II is organized into three sections: an extended overview of the domain; Assessment Tasks; and Instructional Activities. For each chapter, the overview of the domain describes what constitutes students' facility in the domain, details students' strategies and difficulties, summarizes how to assess knowledge of the domain, and sets out a progression of instruction for the domain. The Assessment Tasks and Instructional Activities include detailed notes on student responses and teaching points, which complement and extend the material in the overview of the domain. The inclusion of Assessment Tasks is consistent with the fundamental principle of our approach, that is, that comprehensive assessment precedes instruction. Instruction should be based on very sound understanding of students' current knowledge and strategies.

Part III

Part III (Chapters 9–11) complements Part II, by providing broad overviews of two additional strands of mathematics that relate closely to whole number arithmetic. Chapter 9 focuses on the strand of early algebraic reasoning: what it is, why it is important and how it links closely to the teaching of number and operations. The chapter overviews a range of algebraic topics such as: generalized arithmetic; reasoning about number relationships; equality; patterns and functions; conjecturing and generalizing; and the mathematics of change.

Chapters 10 and 11 focus on the strand of fractions. Chapter 10 addresses key ideas for students' understanding of fractions, including partitioned fractions and quantity fractions, the multiplicative nature of fractions, the importance of coordinating units, models and notations for fractions, fractions beyond one whole, and equivalent fractions. Chapter 11 describes a progression of levels in students' learning of fractions: emergent partitioning; halving; equal partitions; re-forming the whole; fractions as numbers; and multiplicative partitioning. As well, Chapter 11 sets out a teaching sequence and provides detailed descriptions of 13 teaching activities and a set of Assessment Tasks.

Notes to the Reader

Glossary, Appendix and Reference List

This book includes an extensive glossary of technical terms used in the book, an appendix containing descriptions of the key instructional settings used in the book, and a comprehensive list of the works cited in the text (reference list).

Resource CD

Accompanying the book is an extensive Resource CD which includes black line masters of instruction resources mentioned in the book. These resources are designated in the text by this CD Resource icon. A complete list of these resources is provided in the front section of this book. These resources can be used in one-on-one intervention teaching, small-group instruction, classroom learning station instruction, and as home activities in lieu of traditional homework sheets. The CD is organized by chapter. Each resource is available in US 8½ × 11 inch format as well as A4 format. The resources have been rendered as both PDF and XPS files, which will ensure that formatting is maintained. We have also included MS Word versions of resources, to allow teachers to engage in pedagogical engineering by tinkering with materials to meet the needs of their students. Also included on the CD is each Instructional Activity in the book.

Assessment Tasks and Instructional Activities

The chapters in Part II of this book contain many Assessment Task Groups and Instructional Activities. Many of the Assessment Task Groups can be used as Instructional Activities and many of the Instructional Activities could be adapted for use as Assessment Tasks.

Conventions for Reading and Writing Numbers

The readers of our books on the teaching of number (referred to above) are from a range of countries and we are aware that, in these countries, there are differing conventions for reading and writing numbers, and so on. Examples are saying 'one hundred and four' or 'one hundred four'; and writing '3104' or '3,104'. Because our books are published in London, as a general rule we follow the conventions used in the United Kingdom. We trust that, when readers encounter a convention different from the one to which they are accustomed, they will adjust the text accordingly.

PART I

1

Professional Learning for Quality Instruction

Research indicates that the quality of instruction is an important factor influencing student achievement in mathematics and that teacher quality cannot be measured simply in terms of degrees earned by the teachers. We believe that the quality of instruction is critically important and is directly tied to teachers' specialized knowledge of the teaching and learning of mathematics; that is, what is referred to as pedagogical content knowledge (Shulman, 1986). This book aims to be a resource for developing pedagogical content knowledge for teaching arithmetic to 7–11-year-olds. The book is not intended to be a comprehensive curriculum; rather, it provides a fine-grained approach for improving instruction in arithmetic. Critical to our approach is the view of the teacher as a professional practitioner. When teachers are reflective, when teachers engage in professional development, curriculum development, and research, instruction improves. Indeed, we believe that reflective, professional practitioners are the driving force behind improvements in education (Askew et al., 1997; Clarke, 1997; Clarke et al., 1990; Rivkin et al., 2005).

The approach detailed in this book is a major outcome of an extensive programme of research and development over many years. Central to the programme is ongoing, professional collaboration with teachers. We have worked with teachers and instructional leaders in a range of countries including Australia, Canada, New Zealand, Ireland, the United Kingdom and the United States. The research programme derives from an ongoing reflexive relationship between researchers and practitioners working cooperatively to design new approaches to instruction. In this way, our work has been fundamentally influenced by and is deeply indebted to the work of practitioners. We invite teachers to continue to relate to the material in this book as reflective, collegial, professional practitioners. In this chapter, we first discuss ways of using the book for professional learning. We then describe ways of using the book for intervention instruction, for classroom instruction, and for parental involvement (Cobb, 2000; Cobb et al., 2003; Gravemeijer, 1994a; Wright et al., 2007).

Using the Book for Professional Learning and Development

We see teaching as a journey of learning. Teaching thrives when supported by a culture of continual learning, with teachers developing their knowledge of mathematics, as well as their specialized pedagogical content knowledge. For the teacher, the experience of the kind of instruction described in this book is profoundly different from instruction focused on procedures and facts. Learning to teach this way with facility takes several years of dedicated professional development. This book is intended as a resource for such professional development. Professional learning can be accomplished through individual reading, trial and reflection. Learning is typically easier and richer when shared with colleagues

in a group, that is, in a professional learning community (PLC). We encourage readers to seek like-minded professionals with whom they can pursue their learning. Learning in a PLC can be organized in various formats, including as a book study, video-stimulated discussion, or curriculum development. To use this book for professional learning, choose one to three domains from Part II as a focus. Three approaches to learning about a domain are described below: observation to develop awareness; making detailed assessments; and pedagogical engineering (Ball and Bass, 2000; Lord, 1994; Mason, 1998; Munn, 2006; Yoshida, 2008).

Photo 1.1   Using the book for professional development

Developing Pedagogical Awareness

Important professional learning can involve careful observation of student thinking and learning within a domain. The book can serve as a prompt and guide to sharpen awareness. Recommended sources on observation and listening for teaching include Davis (1997), Empson and Jacobs (2008), Mason (2002) and Yackel (2003).

Develop your Awareness of Students' Arithmetic Knowledge and Thinking

Like a naturalist in a forest, be delighted and curious about the variety of students' thinking. Listen carefully, observe closely, take notes. Use the book as a field guide, furnishing details to look for in students' developing arithmetic knowledge: the different ways students think about the number 10, unpacking what knowledge a student uses to do multi-digit subtraction, and so on. Observing your own mathematical thinking helps too.

Develop your Awareness of How Students Learn Mathematics

This book gives some examples of learning moments. Notice when your own students use some new mathematics, for example a more sophisticated strategy 'I did double 8 and 1 more, which is 17' (at the beginning of the term, he only used counting by ones); a new number relationship 'Well 48 is close to 50, so …' (a month ago, she wouldn't have noticed this). Did this new mathematics arise from rehearsing a procedure, or from trying to solve a problem? Did the student accomplish it in the same lesson it was introduced, or many weeks later? Reflecting on your own mathematical learning helps too.

Develop your Awareness of Your Own Teaching

For example, how do you choose the tasks you pose? When a student can't solve a task in a few minutes, how do you respond? Notice when you fish for a particular answer, or when you lead the student through a procedure, or when you adjust the task, or when you leave the student to keep puzzling. What objectives are behind an instructional decision? Listen to yourself on an audio recording, or watch yourself on video. Observing other mathematics teachers helps too.

Making and Using Assessments

For each domain in Part II, exemplar Assessment Tasks are provided with detailed notes about student responses. Use these to develop a profile of student knowledge of a domain. In turn, in conjunction with the descriptions of trajectories of instruction, develop an individual teaching plan for students. This is a powerful approach to using data to drive instructional decision-making. Developing detailed assessment profiles and teaching plans constitutes significant professional learning (Wright, 2002). Recommended sources on using assessment for professional learning include Ellemor-Collins and Wright (2008), Ginsburg et al. (1998), Munn (2006) and Wright et al. (2006a).

Pedagogical Engineering

Many of the Instructional Activities have been designed by teachers to meet the needs of their students. Our approach encourages teachers to be 'tinkerers' (Gravemeijer, 1994a, 2004) with settings and record their observations, conjectures and reflections about student learning in a journal. These journal entries, along with video clips of instruction and assessment, often become the basis of rich discussions among PLCs. The PLCs provide a supportive forum in which teachers share pedagogical innovations, concerns and solutions. In this manner, the practitioners function as pedagogical engineers, designing, tweaking and testing instructional procedures and materials in order to promote improved student learning. We do not propose that every teacher become a researcher. Nevertheless, we believe that reflective practitioners function as researching practitioners when they think deeply about and tinker with settings and tasks. We hope readers will take licence to further develop the tasks and activities in this book. When practitioners engage in dialogue with other teachers and with researchers they can have a profound impact on the profession. Recommended sources on pedagogical engineering include Jacobs et al. (2006), Mason and Johnston-Wilder (2006) and Watson and Sullivan (2008).

Using the Book for Intervention Instruction

Much of the material in this book has been developed in the context of intensive intervention with low-attaining students. For intervention, we have found instruction in one-on-one and small group formats (two or three students) to be highly effective. In those formats the instruction can be closely attuned to the students' current levels of knowledge. An intervention programme of daily or near daily sessions over at least 10 weeks is recommended. For each student, select two to four domains as a focus for initial intervention. Use the Assessment Tasks to develop a detailed profile of student knowledge across those domains. Based on the assessment, target instruction to the cutting edge of the student's knowledge. Address all selected domains in every session: knowledge of the domains can develop concurrently and interdependently. The instruction described in each Domain Overview offers a fine-grained progression appropriate for intervention. Critical to intervention instruction is ongoing close observation of students' thinking and strategies. With such intensive, closely targeted instruction in key domains, low-attaining students can develop robust arithmetic knowledge. For a detailed discussion of the methods of one-on-one assessment and teaching for intervention, the reader is referred to the first two books in this series (Wright et al., 2006a, 2006b).

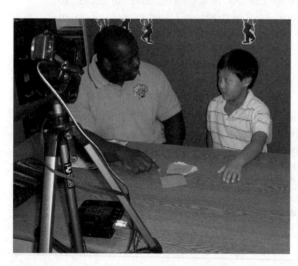

Photo 1.2   Using the book for intervention teaching

Using the Book for Classroom Instruction

Classroom teachers can draw on the book in a range of ways:

- Use select Assessment Tasks with all students in the class or with targeted students.
- Draw on the set of Assessment Task Groups in one chapter to prepare a unit assessment.
- Use an Instructional Activity with the entire class or in small groups within a learning stations format.
- Engage in pedagogical engineering: try an Instructional Activity then develop and refine it.
- Study a Domain Overview as background for understanding students' learning and strategies.

- Tag key tables and figures to refer to during classroom demonstrations or discussions.
- Use the Resource CD to prepare a kit of key instructional settings for a domain.
- Use a whole chapter from Part II as a basis for a unit of work.
- Use the whole book as a map for a course in arithmetic over three or four years.

Our instructional approach is described in detail in Chapter 2. The approach can be applied flexibly to whole classes or small groups of learners. A central challenge of classroom instruction is managing the range of levels of knowledge across the students. The Instructional Activities in the book include notes about differentiating instruction within the classroom. For further discussion of organizing and managing classroom instruction, see Chapter 1 of the third book in the series (Wright et al., 2006c).

Photo 1.3   Using the book for classroom teaching

Using the Book to Promote Parental Involvement

Much has been said about the importance of promoting parental involvement in schools (e.g. Merttens, 1999). Parental involvement is particularly important when attempting to garner parental support for novel approaches to arithmetic. If teachers do not proactively address this, parents feel alienated and can often inadvertently sabotage a teacher's best efforts. This book can be used to promote improved parental knowledge and engagement. The photocopy black line masters of instructional resources contained on the Resource CD can be used in lieu of traditional homework sheets. The activities are engaging and provide a venue for meaningful practice, so most students enjoy the activities and therefore are more likely to complete the assignments. Parents who have experienced this style of homework activity have reported positive feelings about the experience and have stated repeatedly that they wish homework had been like this when they were young. These resources can also be used for activities during family mathematics nights.

Parent academies or workshops are another method for improving home–school relations. This is critical when schools attempt to introduce mathematics that is unfamiliar to the parents. A popular topic for parent academies is alternative algorithms or semi-formal written strategies. Teachers can forearm parents with knowledge of alternative algorithms before introducing them to students in the classroom. This equips parents to reinforce instruction given in school and provides parents with a rationale for using the alternative algorithms. See Chapter 8: 'Written Computation' for more detail on alternative algorithms.

2

Instruction in Arithmetic

The whole numbers are a treasure of puzzles, wonders and satisfactions. Mastering these numbers is a major achievement of each student's schooling. Imagine the numbers 1 to 100 in particular becoming students' familiar mathematical home turf, where their curiosity and confidence in numbers are established. Let students discover the richness of patterns and relationships here, and they will go looking for more in later topics. Let students appreciate efficiency and flexibility here, and they will expect it in later calculations. Let students master addition, subtraction, multiplication and division here, and the knowledge will become the foundation for all further learning in mathematics.

Developing such mastery of arithmetic is within the grasp of virtually every student. However, for virtually every student, mastery requires years of dedicated instruction. Young children's thinking about numbers bears little resemblance to the formal adult arithmetic they can develop over five or six years. In turn, to be meaningful to students, instruction cannot simply be a demonstration of formal arithmetic. Nor can instructional topics be organized the way formal arithmetic is organized. However, the character of instructional developments, from less sophisticated to more sophisticated arithmetic, is entirely consistent with the character of the development of more formal mathematics. This character of development can be called *progressive mathematization* (Freudenthal, 1991; Treffers and Beishuizen, 1999). Thus, arithmetic instruction is a distinctive discipline, yet deeply rooted in the discipline of mathematics.

A great deal is known now about what makes effective mathematics instruction. This chapter describes our approach to instruction in arithmetic, at three different levels. The first section presents the broad organization of instructional topics over ages 7 to 11. The second section characterizes the directionality of instruction, towards the progressive mathematization of students' knowledge. The third section summarizes key elements of an inquiry-based approach to day-to-day assessment and teaching.

Organizing Instruction in Arithmetic

This section presents a view of strong arithmetic knowledge as our instructional aim, and outlines the broad progression of instruction towards that aim. Further, we organize arithmetic instruction into six key domains. These domains are the subject of the six chapters of Part II, and thus are central to the organization of the book.

Aiming for Strong Arithmetic Knowledge

Sometimes the subject of arithmetic is imagined as memorizing the basic facts and mastering the algorithms for the four operations: how to add, subtract, multiply and divide. By contrast, imagine a subject that develops strong integrated mathematical knowledge. We want students to know a lot about numbers – for the number 48, for example, to know what is 1 less, what is 10 more, how far back to 40, how many more to get to 50, where 48 is positioned on a number line, what's half of 48, if 48 is divisible by 2, 3, 4, 5 or 6, and so on. And we want students to be able to solve many kinds of number problems – for example, 48 + 15, but also 48 + ? = 63. *What is the difference between 48 and 63?, what other pairs of numbers sum to 63?, how many such pairs are there? 48 is roughly what fraction of 63?*, and so on. Furthermore, we are convinced that students develop such strong arithmetic knowledge through solving significant arithmetic problems. They learn where 48 is positioned through trying to position 48. They learn what 48 + 15 is through trying to add 15 to 48. Thus, we do not separate learning knowledge about numbers from knowledge of computation. Learning about numbers happens together with calculating and organizing numbers (Anghileri, 2006; Freudenthal, 1991; Heirdsfield, 2001; Pirie and Kieren, 1994; Wright et al., 2007).

A Progression in Mental Computation and Written Computation

Many curricula emphasize the teaching of formal place value and formal written algorithms. There is considerable evidence that early instruction in formal mathematics does not support students' learning of skilful mental computation, and indeed it may hinder their learning. Many students and adults taught in this way rely on written algorithms to solve addition and subtraction tasks. Some curricula include instruction in mental computation, but treat it as a separate topic unrelated to written computation. In accordance with a growing consensus, we have a different approach to teaching computation. We envision the instruction as a single coherent development of computation knowledge, involving both mental and written strategies. The progression of that development can be sketched in five phases, as follows (see Figure 2.1).

1. In most topics, we begin with tasks in settings that are common sense for students. The students solve these tasks using their informal strategies. Informal strategies are typically mental, but also make use of the settings – touching dots, looking at beads, making finger patterns, and so on.
2. Then we begin to distance the settings from the students, until we can pose tasks involving what are referred to as *bare numbers*, that is, involving formal written (or sometimes spoken) arithmetic devoid of any context or setting using materials. The purpose of this is for students to solve tasks mentally without using materials, fingers, and so on. We also begin to introduce informal notations. Many students develop flexible and efficient mental strategies at this stage, and are able to notate their strategies.

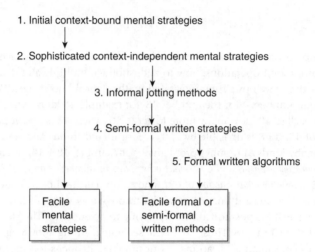

Figure 2.1   A broad progression in the development of mental and written computation

3. For more difficult tasks, students learn to combine mental strategies with informal written jottings.
4. With these mental strategies and jottings as a basis, we then develop semi-formal written computation strategies.
5. If appropriate for the learner, we can develop these strategies further so that students learn the formal written computation algorithms.

Thus, students develop a range of mental computation strategies: some rely on materials, some involve notation, and some are more mathematically sophisticated than others. Developing strong mental strategies is considered important in its own right, and is also considered a basis for developing written strategies. Students develop a range of written strategies, which can be more or less formal. The development of all of these strategies can be closely interconnected. This broad progression in computation knowledge is central to the approach in the book (Anghileri, 2006; Beishuizen and Anghileri, 1998; van den Heuvel-Panhuizen, 2001; Yackel, 2001).

Domains of Arithmetic Knowledge

We find it useful to identify what we call *domains* of arithmetic knowledge (Clarke et al., 2002; Dowker, 2004; Wright et al., 2007). In this book we describe six domains, as the subjects of the six chapters of Part II: *Number Words and Numerals; Structuring Numbers 1 to 20; Conceptual Place Value; Addition and Subtraction to 100; Multiplication and Division;* and *Written Computation*. These six domains have developed over years of our research as substantial coherent topics. For each domain, we can characterize what constitutes facility in the domain; appreciate the significance of that knowledge for students' arithmetic learning; learn how to assess students' knowledge and misconceptions in the domain; and describe a trajectory of teaching and learning towards facility in the domain. Thus, teachers can learn a great deal about any one domain. The domains are described in detail in the overview section of each chapter in Part II. They are outlined below.

Number Words and Numerals

The domain involves knowledge of basic number word sequences and numeral sequences in the range to 1000 and beyond, including sequences by 1s, and by 10s and 100s, and by other multiples such as 2s, 3s, 4s and 5s. The domain also involves reading and writing numerals, up to 5-digit numerals and further.

Structuring Numbers 1 to 20

The domain involves number combinations and partitions in the range 1 to 20, and facility with mental strategies for addition and subtraction that do not involve counting by ones. The domain includes the significant sub-domain of structuring numbers 1 to 10.

Conceptual Place Value

The domain involves flexibly incrementing and decrementing numbers by ones, tens and hundreds. This informal knowledge of ones, tens and hundreds is foundational in mental strategies for multi-digit computation, and can be distinguished from conventional place value knowledge.

Addition and Subtraction to 100

The domain involves facility with mental computation for addition and subtraction in the range to 100, and beyond. The domain includes the sub-domain of higher decade addition and subtraction.

Multiplication and Division

The domain involves facility with mental computation for multiplication and division in the range to 100, and beyond. The domain includes the development of multiplicative reasoning up to multiplication and division as formal arithmetic operations.

Written Computation

The domain involves the development of written methods for the four operations of addition, subtraction, multiplication and division. Methods include informal jotting methods, semi-formal strategies and formal algorithms.

Organizing Instruction with Domains

Teachers can organize instruction in arithmetic around addressing these six domains. Choose two to four domains as a focus for a period of months. Assess students' knowledge of these focus domains. Then teach the focus domains alongside each other, including some time on each focus domain in most lessons. Over time, as instruction in an earlier domain is concluding, a new domain can be introduced. Note that the domains are not seen as discrete topics. Rather, they are interrelated aspects of a coherent developing knowledge of arithmetic. Over the course

Weekly Lesson Plan for _Kym_ _____ (Student)

Teacher: Week: 3

Domain	NWS	Struct 1–20	CPV	Add / Subt	
Plan for Week	FNWS /BNWS 800 – 1200 + beyond Numeral Roll / number track before /after Jumping Reinse 2's, 5's 3's, 4's	Comb → 5 3 verbal Comb →10 Making + reading 1 – 20 Doubles → 10+10 Add / Subt → 20 (Bus Game)	± 10s, 1s → 150 unscreened / screened ± 100s to 1500 ± 100s, 10s, 1s Begin	To /from decade 1–5 6–9	
Reflections	Jumping very confidently	Picked up double / near dable setting very quickly	Good – ± 10, 1s tog other today Getting much better	Add – quick Subt – not so strong.	

Photo 2.1   A teacher's lesson plan organized using domains

of ages 7 to 11 years, the progression from early to late domains is staggered and overlapping. Throughout, teachers seek to develop students' knowledge within each domain. At the same time, teachers recognize how the domains connect, and are increasingly interwoven. For example, within the domain of _Structuring Numbers 1 to 20_, students master knowledge of the partitions of 10, such as solving $7 + \square = 10$. Later, in the domain of _Addition and Subtraction to 100_, this knowledge needs to be extended to higher decades, to solve $47 + \square = 50$ (Askew et al., 1997; Treffers, 1991; van den Heuvel-Panhuizen, 2001).

Related Strands for Instruction

While interweaving the domains within whole number arithmetic, teachers can also address related strands of mathematics. One related strand is early algebraic reasoning. Teachers need to appreciate how, on the one hand, early algebraic reasoning needs to develop in the context of learning arithmetic, and on the other hand, mastery of arithmetic needs to include an increasingly algebraic approach to numbers. Thus, in their arithmetic instruction, teachers need to seek opportunities for algebraic reasoning. A second related strand is knowledge of non-whole numbers, that is, fractions or rational numbers. Developing knowledge of fractions requires a radical reorganization of the ways students think about whole numbers. At the same time, facility with fractions depends on facility with whole numbers. Thus, instruction in fractions is closely related to instruction in whole number arithmetic. These related strands are the subject of the chapters in Part III.

Progressive Mathematization of Arithmetic

This section describes how we view instruction in arithmetic in terms of progressive mathematization. For students, developing strong arithmetic knowledge is primarily a task of advancing in mathematical sophistication. It is tempting to reduce the curriculum to a list of basic facts, or a kit of handy procedures, and in turn base instruction around memorizing facts or rehearsing procedures. However, such approaches lose sight of the advancement in mathematical thinking required, from the student's perspective. By contrast, we need an approach to instruction that emphasizes mathematical thinking. Invite students to problem-solve, visualize, organize, justify and generalize – this is the kind of activity that is likely to help them advance mathematically (Freudenthal, 1991; Fuson, 1992; Goldenberg et al., 2003; Gravemeijer et al., 2000).

Progressive Mathematization

Mathematization means bringing a more mathematical approach to some activity. For example, when a student pushes some counters aside and solves an addition task without them, we say they are mathematizing, since it is mathematically important to reason about relations independent of concrete materials. *Progressive mathematization* means the development of mathematical sophistication over time: for example, developing from adding with counters through to adding bare numbers. It is useful to view the aim of students' learning over a series of weeks as the progressive mathematization of their thinking about arithmetic. The trajectories within each domain, and the broad trajectory through all eight domains, can be understood in terms of progressive mathematization. Below we characterize eight themes of progressive mathematization which recur in many of the domains: structuring numbers; extending the range of numbers; decimalizing; unitizing; distancing the setting; notating; formalizing; and generalizing. These themes are the mathematically significant developments in arithmetic knowledge towards which we aim our instruction. The themes elaborate on how the domains develop and interweave, providing a medium-term view of the instructional approach (Fosnot and Dolk, 2001b; Gattegno, 1988; Gravemeijer, 1997; Treffers and Beishuizen, 1999; Wright et al., 2007).

Theme A: Structuring Numbers

Numbers are often first learned as a list: one, two, three, four, five, and so on. For a 5-year-old, eight may be best understood as the number after seven, and perhaps the number before nine. We seek to structure numbers, that is, to progressively mathematize numbers into richer and more densely organized networks of relations. Students learn to organize the number list into decades (1 to 10, 11 to 20,…); to make sub-lists of multiples (3, 6, 9, 12…); to list pairs adding to 10 (1 + 9, 2 + 8…); to build numbers with 10s (24 is 10 and 10 and 4); to make sets of factors (24 is divisible by 2, 3, 4, 6, 8 and 12); and so on. They need to come to think of eight as double 4, as half of 16, as 5 and 3, as the complement of 2 (to make 10), as a cousin of 18, 28 and 38 (if 8 + 5 = 13, what is 38 + 5?); and so on. These different forms of eight are themselves related: 5 + 3 can be linked with 4 + 4, and with 10 − 2. Thus, for students, numbers increasingly become nodes in networks of relations (Ellemor-Collins and Wright, 2009b; Freudenthal, 1991; Gravemeijer et al., 2000; Treffers, 1991).

The domain *Structuring Numbers 1 to 20* structures the additive relations between the numbers 1 to 20. The domains *Conceptual Place Value* and *Addition and Subtraction to 100* structure the additive relations between the numbers 1 to 100, particularly those relations organized around tens and decuples. The domain *Multiplication and Division* structures multiplicative relations between the numbers 1 to 100, which link closely with the additive relations. The strand of *Early Algebraic Reasoning* raises awareness of relations among numbers, and makes relations more explicit in the form of functions and generalizations. The strand of *Fractions* develops relations between fractional parts and the unit whole, and between different fractional parts.

Theme B: Extending the Range of Numbers

Students first develop arithmetic competence with whole numbers in the range 1 to 5. We seek to progressively mathematize number knowledge to extend it to larger numbers. In a broad sense, this progression in the range of numbers is embedded in the progression of the eight domains: from the range 1 to 20 in *Structuring Numbers 1 to 20*, through to 100 in *Addition and Subtraction to 100*, to 3- and 4-digit numbers in *Written Computation*. *Fractions* can also be seen as an extension beyond whole numbers. More specifically, within every domain, there is a progression in the range of numbers. For example, the domain *Number Words and Numerals* addresses sequences first in the range 1 to 100, then to 1000, then across 1000, and finally beyond 1000. On a still smaller scale, extending the range of numbers can be pursued as a mathematization of any new aspect of number knowledge. For example, as students become fluent with 'ten-plus tasks' (10 + 6 = 16), this can be immediately extended to 20 + 6, 30 + 6 … 100 + 6 … 430 + 6 … 1000 + 6 … Thus, larger numbers are not ignored until they are suddenly encountered as new territory; rather, students are repeatedly making new inroads in their knowledge of larger numbers.

Theme C: Decimalizing towards Base-ten Thinking

In our base-ten numeration system, we organize numbers into 1s, 10s, 100s, 1000s and so on. We express our number words in 1s, 10s and 100s: 'one hundred (and) forty-five'. We organize our numerals into 1s, 10s and 100s using the place value system: in '145' the 1 indicates one hundred, the 4 indicates four tens, and the 5 five ones. We also organize our mental calculations into 1s, 10s and 100s. For example, to add 25 to 47, we might add 10, another 10, then add 5. Formal written algorithms for addition and subtraction exploit the place value system, systematically addressing the 1s, then the 10s, then the 100s, and so on. Essentially, the base-ten system is our means for getting a handle on numbers larger than 20. To make any progress in mathematics, students must be inducted into base-ten thinking, developing a skilful habit of organizing numbers and calculations into 1s, 10s and 100s. Freudenthal emphasized this induction, calling it 'decimalizing' (Freudenthal, 1983; Fuson et al., 1997; Thompson, 2003).

The *Number Words and Numerals* domain develops aspects of base-ten thinking in mastering the sequences of number words and numerals to 1000 and beyond. The *Conceptual Place Value* domain develops the flexible addition and subtraction of 10s and 100s. The *Addition and Subtraction to 100* domain develops mental computation strategies which rely on base-ten thinking. The

Written Computation domain develops these base-ten strategies into written forms, and develops formal place value conventions.

Theme D: Unitizing and Not Counting by Ones

Children's early computation with numbers typically involves counting by ones – 8 + 5 might be solved by counting-on '8 … 9, 10, 11, 12, 13', keeping track of five counts with a nodding pattern; 4 × 5 might be solved by counting out '1, 2, 3, 4, 5; 6, 7, 8, 9, 10; … 20' keeping track of each set of five on one hand, and the four sets on the other. A prominent theme throughout the ages of 7 to 11 years is to progressively mathematize computation towards strategies that do not involve counting by ones – 8 + 5 might be solved by starting with 8, adding 2 to make 10, then 3 more to make 13. This adding-through-ten strategy involves treating 3 as a part of 5, and as a *unit* that can be manipulated as a whole without needing to be built up from a count. *Unitizing* numbers in this way makes it possible to do calculations without counting by ones. It is a significant development in mathematical sophistication (Olive, 2001; Steffe and Cobb, 1988).

The domain *Structuring Numbers 1 to 20* aims to move from counting strategies to non-counting strategies through this unitizing of parts and wholes: combining smaller numbers to make larger numbers, and partitioning larger numbers into smaller numbers. The domains *Conceptual Place Value* and *Addition and Subtraction to 100* develop non-counting strategies through developing ten as a special unit, as discussed in the theme of decimalizing above. The domain of *Multiplication and Division* and the strand of *Fractions* also involve moving from counting strategies to non-counting strategies, requiring the development of numbers as more sophisticated multiplicative units.

Theme E: Distancing a Setting of Materials

Children typically begin making sense of numbers in a setting of concrete materials: fingers, birthday candles, counters, coins, and so on. We seek to progressively mathematize numbers towards independence from materials. That is, we aim for students to understand and solve tasks posed with verbal or written numbers only, without further context, which we call *bare number* tasks. However, if students develop an approach to tasks in a setting of materials, and we remove that setting suddenly, we cannot expect their original approach to transfer to the bare context. Instead, as teachers, we need to be incremental and strategic about distancing a setting from students (Gravemeijer, 1991, 1997; Sullivan et al., 2001).

For example, in the domain *Conceptual Place Value*, tasks of adding by 1s, 10s and 100s are initially posed in a setting of bundling sticks. This setting can be distanced in a progression of four stages: (1) the bundling sticks are visible; (2) the bundling sticks are shown briefly, then screened; (3) the task is posed verbally, with the bundling sticks screened; (4) the task is posed verbally, without reference to the bundling sticks. By removing the setting from the students in stages, the students increasingly develop their visualization and mental organization, until they can solve the tasks independently of any setting. The six domains all involve similar progressions for distancing settings.

Theme F: Notating

Notating is writing a record of some mathematics. For example, Rumi calculates that adding 10 sticks to 24 sticks makes 34 sticks altogether; the teacher notates the calculation as '24 + 10 → 34'. A significant realization of mathematics education research is that mathematical notation and mathematical concepts are learned in tandem. On the one hand, by grappling with some new notation, students can construct a more organized conception of numbers. Consider two examples. Notate with an empty number line – begin mentally sequencing additions. Arrange numerals in columns – gain insight into formal place value. On the other hand, by trying to organize a conception of number, students can make new meaning of some notation. Consider two examples. Establish facts such as 10 + 3 is 13, 10 + 5 is 15 – realize what the 1 and 5 symbolize in the numeral. List the factor pairs of a number, such as 1×24, 2×12, 3×8, 4×6 – use the $\times$ sign to indicate a product relationship, rather than a task requiring calculation. It becomes clear that mathematical notation and concepts are companions that need to be learned together. If too much new notation is introduced without opportunities to grapple with the companion concepts, most students will not make the leap. Instead, the notation remains disconnected from the realm of what makes sense for the students, and becomes a syntactical game following someone else's rules. However, if new notation is not introduced, students' conceptual development will be limited. Ideally, when notation is introduced, we want students to experience this as an invitation to partake of shared tools, which can illuminate their own thinking, rather than as an imposition of someone else's way, which obscures their own thinking. Notating is an important theme in all six domains and the two strands (Carruthers and Worthington, 2006; Fosnot and Dolk, 2001a; Gravemeijer et al., 2000; Gray and Tall, 1994; Sfard, 2000).

Theme G: Formalizing

Students' initial computation strategies are typically mental and informal. We seek to progressively mathematize towards more formal strategies, involving more formal notations. *Formalizing* means investing more significance in form. For example, consider a progression in notating addition strategies. We might first notate a mental strategy for addition on an empty number line. This is an informal notation where we do not care about how the line is drawn or exactly where the numbers are placed. Later we can notate strategies using number sentences, a more formal notation where we do care about how the equals sign is used. A further formal development is to write numbers in columns, a semi-formal notation where we care about getting every digit in the correct column, but don't care exactly how we write out the ensuing calculation. Finally, if we use a formal column algorithm, every single mark we make needs to be in a certain place. Thus, over this learning progression, the form of the notations becomes increasingly significant. The advantage of formalizing is that the form becomes more powerful, and can do more of the work – hence the usefulness of the formal algorithm. The limitation of formalizing is that, without induction into the formalities, the notation is meaningless to us – hence the difficulties many people experience with formal algorithms. Formalizing is involved in all six domains and the two strands. It is particularly important for the domains of *Addition and Subtraction to 100, Multiplication and Division* and *Written Computation* (Anghileri, 2006; Freudenthal, 1983; Gravemeijer, 1997; Pirie and Kieren, 1994).

Theme H: Generalizing

Generalizing is perhaps the most generic form of mathematizing. Mason et al. (2007: 42) challenges us as teachers with the dictum 'a lesson without an opportunity to generalise is not a mathematics lesson'. Generalizing takes many forms. Consider three examples. Having solved 6 + 7 using the double 6 + 6, Sami solves 8 + 9 using 8 + 8, and similarly solves other near doubles. Having established that 24 + 10 is 34, and that 34 + 10 is 44, Toola answers other increments of 10: 44 + 10, 54 + 10, 94 + 10, 104 + 10, 184 + 10, 254 + 10, 1064 + 10, and so on. Uri notices that three multiples of six – 12, 18 and 24 – are each also multiples of both 2 and 3, and conjectures that all multiples of 6 are multiples of both 2 and 3. In each example, some particular cases are established, and the student realizes that other cases can be approached in a corresponding way. In this sense, generalizing is pervasive in arithmetic learning: when students develop number concepts, number relationships, and computation strategies, they are typically generalizing from a few cases to many cases. Generalizing can involve other themes of mathematizing: in the examples above, Sami is structuring numbers (theme A) and Toola is extending the range of numbers (theme B). Generalizing is involved in all domains and strands, and is central to the strand of *Early Algebraic Reasoning* (Gattegno, 1970; Mason and Johnston-Wilder, 2006; Mason et al., 2007).

An Inquiry-based Approach to Instruction

For day-to-day instruction, we advocate an approach based on inquiry, that is, on posing and solving problems (Fosnot and Dolk, 2001a,b; Lambdin, 2003; Treffers and Beishuizen, 1999; Yackel, 2003). In Chapters 2 and 3 of the second book in the series, Wright et al. (2006b), and Chapter 1 of the third book, Wright et al. (2006c), we describe an inquiry-based approach in detail, including discussions of guiding principles of instruction, key elements of moment-to-moment teaching, and characteristics of students' problem solving. In this section we summarize the approach, to complete a coherent account of instruction for the current book. This inquiry-based approach is assumed in the descriptions of instruction for each domain and strand in this book.

Summary of Principles of Instruction

Assessment to Inform Instruction

Careful assessment is fundamental. Assessment involves attentive listening and observation of students solving significant mathematical tasks. Teachers make an initial assessment to develop a detailed profile of students' knowledge and strategies across key domains of instruction. As well, teachers make ongoing assessment throughout the course of instruction. Regular assessment to inform instruction becomes a class norm.

Teaching Just Beyond the Cutting Edge

Based on their assessment of students' current levels of knowledge, teachers pitch instruction just beyond the cutting edge of students' learning. In this way, tasks are at a level that makes sense to the students in terms of their current knowledge, but typically to solve the task, students need to reorganize their approach, develop new strategies, or gain new insights. This activity beyond the cutting edge leads to learning. Teaching just beyond the cutting edge requires that, in moment-to-moment teaching, teachers closely observe students' activity and finely adjust tasks. Classroom teachers can be aware of what strategies and forms of reasoning have become accepted practice within the class as a community, and thus pitch teaching tasks at the communal cutting edge of the class. At the same time, in interactions with each student, the teacher can tune particular questions or task modifications to the cutting edge of the individual. Posing challenging tasks becomes a class norm.

Solving Genuine Problems

By pitching instruction just beyond the cutting edge of students' knowledge, students are regularly solving tasks that for them are genuine problems – that is, the tasks are challenging. Nevertheless there is a good likelihood that students will solve them given a supportive learning environment. To work on these tasks, students are given time for sustained, hard thinking. Students gain intrinsic satisfaction from thinking hard and solving genuine problems. Teachers gain satisfaction from making and preserving extended thinking time for students. Sustained thinking becomes a class norm.

Reflecting on Problem Solving

When students respond to tasks, it is the students' responsibility to verify their answers. An individual can self-verify, by using a less sophisticated strategy to check a solution, for example, by counting with materials to check the answer from a mental strategy. Also, the class can discuss and determine as a group which solutions are justified. Teachers can notate students' solutions, creating a record that supports further reflection and discussion. Sustained reflection on solutions and discussion of solutions become class norms.

Photo 2.2 Teacher and students discuss a solution to a task

Emphasizing Mathematical Thinking

Through all this Instructional Activity of assessment, posing tasks, solving tasks and reflecting on solutions, the teacher keeps activity oriented towards mathematization. In posing and adjusting tasks, teachers are aware of directions for progressive mathematization. Tasks are often amenable to extension in three directions:

1. Extending the range of numbers, for example, from 1–5, to 1–10, to 1–20.
2. Increasing the arithmetic complexity of tasks, for example, from saying number of dots on a ten-frame, to saying complement to ten, to totalling dots on two frames.
3. Distancing the setting and formalizing the task, for example, from showing materials, to screening materials, to presenting with bare numbers.

Also, in observing students' strategies, the teacher pays attention to mathematical sophistication. Teachers show a preference for students' non-counting strategies rather than counting strategies. They draw attention to students' organizing of numbers using tens, but away from a focus on particular procedures. Teachers offer a more formal symbolization. Thus teachers act as a compass towards mathematical sophistication, away from proceduralism. Teachers also establish the practice of students explaining and justifying their thinking, and verifying their solutions. The importance of thinking mathematically is an established norm in the class. A major aim of this book is to detail, for each domain, how to pursue progressive mathematization in these ways (Goldenberg et al., 2003; Mason and Johnston-Wilder, 2006; Stephan and Whitenack, 2003).

Using Instructional Settings

Materials, such as numeral rolls, ten-frames, and bundling sticks, are used as settings for posing tasks. A well-designed setting is amenable to students' initial informal approaches. At the same time, the setting provides a context for students to reflect on and further organize their thinking. We make use of colour coding in settings to help structure the materials, such as partitioning 10 dots into dots of two colours. We also use flashing and screening of settings. Flashing is showing the setting for a short time, say 1–2 seconds, then screening it. Use of flashing and screening are part of the progression of distancing students from the setting, challenging students to rely increasingly on visualization and mental strategies (Gravemeijer, 1997; Wright et al., 2007).

We distinguish this inquiry-based use of materials as a setting for posing and solving problems, from other uses of materials. In some instructional approaches, teachers use materials to demonstrate a way of thinking about a task, for example, *I think of splitting the ten and adding it to thirty, like I pick up this bundle and move it here.* Another approach is to teach students particular procedures with the materials, for example, to arrange bundling sticks in certain ways on a place value mat. However, training in procedures with materials doesn't bring students closer to sophisticated mental strategies. These instructional approaches assume a correspondence between the materials and the mathematical thinking, expecting students to see mathematical relationships based on relationships in the materials. However, students have rarely constructed such a correspondence. Students are unlikely to see the

Photo 2.3   Screening the setting to pose a task

Photo 2.4   Unscreening to verify the solution

mathematical relations in the materials; rather, they will see the materials from the perspective of their own informal reasoning (Cobb, 1991; Gravemeijer, 1991; Wright, 1992).

Inquiry Mode and Rehearsal Mode

While students need to solve challenging tasks to advance in mathematical sophistication, they also need to rehearse their knowledge and strategies to develop facility. Thus, it is helpful to distinguish two productive modes of work students can adopt: inquiry mode and rehearsal mode. *Inquiry mode* occurs when students are trying to solve a novel problem, exploring some new material, generating further examples. It is activity that produces something 'new' for the student, that breaks new mathematical ground. *Rehearsal mode* involves rehearsing something that has been introduced before: identifying some numerals, naming some figures, reciting some number word sequences. It is a practice that repeats something with which the student is acquainted, with the intention of increasing familiarity and ease, and perhaps working towards automatization. Successful inquiry and rehearsal have distinctive qualities, as suggested in Table 2.1.

It behoves a teacher to be mindful of these distinctive qualities of activity. If an inquiry task is set, but the teacher also provides an approach to solving it, then students may not make sense of the task for themselves, and may not establish interest in solving it. If an inquiry task is set, but the teacher intervenes whenever the pace stalls, the students may never fire up their puzzling mind. On the other hand, if a rehearsal session includes a difficult task, it will confuse and dishearten the student. If a rehearsal session is frequently interrupted for discussion, students may lose attention, and not effectively rehearse their knowledge.

An instructional task will be suited to one or other of these modes, depending on the knowledge of the student. For example, for Anya, the task 'write down all the ways of making ten' is an inquiry task, requiring thinking time, scribble room, and some follow-up inquiries – 'Convince me that you have found them all'. For Ben, and indeed for Anya two weeks later, the same task is a *rehearsal* task, requiring about one minute, just six orderly lines of writing, and a

Table 2.1 Inquiry mode and rehearsal mode

	Inquiry mode	**Rehearsal mode**
Challenge	Tasks need to be challenging but solvable	Tasks need to require just a moment's thought, mostly involving recall
Engagement	Student engagement and energy arise from thinking hard, taking initiative and discovery	Student engagement and energy arise from the brisk pace of the task, and the regularity of success
Autonomy	Students need autonomy in approaching the task, and preferably autonomy in checking their solutions	The task is mostly externally directed – for example, by a teacher, a game, a computer, or a worksheet. Answers are checked immediately
Room	Students need room to expand their activity: desk space to lay out materials, blank paper for jottings, sufficient quiet to leave mental room for thinking hard	Students may need less room: just room to chant, or to see flash cards, or to write short answers, or to set up a game
Time	Time needs to be relatively long, long enough to exercise students' persistence and initiative	Time needs to be relatively short, sufficient to practise without getting tired or distracted
Pace	Pace varies with the ebb and flow of students' inventions and puzzling	Pace is kept fairly brisk and even
Follow-up	Inquiry work is well served with follow-up sharing, discussion and debate, to bring communal mathematical reasoning to bear on students' work	Rehearsal work can be followed-up with revisiting two or three of the items that caused difficulty

quick self-check against the answer made the previous week. Each student will benefit from a mixed diet, with plenty of inquiry, and some regular rehearsal. In a class with varied knowledge – that is, in any class – arranging a mixed diet for all students is not straightforward.

PART II

3

Number Words and Numerals

DOMAIN OVERVIEW

Knowing the words we say for numbers and the numerals we write for numbers is important basic number knowledge. Number words are typically learnt in sequences: from one to ten, from one hundred backwards, and so on. Sometimes students say a sequence in the context of counting things – counting flowers or spots or fingers; but students also say a sequence simply as a sequence of words to recite –'one, two, three, four…'; or 'one hundred, ninety-nine, ninety-eight …'. These are quite different activities. To maintain this distinction, we talk about the former as *counting*, and the latter as simply saying a *number word sequence* (NWS). In a parallel fashion, students can read numerals in the context of quantities – '6' beside six flowers, '100' beside a pattern of 100 spots; but students can also learn to read numerals as bare marks, somewhat like learning to read sight words in literacy instruction – 41 is read 'forty-one', 306 is read 'three-hundred (and) six'. The rudimentary knowledge of NWSs and numerals without a context of quantities is an important domain of students' developing number knowledge, and it requires explicit instruction (Hewitt and Brown, 1998; Steffe and Cobb, 1988; Wright et al., 2006a, 2007). In this overview, we first explain the significance of this domain for 7–11-year-olds. We then describe learning in this domain, including detailing student difficulties with number words and numerals. A brief section summarizes assessment of the domain. Finally, we describe approaches to instruction in the domain.

Significance of Knowledge of Number Words and Numerals

Learning to say NWSs and to read numerals in the range 1 to 100 is a feature of students' early development of number knowledge. Students' early difficulties are well documented, such as: confusions between –teen and –ty number words; knowing sequences forwards but not backwards; and mis-reading teen numerals (e.g. Fuson et al., 1982; Wright, 1994). Typically, considerable attention is given to instruction in number words and numerals in the early years of school. In the middle years of primary school, by contrast, instruction in number words and numerals often decreases. Yet there is a deal more to learn in these years, and many students encounter new difficulties. Students need to learn:

- NWSs to 1000 and beyond, forwards and backwards
- the NWSs of decuples, centuples and thousands
- NWSs by tens off the decuple, such as '24, 34, 44 …' which become useful in developing jump strategies for addition and subtraction
- NWSs by 2s, 3s, 4s, and so on, which become central to developing strategies for multiplication and division
- reading and writing numerals up to at least 5 digits.

There is evidence that students who lack this facility with number words and numerals struggle to progress with further arithmetic knowledge. For example, if students do not know the NWS from 305 backwards across 300, how can they make sense of a task such as ten less than 305? Students can and should learn number word sequences and numerals in a number range well in advance of learning to add and subtract in that range. Familiarity with a range of numbers establishes a basis for meaningful arithmetic (Denvir and Brown, 1986; Ellemor-Collins and Wright, 2007; Hewitt and Brown, 1998; Wigley, 1997; Wright et al., 2007).

Learning Number Word Sequences

To become facile with a NWS, students need to be able to say the sequence forwards (FNWS) and backwards (BNWS), without hesitations. Students also need to be able to say the number word immediately before or after a given word. For example, when asked *what is the number after 99?*, students need to be able to answer 'one hundred', without reciting 'ninety-one, ninety-two …' to find the answer. To appreciate what facility with NWSs involves, it is useful to observe students' difficulties while learning NWSs. Tables 3.1, 3.2 and 3.3 present examples of student difficulties. These examples are discussed below.

Learning Number Word Sequences by 1s

In early number learning, the NWS from 'one' to 'ten' needs to be memorized. In English and many other languages, the NWS from 'eleven' to 'twenty' and the NWS of decuples 'ten, twenty, thirty, … one hundred' do not build transparently from the basic sequence of 'one' to 'ten', so they also need to be memorized. Students then learn how to link these sequences together to say the NWS from 'one' to 'one hundred', forwards and backwards. For more detail on early learning of number words, see Wright et al. (2006c). Typically, facility with the NWS to 100 is accomplished in the first two years of school, but there may be 7–8-year-olds who still have difficulties. Persistent difficulties can be: the teen numbers, knowing the number word after 99, and knowing the BNWS across decuples (see Table 3.1).

Table 3.1 Examples of student difficulties with number word sequences (NWSs) by 1s

Hurdling a decuple	'52, 51, **40**, 49, 48 ...'
	'52, 51, ∧ 49, 48 ...'
	'52, 51, 50, **89**, 88 ...'
	'52, 51, 50, **59**, 58 ...'
Hurdling 100	'98, 99, 100, **ten hundred**'
	'98, 99, 100, **200, 300** ...'
	'102, 101, ∧ 99, 98 ...'
Hurdling 110	'108, 109, **1000**, 1001 ...'
	'108, 109, **200**, 201, 202 ...'
	Number word after 109: '**1000**'
Hurdling 200	'198, 199. That's all I know.'
	'198, 199, **1000**, 1001 ...'
	'198, 199, ∧ 201, 202 ...'
	'202, 201, ∧ 199, 198 ...'
Hurdling 1000	'998, 999 ... I don't know.'
	'998, 999 ... **ten hundred**?'

Note: Errors are marked in **bold**, omissions are marked with '∧'.

To learn the NWS to 'one thousand' and beyond, students learn the sequence of centuple words. 'One hundred, two hundred ... nine hundred' is straightforward. The substantive new learning is the sequence 'nine hundred, one thousand, one thousand one hundred, one thousand two hundred ...'. Students also learn to treat each sequence of 'one' to 'ninety-nine' as a chain, and learn how to link each chain together through the hundreds. Common difficulties are FNWS across 110, 200, 1000, and 1100, and BNWS across any centuples (see Table 3.1). These difficult points in the sequences can be referred to as *hurdles*. Even when students manage hurdles correctly, they may be hesitant, and require regular practice to achieve robust facility (Ellemor-Collins and Wright, 2007; Skwarchuk and Anglin, 2002).

Through learning NWSs by 1s, students are implicitly learning our system for naming numbers. This system works much like the dials of an odometer. It could be described as follows. In a forward NWS, the larger number words stay fixed while the last word ticks through 'one' to 'nine', as in 'three hundred (and) seventy-one, three-hundred (and) seventy-two ... three-hundred (and) seventy-nine'. After a 'nine' the decuple increments by one, 'three-hundred (and) eighty'. The centuple word only increments after 99; and the thousands word only increments after 999. In a sense, the student who says '1008, 1009, 2000' has not learnt that the thousand word stays fixed until the centuple words have gone through nine hundred. As students name numbers beyond 2000, this number naming system needs to become more explicit for them. *What is the number after 39,199? What is the number before 750,000?* Of course, the number naming system has a quantitative logic. If we count dots up to 1009, then count one more dot, we will have 1000 dots and another 10 dots. We won't have two lots of 1000 dots. So it makes sense to call the number 'one thousand (and) ten', not 'two thousand'. However, students can learn that the number after 1009 is 'one thousand (and) ten' by learning the naming system of numbers, before they explicitly understand the quantitative sense of the numbers.

Learning Number Word Sequences by 10s and 100s

Students learn the number words for decuples and centuples while learning the basic NWS by 1s. They need to explicitly learn the NWSs by 10s and 100s. Table 3.2 presents examples of student difficulties with NWSs by 10s. The BNWS by 10s from 'one hundred' back to 'ten' is sometimes still unfamiliar to 7–8-year-olds leading to hesitations and odd errors. NWSs by 10s off the decuple are frequently unfamiliar. On their first attempts, students typically count each ten by ones, or use an incorrect system of number words. With practice, students can pick up the basic pattern easily enough. Sequences through the teen numbers require particular attention, as there are distinctive irregularities in the teen number words. NWSs by 10s in the range to 1000 encounter hurdles at centuples. Difficulties with teen numbers also persist. The error in the sequence '430, 420, 410, **300**, 390, 380 ...' is analogous to a common error in younger students when counting backwards by 1s, for example '43, 42, 41, 30, 39, 38 ...', and highlights the difficulty of linking the basic chains correctly when going backwards (Ellemor-Collins and Wright, 2007).

Learning Number Word Sequences by 5s, 2s, 3s and 4s

Once students know the basic NWS by 10s, they readily pick up the NWS by 5s, which seems to have a catchy beat 'five, *ten*, fifteen, *twenty*, twenty-five, *thirty* ...'. The NWS by 2s is also usually picked up readily. While most students will learn these NWSs forwards in the first years of school, fewer will be facile with them backwards. Most students learn the NWSs by 3s and 4s,

Table 3.2   Examples of student difficulties with number word sequences (NSWs) by 10s

10s on the decuple	'40, 30, 20, **15**, 10.'
10s off the decuple	'24, **25, 20** ... 24, **25, 20**?'
	'24, **30, 34, 40** ...'
10s and teen numbers	'42, 32, 22, ∧ 2.'
	'42, 32, 22, **14**, 4.'
	'42, 32, 22, **10, 1**.'
10s in range to 1000	'167, **267, 367, 467** ...', i.e. by 100s, not 10s.
	'177, 187, 197, one hundred and- **297**, 207, 217 ...'
	'430, 420, 410, **300**, 390, 380 ...'
	'436, 426, 416, **414**, 406, **404**.'
	'436, 426, 416, ∧ 397 – no 396.'
	'436, 426, **326**, ∧ 306, **three hundred and zero**, 296, 286 ...'

Table 3.3 Examples of student difficulties with number word sequences (NWSs) by 3s

Errors in pattern	'3, 6, 9, 12, 15, ∧ 21, I don't know anymore.'
	'3, 6, 9, 12, 15, 17, 20, 23, 26, 28, 31.'
Making up own pattern	'3, 6, 9, 13, 16, 19, 23, 26, 29, 33, 36, 39.'
	'3, 6, 9, 12, 14, 16, 18, 20.'

forwards and backwards, later than the first years of school. Students often know the first few terms – 'three, six, nine, twelve' – but later terms are more challenging. Table 3.3 presents some examples of student difficulties with the FNWS by 3s. Students may count each three by 1s, and may need to use rhythmic counting or fingers to manage this successfully. They may make errors while apparently trying to follow the pattern of 3s. Or they may make up their own pattern. Learning NWSs by 3s and 4s and other factors involves using additive knowledge: three more than 12 is 15, three more than 15 is 18, and so on. Nevertheless, with rehearsal, these NWSs can be automatized like earlier NWSs.

Learning to Read and Write Numerals

This domain is concerned with students learning to read and write numerals. To be considered facile in a range of numerals, students need to be able to identify any numeral presented to them and write any numeral requested. Most students become facile with identifying and writing 2-digit numerals in the first years of school. Confusions with teen numbers may persist (see Table 3.4). Also, students' development of handwriting varies markedly in the early years of school. For example, some 7–8-year-olds may still write some digits back to front (Wright, 1998).

Facility with 3-digit numerals usually follows readily from facility with 2-digit numerals. Students can come to know that a 3-digit numeral is a hundreds number. Reading a numeral such as '5 _ _' always begins 'five hundred (and) …', while writing a number such as 'five hundred (and) …' always begins '5 _ _'. And, 4-digit numerals are equally transparent. Reading a numeral such as '6 _ _ _' always begins 'six thousand …', while writing a number such as 'six thousand …' always begins '6 _ _ _'. Students can and should learn such implicit rules for reading and writing numerals before they learn formal place value in numerals. While students are developing facility, numerals with 0s can present difficulties for reading and writing, particularly in 4-digit numerals – see Table 3.4 (Cayton and Brizuela, 2007; Hewitt and Brown, 1998; Wright et al., 2007).

Students need to learn to read and write numerals up to at least nine digits. Learning to read and write numerals with more than four digits usually involves learning more explicit rules about grouping digits in threes, and naming the number of millions (up to hundreds of millions), then the number of thousands (up to hundreds of thousands) and the final 3-digit number. For example, the numeral 17,026,803 is parsed into three separate parts or periods – <u>17</u> million, <u>026</u> thousand, <u>803</u> – and read '17 million, 26 thousand, 8 hundred (and) three'.

Table 3.4   Examples of student difficulties with numerals

2-digits	12	'twenty' or 'twenty-one'
	15	'fifty'
	for 12	writes '21'
3-digits	306	'three hundred (and) sixty'
		'thirty-, no three hundred (and) six'
		'three zero six'
	for 270	writes '217'
4-digits	1000	'ten hundred'
	8245	'eighty-two hundred (and) forty-five'
	6032	'six hundred (and) thirty-two'
		'sixty thousand (and) thirty-two'
		'six thousands, zero hundreds, (and) thirty-two'
	3406	'thirty-four hundred (and) sixty'
		'thirty-four thousand (and) six'
	1300	'thirty hundred' or 'thirteen hundred'
	3010	'thirty thousand (and) ten'
	for 1005	writes '10005'
5-digits	10,000	'one million' or 'one thousand'

Assessment of Number Words and Numerals

Assessment of Number Word Sequences

Ask students to say select sequences, and closely observe their facility. Also, ask students to say the number word after or before select hurdle numbers. Assess:

- in the ranges to 100, to 1000, across 1000, and beyond 1000
- hurdles such as decuples, centuples, 1000
- backwards as well as forwards.

Assess sequences of multiples:

- by 10s, on- and off- the decuple
- by 100s
- by 5s, 2s, 3s and 4s.

Sequences need not be long: five to 15 numbers. It can be efficient to assess a sequence backwards first: if students are facile backwards, they are likely to be facile with the same sequence forwards. Knowledge of number word sequences, by and large, is not conceptual, so an assessment simply determines, for a given sequence, whether a student is (a) facile, (b) successful but with hesitations or self-corrections, or (c) unsuccessful. Noting students' particular difficulties is important.

Assessment of Reading and Writing Numerals

Assess knowledge of numerals by presenting numerals for students to identify, and by asking students to write particular numerals. Assess:

- 2-digit, 3-digit, 4-digit, 5-digit numerals and beyond
- numerals without teen numbers or zeros
- numerals with teen numbers
- numerals with zeros.

Instruction in Number Word Sequences

Number word sequence instruction is well served by regular brief instructional sessions. Keep advancing the level of the sequences selected in order to challenge the students:

- focus on hurdle numbers
- shift from FNWS to BNWS
- shift the range from 1–100, to 1–200, 1–1000, across 1000, beyond 1000
- shift from 10s on the decuple to 10s off the decuple
- shift from sequences by 1s to sequences by 2s and 5s
- shift from sequences by 2s and 5s to sequences by 3s, 4s and other multiples.

For a given range of NWS, say 1–200, early instruction works well in the context of the sequence written out in numerals, as on a numeral roll (see Appendix) (Wright et al., 2006b, 2007). The numeral sequence constitutes the reference for the correct sequence, rather than the teacher. Initially, students can simply read the sequence. A progression of four task types is particularly effective. First, cover the numeral roll and uncover the numerals one at a time. The students' task is to say each number in turn after seeing the numeral. Second, when the sequence is more familiar, the students' task is to say each number in turn *before* seeing the numeral. In this case, seeing the numerals enables self-verification. In shorthand, the first task is known as 'See then say', the second as 'Say then see'. Third, focus on the sequence backwards, both see then say, and say then see. Fourth, place the numeral sequence under a device with lids for each numeral, such as a multi-lid screen (see Appendix). Open one lid, then point to other lids for the students to name: the number before, the number two after, and so on (see Figure 3.1). After students answer, the lids can be opened to check. These four tasks are summarized in Box 3.1. In this setting of the numeral roll, the students' developing facility with NWSs and their developing facility with numerals are mutually supportive. The use of covering and lids allows incremental internalization of the sequence. The covering and lids also help a teacher to monitor students' specific difficulties, and to finely adjust the tasks to the cutting edge of their learning.

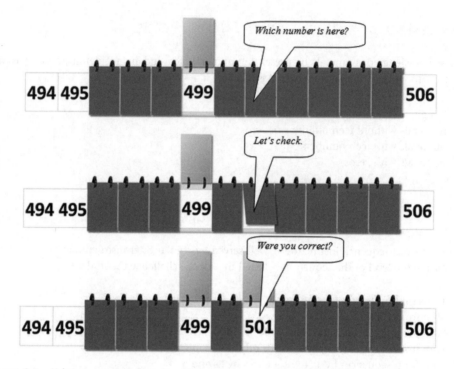

Figure 3.1 Using a numeral roll and multi-lid screen

Once students have consolidated their knowledge of a NWS, rehearsal mode instruction is useful to habituate the sequence. Lead regular brisk sessions simply chanting a few sequences. Also, ask students to write out sequences in numerals. A numeral ladder is a simple organizer for this task. Students sketch a ladder of 10–20 rungs and write the given start number at the bottom rung. They can then continue the sequence forwards up the ladder, placing the numerals on successive rungs. Backwards sequences begin at the top rung, and continue back down the ladder. Students can also practise their knowledge of number word and numeral sequences in useful contexts: look up given page numbers in a large reference book; mark given measurements on a measuring tape; find particular years on a long timeline. Several NWS rehearsal activities are described in detail in the Instructional Activities section. Note that, as students recite or write a sequence, they may need time to organize their thinking when going past a hurdle. On the other hand, if a student simply can't remember what word comes after 199 for example, they might not have any means to work it out, and so telling them is appropriate.

Instruction with the numeral roll, chanting, numeral ladders, and so on, does not involve students reasoning about quantities. In this domain, we work at the level of aural patterns and numeral patterns. We will also want students to work with quantities. The *Conceptual Place Value* domain in Chapter 5 addresses sequences by 1s, 10s and 100s in the context of quantities. The *Multiplication and Division* domain in Chapter 7 addresses sequences by 2s, 3s, 4s and 5s in the context of quantities.

Photo 3.1 Student writing numerals in a numeral ladder

Instruction in Numerals

Arrow cards are a useful instructional setting (see Appendix), developed by Gattegno (e.g. 1988), and also by Montessori (e.g. 1912/1964). Each student needs access to a set of arrow cards. Present a numeral built with arrow cards, and ask students to read it (see Figure 3.2). Since each card shows a part of the numeral – 4000, 50, 6 – the cards can support students in saying the corresponding number words – 'four thousand (and) fifty-six'. Conversely, ask students to build a number with arrow cards. Take time to reflect on zeros: how do they figure in the numeral and in the number word?

Digit cards are also a useful instructional setting (see Appendix). Each student needs access to a set of digit cards. Unlike arrow cards, digit cards have no place value structure built in, so they demand more facility with reading and writing numerals. Have students read a numeral built in digit cards. Conversely, say a number for students to build with digit cards. Digit cards can also be used in conjunction with arrow cards: students build a given number first with arrow cards then with digit cards, or vice versa. Digit cards serve well for presenting useful

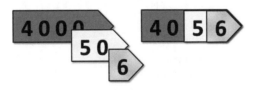

Figure 3.2 4056 built with arrow cards

Photo 3.2   Using arrow cards with digit cards

comparisons: For example, compare reading the numerals 360, 306 and 603; compare building the numerals 400, 410 and 420.

Finally, ask students to read and write numerals without using any instructional setting such as the arrow cards or digit cards. If students are having difficulty writing numerals, ask them first to picture the numeral mentally – how many digits does it have, what is the first digit, are there any zeroes – then to write the numeral. For numerals of more than four digits, students need to learn the numeration system: right to left, there are the initial three digits, then up to three digits for the thousands, then up to three digits for the millions. The Place Value Houses activity IA3.3 offers a straightforward approach to instruction in this system.

Give students opportunities to read and write numerals in realistic contexts. Newspapers are a bountiful source of meaningful numerals. Old financial records and forms can be surprisingly engaging for young students. Reference books on topics of interest will have interesting numbers: statistics on sports, dinosaurs, social demographics, the human body. Astronomy offers many astounding large numbers. The *Guinness Book of World Records* can be a particularly enjoyable source of numbers to read and write.

When students struggle with reading and writing numerals, there can be a temptation to help by teaching formal place value. However, formal place value at this point is unnecessary, and can be counterproductive. Students can and should learn to read and write numerals initially by more rudimentary implicit syntactic rules (Gattegno, 1988; Wigley, 1997). In the *Conceptual Place Value* domain in Chapter 5, we describe instruction involving numerals in the context of quantity, and making correspondences between numerals and materials organized into ones, tens, hundreds and thousands. Instruction in conceptual place value and instruction in number words and numerals complement each other.

ASSESSMENT TASK GROUPS

List of Assessment Task Groups

A3.1: Numeral Identification
A3.2: Writing Numerals
A3.3: Number Word Sequences by 1s
A3.4: Number Word Before, Number Word After
A3.5: Number Word Sequences by 10s on the Decuple
A3.6: Number Word Sequences by 100s on the Centuple
A3.7: Number Word Sequences by 10s off the Decuple

TASK GROUP A3.1: Numeral Identification

Materials: Numeral cards with 2-digit, 3-digit, and 4-digit numerals.

What to do and say: Show the numeral cards in turn. *What number is this?* For 2-digit numerals, include teen numbers. For 3-digit and 4-digit numerals, include numbers without zeros, and numbers with all possible arrangements of zeros. A sample set of 3-digit numerals is: 268, 314, 400, 520, 604, 101.

Notes:

Photo 3.3   Reading numeral cards for numeral identification

- Using numeral cards makes administering the task crisp, and easy to repeat. Writing the numerals in a list is an alternative, but display only one numeral at a time, so that the other numerals do not provide a clue.
- Some students may still read teen numbers as decuples: for example, 13 as 'thirty'.
- Identifying 12 as 20 or 21 is quite common. Also 21 is sometimes identified as 12.
- 730 may be identified as seventy-three hundred, or seven-hundred and three.
- 306 may be identified as thirty-six, or three-hundred and sixty, or three-zero-six.
- Observe hesitations and self-corrected slips, as well as outright errors. Students need to become fluent at numeral identification.
- If a student struggles with identifying 2-digit numerals, persist with posing 3-digit numerals. In some cases these will be easier to identify.
- 5-, 6- and 7-digit numerals may all be of interest too.

TASK GROUP A3.2: Writing Numerals

Materials: Paper and pen.

What to do and say: *Write the number that I say.* Pose 2-digit, 3-digit and 4-digit numbers, without and with zeros as per numeral identification task A3.1.

E.g. 6, 12, 17, 92, 517, 270, 306, 1000, 6005, 2020, 4940.

Notes:

- If students cannot write 3-digit numerals, do not ask them to write 4-digit numerals.
- 306 may be written 3006. 6005 may be written 60005.

- If possible, observe the order of students' writing closely. For teen numbers, some students write the ones-digit first. Thus when writing 17, the 7 is written before the 1 is written. For 306, the student may write a 3, leave a space, write the 6, then finally write the 0. This is likely to occur because the student is unable to visualize the numeral, prior to writing it.

TASK GROUP A3.3: Number Word Sequences by 1s

Materials: None.

What to do and say: *Count backwards from 103. I'll tell you when to stop.* Stop the student at 95. *Count forwards from 296. I'll tell you when to stop.* Stop the student at 313. Similarly, pose other forward and backward sequences across the main hurdle numbers: decuples, centuples, 1000.

Notes:

- Keep sequences short: 5 to 20 numbers. When reciting long sequences, students tend to lose rhythm and attention.
- Consider posing backward sequences first. If a student is fluent with backward sequences she is probably fluent with forward sequences in the same range, so assessing forward sequences can be omitted.
- Students might say a forward sequence subvocally, to figure out a backward sequence.
- Listen carefully for omissions, errors and awkwardness in saying any number words.

TASK GROUP A3.4: Number Word Before, Number Word After

Materials: None.

What to do and say: *Say the number that comes just before 20.*

Similarly, the number before: 30, 55, 81, 100, 170, 201, 300, 1000, 1100, 2000.

Say the number that comes just after 39. Similarly, the number after: 50, 89, 144, 109, 1000, 359, 610, 999.

Notes:

- Number word before and after tasks require handling the hurdle points in the number word sequence without overtly saying a sequence. Students might say a forward sequence subvocally, to figure out the number word before a particular number word.

- Students might attempt to visualize a numeral sequence in order to solve some of these tasks.
- Students may confuse number word after with number word before. A hand gesture may help, indicating a jump to the right for number after, or to the left for number before.
- A variation is to present numbers on numeral cards, ask the student to read the number, and then ask for the number before or after. Students may find it easier to answer when they are able to see the numeral.

TASK GROUP A3.5: Number Word Sequences by 10s on the Decuple

Materials: None.

What to do and say: *Count backwards by 10s, starting at 140.* If this is too difficult, try forwards: *Count forwards by 10s, starting at 10.* Stop the student at 130.

Notes:

- Memorizing the sequence of decuples is important.
- Students may be much less familiar with the backwards sequence, hesitating between some numbers.
- If a student is unfamiliar with the task of 'counting by 10s', give the first three terms of the sequence to get them started.
- Students may say, going forwards, '… 80, 90, 100, 200'.

TASK GROUP A3.6: Number Word Sequences by 100s on the Centuple

Materials: None.

What to do and say: *Count by 100s, please.* Stop the student at 1400.

If this is an unfamiliar task, give the beginning of the sequence: *100, 200, 300.*

Notes:

- The sequence to 900 is usually very easy, even for students unfamiliar with counting by hundreds.
- The terms beyond 900 are of interest. Students may not know what comes after 900, or after 1000. Students may say '… 900, ten hundred, eleven hundred, twelve hundred'; '900, ten hundred … oh, one thousand'; '900, 1000, 2000'.

TASK GROUP A3.7: Number Word Sequences by 10s off the Decuple

Materials: None.

What to do and say: *Count by 10s, starting from 24.* Stop the student at 124. Similarly with other sequences off the decuple in the range to 1000, forward and backward.

Notes:

- Students may be unfamiliar with these sequences, and not know how to proceed.
- Students may make ten counts by ones to find each term. Watch closely for finger, lip or head movements.
- Students may count to find the first terms of the sequence, then recognize the pattern, and continue the sequence without counting by ones.

 INSTRUCTIONAL ACTIVITIES

List of Instructional Activities

IA3.1: Arrow Cards Draw for Numeral Identification
IA3.2: I Read, You Write, We Check, We Build
IA3.3: Place Value Houses
IA3.4: Choral Chanting
IA3.5: What Comes After Nine?
IA3.6: Disappearing Sequences
IA3.7: Bare Numeral Roll
IA3.8: Numeral Roll with Window or Multi-lid Screen
IA3.9: Numeral Grid Sequences
IA3.10: Numeral Ladder
IA3.11: The Four Kings Game
IA3.12: Lovely Lucy

ACTIVITY IA3.1: Arrow Cards Draw for Numeral Identification

Intended learning: To identify numerals.

Instructional mode: Shorter, rehearsal mode for partners.

Materials: One set of arrow cards for each group.

Description: Place all tens and ones arrow cards numerals face-down on the table top. Each student draws one of each colour arrow card: a tens card and a ones card. Students build the number with the arrow cards. Each student reads his or her number. Students 'expand' the arrow cards to verify the numeral identification.

Responses, variations and extensions:

- This task is designed to build facility with numeral identification. If needed, this activity may be combined with building the number with base-ten materials for additional scaffolding.
- Repeat activity with hundreds, tens and ones arrow cards.
- Repeat activity with thousands, hundreds, tens and ones arrow cards.
- This activity builds capacity for expressing numbers in expanded notation. Students may literally place a plus symbol between the arrow cards to form the expanded form of the number. Use the term 'expand' with students intentionally to facilitate this connection.
- Activity may be done without the zero place holder arrow cards (0, 00, 000, 0000).
- Students tend to struggle with reading numerals with zero place holders, numerals with teen numbers, and the left–right orientation for tens and ones.

ACTIVITY IA3.2: I Read, You Write, We Check, We Build

Intended learning: To build facility with reading and writing numerals.

Instructional mode: Shorter, rehearsal mode for pairs.

Materials: Numeral cards, arrow cards, paper and pencil.

Description: Students work in pairs. The first student draws a numeral from a collection of numeral cards. That student reads the numeral without the partner seeing the numeral. The other student then writes the numeral on paper. The partners then compare the numerals to check and then build the numeral from arrow cards to further confirm their reading of the numeral. Partners then exchange roles for another numeral.

Responses, variations and extensions:

- This activity may be done with 2-digit, 3-digit, 4-digit numerals, or a mixture of 2- to 4-digit numerals.
- The activity may be extended beyond 4-digits by eliminating the last step in the process (i.e., building the numeral with arrow cards). Rather the students would use digit cards to build the numeral on the place value houses graphic organizer (Figure 3.3) to confirm the reading of each period.
- A link to conceptual place value can be made by having the other student build the number with base-ten materials.

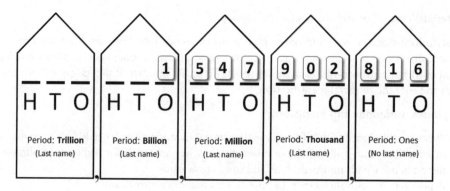

Figure 3.3   Place value houses graphic organizer

ACTIVITY IA3.3: Place Value Houses

Intended learning: To build facility with reading large numerals.

Instructional mode: Shorter, inquiry mode to rehearsal mode for individuals or whole class.

Materials: Place value houses graphic organizer, digit cards (15 copies of each digit).

Description: The place value houses graphic provides students with a simple organizer for developing the knowledge of how large numerals are read. The graphic consists of several 'houses', each representing each period, with three line segments functioning as place holders for the ones, tens, and hundreds of each period. The teaching procedure involves displaying the place value houses graphic and saying, *Today we are going to learn an easy method to read large numerals. This* [indicating the graphic with digit cards on each place] *is called the place value houses graphic organizer. This graphic is used to help us learn how to read numerals with more than three digits. The houses on this graphic represent each period of a number. To read a large number, read the three-digit number within each house and then say the house's last name. Start with the left-most house and read each house left to right.*

Responses, variations and extensions:

- This activity is appropriate only after students can read three-digit numerals with facility.
- There is an American version of this graphic that has a comma separating each period. Students can be told to say the name of the period each time they reach the comma.

ACTIVITY IA3.4: Choral Chanting

Intended learning: To build facility with number word sequences.

Instructional mode: Shorter, rehearsal mode for individuals, pairs or whole class.

Materials: None.

Description: The purpose of this activity is to build facility with different number word sequences. Students chant the sequence to a rhythm or cadence.

Responses, variations and extensions:

- One variation is to display the sequence as it is chanted.
- A PowerPoint slide show can be used to illustrate the sequence as it is chanted.
- Students may also do a round robin chant in which they take turns saying each number in the sequence.
- Teachers should monitor student participation carefully.

ACTIVITY IA3.5: What Comes After Nine?

Intended learning: To build facility with hurdling the decuple, centuple and thousands milestones in the forward number word sequence by 1s.

Instructional mode: Shorter rehearsal mode for individuals, small groups or whole class.

Materials: None.

Description: This oral activity is designed to focus instruction on the numbers that come right after any number ending with a 9 in the ones place. The leader asks, *What comes after 9? What comes after 39? What comes after 99? What comes after 129? What comes after 249? What comes after 999?*

Responses, variations and extensions:

- Typically, older students are facile in producing the forward number word sequence within a decade, but struggle crossing decuple, centuple and thousands numbers.
- The range of numbers can be limited to accommodate students' emerging knowledge of forward number word sequences.
- A variation would be to focus on backward number word sequences by asking, *What comes right before 10? What comes right before 40? What comes right before 100? What comes right before 290? What comes right before 1000?*

ACTIVITY IA3.6: Disappearing Sequences

Intended learning: To build facility with any forward or backward number word sequence.

Instructional mode: Shorter, rehearsal mode for individuals, partners or whole group.

Materials: Scrap paper and pencil or white board and marker.

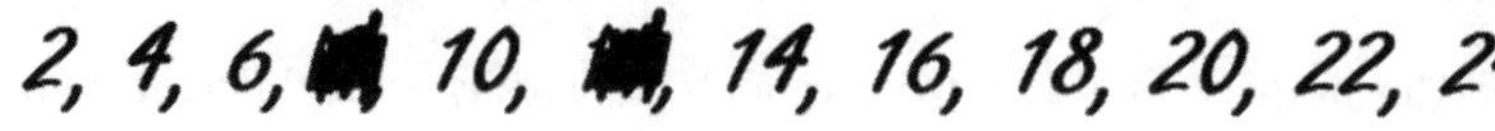

2, 4, 6, ▮ 10, ▮, 14, 16, 18, 20, 22, 24

Figure 3.4 A disappearing sequence for multiples of two

Description: This activity is a means of automatizing any number sequence. On a piece of paper or a white board, write out the first twelve terms in the desired sequence in order in a straight line, left to right. Make sure that the sequence is accurate. For example, if working on the multiples of three, students would write: 3, 6, 9, 12, 15, 18, 21, 24, 27, 30, 33, 36. Have the students recite the sequence as you touch each numeral until they can say the sequence with facility. After students have recited the sequence several times, ask for a volunteer to select a number to be covered. Cover the numeral with a sticky note, or scratch it out, such that it cannot be read but its place in the sequence is still marked (see Figure 3.4). Have students recite the sequence again as you point to each numeral, including the covered number. This facilitates students visualizing the sequence. Continue to ask for volunteers to select a term to be covered and then have the whole group recite the full sequence. That is, have students recite the full 'disappearing' sequence each time a numeral is removed. Repeat the process until all twelve numerals have 'disappeared'. Recite one final time, touching the spots in which each numeral used to be.

Responses, variations and extensions:

- This activity is designed to build facility with any number word sequence, forward or backward, by 1s, 10s or other multiples. For example, by tens off the decuple – 4, 14, 24, 34 …; or by threes – 3, 6, 9, 12 ….
- It is critically important to make sure students begin with a correct sequence.
- Before students begin reciting the sequence, the teacher might have students use the constant function of the calculator to check their sequence. For most calculators used at the primary level, the = sign can function as a constant key. For example, students would press the following sequence of keys to check for the sequence of multiples of 3: <0> ,<+>, <3>, <=>, <=>, <=>, <=>, <=>, <=>, <=>, <=>, <=>, <=>, <=>, <=>
- A variation is to have students write the sequence on both sides of their paper. One side is used for the disappearing sequence. The other side can be used to check if a student gets stuck on producing the sequence.
- Another variation is to use numeral tracks. Rather than scratching out the term, a lid is closed. In this fashion, students may easily check to verify that their sequence is correct.

ACTIVITY IA3.7: Bare Numeral Roll

Intended learning: To build facility with forward and backward number word sequences.

Instructional mode: Shorter, inquiry mode for individuals or small groups.

Materials: Numeral roll (see Appendix).

Description: This activity is typically used when initially introducing the numeral roll as an instructional setting. Ask questions to guide the students' examination of the setting. *This is called a numeral roll. What do you notice about this? What patterns do you see? Tell me what you notice about the colours. These numbers are called the ones* (gesturing to first decade). *These numbers are called the teens* (gesturing to the teen numbers). *These numbers are called the twenties* (slide roll to reveal the twenties). *Someone has called these groups of numbers families: the teens family, the twenties family. What do you think people might call the next family? Which family do you think will come after the sixties family? Which family do you think will come before the nineties family?*

ACTIVITY IA3.8: Numeral Roll with Window or Multi-lid Screen

Intended learning: To build facility with forward and backward number word sequences.

Instructional mode: Shorter, rehearsal mode for individuals or small groups.

Materials: Numeral roll for selected sequence, and multi-lid screen or numeral roll window (see Appendix).

Description: The teaching procedure involves: (1) presenting the numeral roll without any screens and having the student(s) identify patterns, say the numbers in a section of the sequence while pointing to each numeral as the corresponding number is said; (2) positioning the multi-lid screen over the section of the roll of interest and opening each lid in order to reveal each numeral in the sequence as the student says each number (see then say); (3) closing each lid after the number is stated; (4) pointing to the lid to prompt for the number and then opening the lid to confirm the response (say then see); (5) selecting any lid on the track to open and then asking the student to supply either the number just before, just after, two after, or two before the revealed numeral.

Responses, variations and extensions:

- Sequences by 1s, 10s, 100s; 5s, 2s, 3s, 4s all work well with the numeral roll and multi-lid screen. Sequences might begin with any number.
- This device can be used in a similar manner as the numeral track (Wright et al., 2006c). The advantage of the numeral roll is that it easily accommodates longer sequences.
- The numeral roll may also be used with a single-window screen with which the teacher can isolate a section of the

Photo 3.4 Using the numeral roll with a window

roll while revealing a single numeral. This is particularly useful with focusing solely on the number immediately before or immediately after a given number.

- Students typically struggle with hurdling the decuple and centuple.
- Students frequently reveal a lack of knowledge of the patterns of the system of number names.
- Examples of common student difficulties are given in Tables 3.1, 3.2 and 3.3.

ACTIVITY IA3.9: Numeral Grid Sequences

Intended learning: To build facility with forward and backward number word sequences.

Instructional mode: Shorter, rehearsal mode for individuals.

Materials: Numeral grid with blank grid on the reverse, 1 red translucent chip, 1 green translucent chip.

Description: This activity allows the student to rehearse a relatively short sequence of numbers (typically ten or less terms) with an intentional fade of scaffolding. The activity is designed to do all the steps in one session in order to promote visualization. Follow the steps below.

1. Place the green and red chips respectively on the first and last numeral in the sequence (see Figure 3.5).

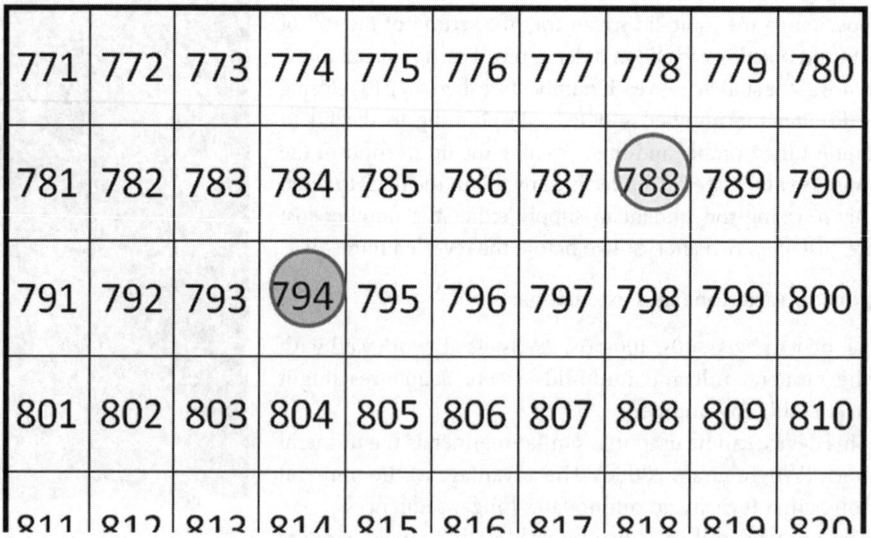

771	772	773	774	775	776	777	778	779	780
781	782	783	784	785	786	787	788	789	790
791	792	793	794	795	796	797	798	799	800
801	802	803	804	805	806	807	808	809	810
811	812	813	814	815	816	817	818	819	820

Figure 3.5 A numeral grid with chips marking beginning and ending of sequence

2. The student begins with the number covered by the green chip and says each number in the sequence while touching the numeral on the grid. The student stops upon reaching the red chip.
3. The student repeats step 2 until he or she can say the sequence smoothly.
4. Turn the grid over to the 'blank' side. Place the chips in the squares that would correspond with the first and last numbers of the sequence if the numerals were visible on the blank grid.
5. The student says the sequence and points to the empty squares. The structure of the grid will provide a scaffold for students in that the student quickly realizes that the square at the right margin of the grid will be a decuple number. If a student makes a mistake, the structure will prompt the student to correct the mistake without the teacher needing to intervene.
6. Once the student can say the sequence while touching the blank side, the grid is removed completely from sight. The student is then prompted to think about the grid and point to the tabletop while repeating the sequence. If the student struggles, the grid can be resupplied in order for the student to check.
7. Finally, the student is asked to close his or her eyes to say the sequence.

ACTIVITY IA3.10: Numeral Ladder

Intended learning: To build facility with forward and backward written number sequences.

Instructional mode: Longer, rehearsal mode for individuals or small groups.

Materials: Paper, or a printed numeral ladder, and a pen or pencil.

Description: A numeral ladder is a simple graphic organizer consisting of two long vertical lines crossed with horizontal rungs (see Figure 3.6). The teacher can prepare the activity using printed

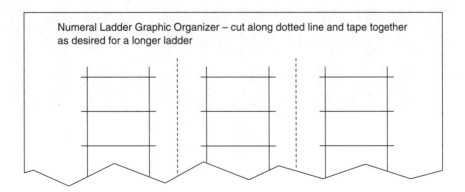

Figure 3.6   Blank numeral ladders

numeral ladders. Alternatively, ladders can be drawn easily on a white board or by students in their workbooks. Write a numeral on the bottom rung of a ladder. The students' task is to continue the sequence forwards, writing a numeral on each rung of the ladder. Alternatively, write a numeral on the top rung, for students to continue the sequence backwards.

Responses, variations and extensions:

- Sequences by 1s in higher centuries and millennia work well with numeral ladders.
- Additional scaffolding can be provided by initially supplying more numerals periodically along the ladder.
- A variation is to draw the ladder on the white board. A small group of students, each with a different colour of marker, take turns writing numerals to continue the sequence.

ACTIVITY IA3.11: The Four Kings Game

Intended learning: To build facility with number word sequences. To sequence numerals.

Instructional mode: Longer, rehearsal mode for individuals or partners.

Materials: One deck of Four Kings cards.

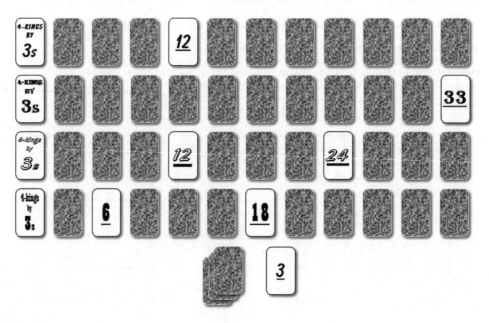

Figure 3.7   A Four Kings game underway, using a sequence of 3s

Description: The Four Kings deck contains four sets of a number sequence of about ten terms, each set in a different font. A font card heads each of the four rows. All but four cards are dealt in four equal rows, with cards face down (see Figure 3.7). Each row should be one less in length that the number of terms in the sequence. The four cards not dealt constitute the draw pile. The last number in the sequence constitutes the 'stopper'. The object of the game is to correctly sequence each card in its matching font row before uncovering the fourth stopper. Play begins with the player drawing the top card on the draw pile. The player matches that card to the appropriate font row and then in the appropriate spot for that term in the sequence. The player replaces the face-down card in that spot with the 'draw' card in its proper place in the sequence face up. The card replaced in the row then becomes the card to be placed. If the card is the last card in the sequence (the stopper), it is placed on the bottom of the draw pile face-up. A new card is drawn from the draw pile and play continues until all cards are in their proper sequence or all four stoppers have been uncovered.

Responses, variations and extensions:

- This task is designed to give players repeated practice saying a relatively short sequence of numbers. Students can think about the number that comes before or after a visible number in order to place each numeral card.
- If a student makes a mistake in placing the card, the mistake will likely be corrected during a future turn as the student attempts to place other numerals.
- Four copies of any sequence of numbers, each in a distinctive font or color, can constitute a deck. See CD reference for the Four Kings deck sample and template. Simply substitute the terms in the desired sequence for the numerals 1–12 as they appear in the template.
- This activity works well with sequences of multiples and sequences students use to increment. For example, by tens on and off the decuple and by hundreds on and off the centuple.
- If a student consistently omits a number from a sequence, have that number function as the 'stopper' in the game.
- An enrichment activity is to allow students to modify the template to create their own new deck.

ACTIVITY IA3.12: Lovely Lucy

Intended learning: To build facility with forward and backward number word sequences. To sequence numerals.

Instructional mode: Longer, rehearsal mode for individuals or partners.

Materials: One deck of standard playing cards.

Description: Shuffle cards well. Deal all 52 cards face up in 17 overlapping triads with one single card (see Figure 3.8a). Move one card at a time. Cards may be played in a descending order by suit on another stack or in ascending order, A, 2, 3, … K, in a new stack (see Figure 3.8b). Ascending stacks are 'safe'. The goal is to move progressively all cards onto the appropriate ascending stack. Descending stack cards may be shuffled and dealt again twice in an attempt to

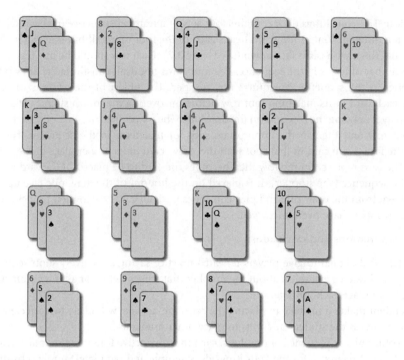

Figures 3.8a Lovely Lucy card layout

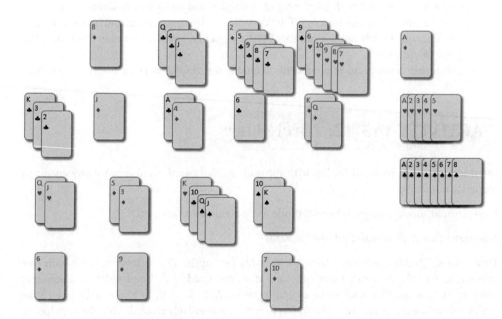

Figures 3.8b Lovely Lucy game underway

move all cards to the ascending stacks. One *merci* move is allowed during the last round. This involves extracting any card from a descending stack to play it on any stack. See Resource CD for detailed directions sheet.

Responses, variations and extensions:

- This game may be played with any Four Kings deck. For less challenge when playing with multiples decks, descending stacks need not follow suit. For greater challenge, all stacks must follow suit.
- Strategy and logic play a large part in being successful with this game.
- Partners may discuss strategy while cooperatively playing the game.
- A hint for success with the game is to begin the stack with the highest card possible, since once a card of a lower value is played in descending order, the sequence cannot be moved except to play each card individually on the ascending stack.

Reference: 'La Belle Lucie', from *The Encyclopedia of Games*, edited by Brian Burns (1998). London: Amber Books Ltd. pp. 23–27.

4

Structuring Numbers 1 to 20

DOMAIN OVERVIEW

Students' early arithmetical strategies are typically based on counting by ones. Greta, a relatively sophisticated counter, solved the task 7 + 6 by counting-on six counts from 7, '7: 8, 9, 10, 11, 12, 13' while using her fingers to keep track of the six counts. Students need to develop much more facile and knowledgeable ways of adding and subtracting small numbers. A year later, Greta solved the same task by thinking '6 and 6 is 12, and one more is 13'. This more sophisticated strategy does not involve counting by ones. Rather, it involves partitioning 7 into 6-and-1, reorganizing 6 + 7 as 6 + 6 + 1, and knowing the combination 6 + 6 without calculation. We refer to this kind of thinking as *structuring numbers*: giving numbers more structure by seeing numbers as constructed of smaller parts, by organizing numbers to make them easier to work with, and by recognizing common combinations (Ellemor-Collins and Wright, 2009b). It is critical that students' early arithmetical thinking progresses from being based on counting by ones to being based on structuring numbers (Bobis, 1996; Fuson, 1992; Steffe and Cobb, 1988; Wright, 1994; Young-Loveridge, 2002).

Facility with Addition and Subtraction in the Range 1 to 20

As another example of facile calculation based on structuring numbers, Harry explained his approach to 7 + 6 as: '7 and 3 is 10, and there's 3 left, which makes 13'. Greta's approach can be labelled a *near-doubles* strategy, Harry's an *adding-through-ten* strategy. Unpacking non-counting strategies like Greta's and Harry's, can help us appreciate the arithmetic knowledge students need to acquire. We identify three aspects of facile calculation: (a) knowledge of key number combinations and partitions; (b) a part–whole constructions of number; and (c) relational thinking (Ellemor-Collins and Wright, 2009b).

(a) Knowledge of Key Number Combinations and Partitions

The student has some useful combinations and partitions as known facts, requiring no calculation, such as 6 + 6 is 12, 10 + 3 is 13, 7 is 6 + 1, 10 is 7 + 3. There are three families of combinations commonly relied on by facile calculators (Treffers, 1991):

- the doubles and halves $(2 = 1 + 1, 4 = 2 + 2, \ldots)$
- the combinations with 5 $(6 = 5 + 1, 7 = 5 + 2 \ldots)$ and with 10 $(11 = 10 + 1, 12 = 10 + 2 \ldots)$
- the partitions of 5 $(1 + 4, 2 + 3)$ and of 10 $(1 + 9, 2 + 8, 3 + 7, 4 + 6, 5 + 5)$.

(b) Part–Whole Constructions of Number

Harry takes for granted that adding 3, and another 3, amounts to adding 6. We might say that, for him, the composition of 3-and-3 as 6 is transparent. Similarly, Greta is happy to drop 1 off the 7, and add it back on later: she is sure that, in the end, she has included 7 in her total. These students have developed a part–whole construction of number: for them, a number can be composed of smaller numbers, and the parts and whole can be conceived of simultaneously. When a student relies on counting by ones, she does not operate with numbers in this way. For such a student, the sum of 3 and 3 is found by counting, and once 6 is arrived at, there is no way to see the two threes there 'in the six': the threes are lost in the act of counting, as it were. Similarly, 7 would be established by making seven consecutive counts: adding six and then one more later on would not amount to 7 for such a student (Resnick, 1983; Young-Loveridge, 2002).

(c) Relational Thinking

The student sees relationships between numbers and other numbers, and reasons in terms of number relationships. Greta probably began solving $7 + 6$ by noticing that it is close to $6 + 6$. She was also able to reason that her answer is one more than 12, perhaps by thinking 'bring one from the 7' or 'compensate one less there with one more here'. When Harry saw $7 + 6$, he may have associated 7 with 3 – as the familiar partition of ten – and noticed he also associates 6 with 3 – as the double – and before he knew it, he was solving the task. We call this type of noticing and reasoning *relational thinking*. Of course, it is difficult to know what Greta or Harry noticed, because such thinking can be so quick and implicit. Relational thinking can be more conspicuous in its absence. Isabel, having just rehearsed her knowledge that double 6 is 12, was posed $7 + 6$, and still used a counting strategy. She seemed to see $7 + 6$ as an instruction to carry out a counting procedure, rather than as numbers that can be related to other numbers and reorganized to suit her calculations. Research into facile mental calculation suggests that relational thinking is critical (McIntosh et al., 1992; Threlfall, 2002).

Thus, facile calculators structure numbers. They work in the range 1 to 20 as if it were a familiar neighbourhood, recognizing a richly organized network of number combinations, partitions and relationships (Greeno, 1991). They know a lot about the numbers: 7 is close to 6, less than 10, not an even double, it equals 5 and 2, $3 + 3 + 1$, 10 less 3, half of 14. For facile calculators, adding and subtracting in the range 1 to 20 is mostly about structuring numbers in terms of this network of arithmetic knowledge: $6 + 3$ is solved as one less than $6 + 4 = 10$, or it is three 3s; $8 + 9$ is solved as $8 + 8 + 1$, or $10 + 8 - 1$; $13 - 5$ is solved as $13 - 3 - 2$, or $(10 + 3) - 5 \rightarrow (10 - 5) + 3 \rightarrow 5 + 3 \rightarrow 8$; $17 - 15$ is solved knowing that 5 and 2 makes 7. Ultimately, most additions and subtractions in the range 1 to 20 become memorized or automatized.

Significance of Structuring Numbers 1 to 20

Learning to structure numbers 1 to 20 is significant for students. Students who can structure numbers experience the great satisfaction of mastering a real adult skill – addition and subtraction in the range 1 to 20. Also, there is a lot more fun and fascination to discover in numbers once you can structure them. Furthermore, the most commonly observed characteristic of low-attaining mathematics students is a persistent dependence on counting by ones. When students do not structure numbers, it seems that they cannot progress. It is worth considering why (Denvir and Brown, 1986; Gray, 1991; Wright et al., 2007).

(a) Knowledge of Key Number Combinations and Partitions

Facility with number bonds in the range 1–20 becomes important for calculations beyond 20. This is part of what we imply when we call them 'the basic facts'. For example, solving a two-digit sum such as 37 + 16 using a non-counting strategy requires subtotals calculated in the range 1–20: knowing 7 and 6, or 10 and 3, or 3 and 1. Students who cannot calculate such subtotals with speed and ease, will not succeed with multi-digit addition and subtraction (Heirdsfield, 2001; Treffers, 1991).

(b) Part–Whole Constructions of Number

The part–whole construction of numbers is a major achievement in students' early number learning. Treating numbers as made up of other numbers is a large conceptual advance on treating numbers as made from counts. Further advances in number concepts depend on the part–whole construction: a view of multi-digit numbers as made of ones, tens, hundreds, and so on; a multiplicative view of numbers as multiples of factors; a view of fractions as parts of a whole number. A student who is constrained to thinking of numbers by counting will struggle to make meaning of these more advanced number concepts (Bobis, 1996; Resnick, 1983; Young-Loveridge, 2002).

(c) Relational Thinking

The importance of relational thinking is less often recognized. A mathematics programme that does not demand relational thinking can be teased along for a while – memorize the basic facts, train up the four written algorithms, don't test any task that hasn't been practised beforehand. But at some point, the students will confront a novel problem, or be unable to recall a basic fact, or begin work on algebra in earnest, and their underdeveloped relational thinking will fail them. Students' arithmetic learning, including proficient number sense, flexible mental computation, and the ability to apply mathematics in novel contexts, requires the development of relational thinking (McIntosh et al., 1992; Threlfall, 2002).

Some students appear prone to procedural thinking rather than relational thinking with numbers (Gray and Tall, 1994). It is important to assert that students can learn relational thinking, they can develop strong knowledge of structuring numbers. The instruction they receive makes a significant difference in their learning (Ellemor-Collins and Wright, 2009b). Some knowledge of structuring numbers may be established early for students, such as subitizing small numbers, knowing some doubles, and making combinations with five in finger patterns. Our experience suggests, however, that some students do not develop or use knowledge of these structures without dedicated instruction. Hence we see structuring numbers as a key instructional topic for developing arithmetic knowledge.

Assessment of Structuring Numbers 1 to 20

We can assess students' knowledge of structuring numbers 1 to 20 by considering the three aspects of facile calculation identified above, and observing the students' strategies for solving additive tasks. The section of Assessment Task Groups describes appropriate tasks.

- **Knowledge of key number combinations and partitions**
  Which key number bonds has the student automatized: small doubles, big doubles, combinations with 5, combinations with 10, partitions of 10?
- **Part–whole construction of number**
  Is the student constrained to making numbers by counting, or can she spontaneously partition a number into parts, and treat parts as transparently equivalent to the whole?
- **Relational thinking**
  Are the student's strategies restricted to rehearsed procedures, or is there evidence of solving tasks by noticing or making relationships between numbers? What number relationships does he notice and make?
- **Additive strategies**
  Does the student rely on counting strategies? If not, what non-counting strategies are used?

Outline of Instruction in Structuring Numbers 1 to 20

The approach to instruction in structuring numbers builds on the work of Treffers (1991, 2001), Gravemeijer (1994b), Gravemeijer et al. (2000) and Wright et al. (2006b, 2006c). Instruction in structuring numbers seeks to cultivate the three aspects of facile, knowledgeable calculation characterized above. Using instructional settings such as ten-frames and the arithmetic rack, students develop facility with number combinations and partitions. Through inquiry and discussion, the teacher draws attention to part–whole constructions, working with numbers as parts of other numbers, and to relational thinking, making relationships between numbers. The instructional settings enable students to reason arithmetically in ways that transcend counting by ones, and thereby develop facility with structuring numbers. As facility develops, the students are weaned off the settings, towards solving verbal and written tasks (Ellemor-Collins and Wright, 2009b).

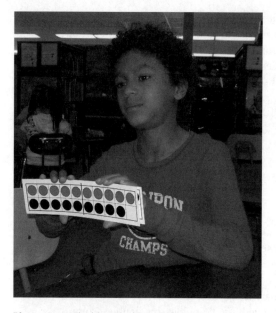

Photo 4.1 Flashing double ten-frames

Instruction is organized broadly into two ranges: structuring 1 to 10 with ten-frames, then structuring 1 to 20 with the arithmetic rack (see the Appendix for descriptions of these instructional settings). These are not discrete phases of instruction, but teachers have found it helpful to think in terms of these two ranges, and to focus on establishing a student's facility with 1–10 before moving the focus to 1–20. Within these ranges, instruction is organized around subsets of number combinations, beginning with an emphasis on the key double, 5 and 10 combinations. The subsets provide a focus for instruction, and support students' practice towards automaticity. As facility develops, instruction involves larger and larger sets of combinations, building towards the aim of students working in the whole range 1 to 20 as a richly organized network of number combinations, partitions and relationships.

Instruction in Structuring Numbers 1 to 10 Using Ten-frames

Instruction in structuring numbers 1 to 10 should begin in preschool and the early years of school. Students work with finger patterns, and five-frame and ten-frame settings, to make and read patterns for numbers up to ten, show eight fingers in different ways, find 4 + 3 without counting by ones using finger patterns, and so on. Some 7–11-year-olds need further work on structuring numbers 1 to 10. Instruction progresses through three subsets of combinations, with increasing complexity of structuring. Ten-frame cards are a useful setting for this learning.

Progressing through Three Subsets of Combinations

1. Patterns for Numbers 1 to 10

Students begin with work on identifying each card of a regular set of ten-frame cards: *How many dots?* These tasks build knowledge of two families of key number bonds: the combinations with 5 (5 + 1, 5 + 2 … 5 + 5) from the five-wise patterns (see Figure 4.1a), and the doubles combinations (1 + 1, 2 + 2 … 5 + 5) from the pair-wise patterns (see Figure 4.1b). Working with these subsets of cards separately at first can facilitate establishing the pattern recognition. As students consolidate facility, the task can be extended to *How many dots? And how many more to make ten?*

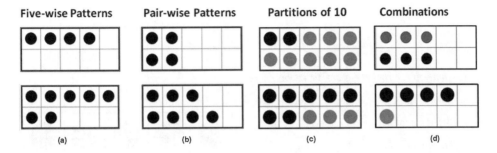

Five-wise Patterns	Pair-wise Patterns	Partitions of 10	Combinations
(a)	(b)	(c)	(d)

Figure 4.1   Examples of ten-frames: five-wise patterns, pair-wise patterns, partitions of 10, combinations

2. Partitions of 10

Introduce the set of partitions of 10 ten-frames (see Figure 4.1c) to work explicitly on a third family of key number bonds: the partitions of ten (10 + 0, 9 + 1, 8 + 2, 7 + 3, 6 + 4, 5 + 5). *How many dark dots? How many light dots?*

3. Combinations in the Range 1 to 10

Introduce the set of combination ten-frames (see Figure 4.1d) to present small combinations, 0–5 light dots combined with 0–5 dark dots. *How many light? How many dark? How many altogether?* This task can be extended with the question … *And how many more to make ten?*, forming a quartet of questions for each card that makes for a rigorous and productive work-out on structuring numbers 1 to 10. These cards can also be viewed as partitions of numbers up to ten, which could be emphasized with a shift in the questions: *How many dots (altogether)? … Made of (what two parts)?*

Photo 4.2 Organizing partitions ten-frames

Progressing from Ten-frames to Mental and Written Tasks

Do not address these three subsets as detached topics. Rather, as the first is being consolidated, introduce the second; and as the second is being consolidated, introduce the third. With each new set of ten-frame cards, begin in inquiry mode. Students may benefit from an opportunity to make the patterns themselves, using counters in an empty frame. Students could arrange the set of cards in an order, and describe relations between the cards: *How does the 7 card relate to the 8 card; the five-wise 8 to the pair-wise 8; the 8 to the 2?* Screen or flash each card, to strengthen visualizing of the pattern. Thus encourage students to structure the patterns into partitions (see Box 4.1). Initially, some students apparently will need to count dots by ones but ultimately students should be encouraged to reason without counting by ones.

BOX 4.1   INSTRUCTIONAL INQUIRY ENCOURAGING STRUCTURING

How did you see that there are eight dots there?

– There's 5 in that row, and 3 in that row, and 5 and 3 is eight.

Yes. What's another way to see eight there?

– We could count 1, 2, 3...

Yes, but how can we do it without counting?

– Um. There's six, and two more.

Yes. How did you see that group as six?

– Three and three.

OK. Another way to see the eight?

– Um. There's, um, two missing from the whole ten.

Nice. Another way to see the eight? ...

Work towards automatization with rehearsal mode activities. Work through a set of ten-frame cards as flash cards daily. After each flash and answer, showing the card again allows students to self-check. Continue to pause occasionally to inquire about students' structuring of the dot patterns. As the students master the partitions of 10 and combination sets, the cards can be put aside, and tasks can be posed verbally: *I'll say a number, you say how many more to make 10*, and *I'll say two numbers, you say the sum*. Finally, shift to presenting tasks as written expressions using the + and – symbols. A set of expression cards showing all the expressions with sums up to 10 works well. Students can write their own expressions too. Working with subsets of the sums gives focus to instruction, and can support students' structuring efforts: the doubles and near-doubles; the partitions of 9; sums involving 6, 7 or 8.

Instruction in Structuring Numbers 1 to 20 Using the Arithmetic Rack

When students have facility with structuring numbers 1 to 10, they are ready to extend this to the range 1 to 20. The arithmetic rack is a useful instructional setting. The double ten-frame is an alternative to the arithmetic rack. Instruction progresses through three main phases:

1. making and reading numbers 1 to 20
2. adding two numbers in the range 1–10
3. adding and subtracting in the range 1–20.

Instruction Phase 1: Making and Reading Numbers 1 to 20

The arithmetic rack has standard patterns for the numbers 1 to 20. The patterns are described below, and illustrated in Figure 4.2.

- **Ten-wise**
  Make patterns by filling the upper row then the lower row. Numbers 1–10 have all beads on the top row. Numbers 11–20 have ten on the upper, and the remainder on the lower row.
- **Five-wise**
  Make patterns by filling upper five, lower five, second upper five, second lower five. For numbers 1–5 and 15–20 the five-wise pattern is the same as the ten-wise pattern. For numbers 9, 10, 11, the five-wise pattern is the same as the pair-wise pattern. So only 6, 7, 8 and 12, 13, 14 have three standard patterns altogether. In the five-wise pattern for 10–15, the ten dark beads can be seen as a block of ten.
- **Pair-wise**
  Make patterns by adding beads alternately from upper and lower rows. An even number has half the beads on one row, half on the other – a *double*. An odd number has one more bead on one row than the other – a *near-double*.

Students need to learn the standard patterns for the numbers. Learning these patterns builds experience with some useful combinations and this learning is a prerequisite for solving other additions and subtractions in the arithmetic rack setting. Introductory tasks involve copying the standard patterns made by the teacher. Instruction then mostly involves rehearsal of two skills: (a) making the pattern for any number called; and (b) reading the number of any pattern flashed. For making, the teacher calls a number, and the students are to make a pattern of beads. The goal is for students to make the numbers in one or two quick movements, rather than moving

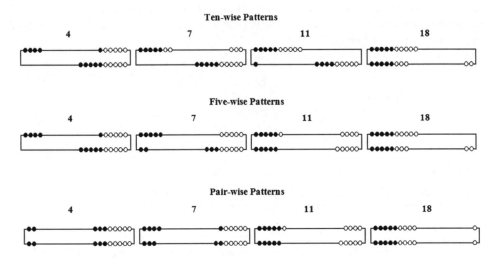

Figure 4.2 Examples of standard patterns on the arithmetic rack

beads one at a time. For reading, the teacher screens the rack while making a pattern, then flashes (briefly displays) the pattern, and the students are to say the number displayed on the rack. Initially, work separately on the three families of patterns: ten-wise patterns, five-wise patterns and pair-wise patterns. Later, these can be done together *Make 11. Now make 11 another way.*

Instruction Phase 2: Adding Two Numbers in the Range 1 to 10

Phase 2 involves posing additive tasks with both addends in the range 1 to 10. When initially using the arithmetic rack with such tasks, both addends can be made on the rack. Make the first addend on the upper row and the second addend on the lower row. *How many altogether?* Allow for flexibility in the way students calculate rather than imposing a strict procedure to follow. Students learn that sometimes it is helpful to exchange beads on the upper row for an equal number of beads on the lower row. In other instances they can determine the sum without the need to move any beads. In many instances there are several ways the sum can be determined – encourage students to describe a variety of ways. Tasks can be extended with *And how many more to make 20?*

There are several common ways to add two numbers in the range 1 to 10. These are often described as 'thinking strategies' or 'non-counting strategies' with names like 'doubles and near-doubles', 'adding through ten', 'compensation'. Training students in these strategies can be tempting: show the steps, ask the student to try examples, and prompt them through the same steps. Resist this temptation. Such training diverts students' attention from their own reasoning to someone else's procedure. Students need to be paying attention to numbers and number relationships, and to their own efforts to solve problems and make meaning. Showing an example strategy can help focus students' attention on number relationships they were not seeing. But training and re-prompting a set of procedural steps is unlikely to achieve the larger goal of facile addition and subtraction.

Instruction in phase 2 can progress through different subsets of sums, from smaller numbers and more familiar combinations, through to larger numbers and less familiar combinations. Subsets of sums are described in Box 4.2, and illustrated in Figure 4.3. Instruction in phase 2 also progresses from the arithmetic rack to verbal and written tasks. This progression is described further in a separate section below.

BOX 4.2   ARITHMETIC RACK: SUBSETS OF SUMS WITH ADDENDS IN THE RANGE 1 TO 10

Addends in range 1–5

Small doubles: 1 + 1 to 5 + 5

These should be straightforward, as they are equivalent to standard pair-wise patterns. For example, students can realize that 3 + 3 can also be regarded as a pattern for six.

Five-plus sums: 5 + 1, 5 + 2 ... 5 + 5

Similarly, these are equivalent to standard five-wise patterns. For example, 5 + 3 can be regarded as a pattern for eight.

Two addends in the range 1 to 5

These combinations (which include the subsets above) should also be straightforward because the students already have facility with structuring numbers in the range 1–10.

Sums with standard patterns

Big doubles: 6 + 6 to 10 + 10

These are equivalent to pair-wise patterns for 12, 14, and so on. Students can realize that 6 + 6 on the rack can be regarded as 12. Students can also transform these into alternative patterns, for example 6 + 6 becomes 10 + 2.

Ten-plus sums: 10 + 1, 10 + 2 ... 10 + 10

These are equivalent to ten-wise patterns for 11 to 20. A pattern can be regarded alternatively as 10 + 6 and as 16.

Larger five-plus sums: 5 + 6, 5 + 7 ... 5 + 10

These are equivalent to the five-wise patterns for 11 to 15. The pattern for 5 + 8 can be seen as 10 dark beads and 3 light beads, and so be regarded as 13. Students can also transform these, for example 5 + 6 becomes 10 + 1; 5 + 7 becomes 10 + 2.

Other sums

Partitions of ten: 9 + 1, 8 + 2, 7 + 3, 6 + 4, 5 + 5

The partitions of ten should be familiar from students working in the range 1–10. They present slightly differently on the arithmetic rack than in a ten-frame. Students can also transform these, for example 6 + 4 becomes 5 + 5; 8 + 2 becomes 10.

One addend in the range 6 to 9 and one addend in the range 1 to 4

Additions of this kind can be solved by transformations such as the following:

6 + 1 → 7	(swap one bead)	8 + 1 → 9	(swap one bead)
6 + 3 → 5 + 4	(swap one bead)	8 + 4 → 10 + 2	(swap two beads)
7 + 2 → 9	(swap two beads)	9 + 2 → 10 + 1	(swap one bead)
7 + 4 → 5 + 5 + 1	(swap one bead)	9 + 3 → 10 + 2	(swap one bead)

Two different addends in the range 6 to 9

Additions of this kind can be solved by transformations such as the following:

6 + 7 → 5 + 5 + 3	(swap one bead)	7 + 8 → 5 + 10	(swap two beads)
6 + 8 → 5 + 5 + 4	(swap one bead)	7 + 9 → 6 + 10	(swap one bead)
or → 7 + 7	(swap one bead)	or → 8 + 8	(swap one bead)
6 + 9 → 5 + 10	(swap one bead)	8 + 9 → 7 + 10	(swap one bead)

Instruction Phase 3: Adding and Subtracting in the Range 1 to 20

Phase 3 develops facility with the full variety of additive and subtractive tasks. Students need to solve problems presented in different forms, such as combining, partitioning, taking away,

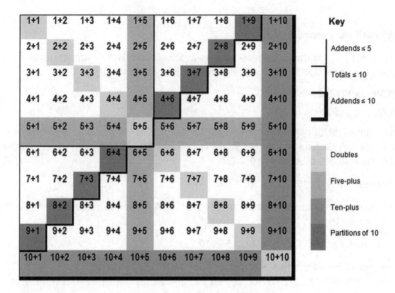

Figure 4.3   Table of additions marking subsets of sums

finding a difference, finding a missing addend and finding a missing subtrahend (see Box 4.3). As with phase 2, allow for flexibility in the way students calculate, and pay attention to their efforts to structure the numbers. Instruction progresses from using the arithmetic rack through to formal written tasks – see the section below.

BOX 4.3   ARITHMETIC RACK: A VARIETY OF TASK TYPES IN THE RANGE 1 TO 20

In all task types here, the task needs to be posed verbally or in horizontal written format, alongside the presentation on the arithmetic rack. When checking or discussing an answer, it can help to slightly separate the beads corresponding to the partition in the task, so that each part, as well as the whole, can be readily visualized.

Addition with one addend >10

E.g. 12 + 5, 13 + 3, 18 + 2. Present the large addend only on the rack. Pose the task: *What is five more?*, *What is 12 plus five?*, *12 + 5.*

Missing addend

E.g. 12 + ? = 17, 8 + ? = 15, 18 + ? = 20. Present the first addend only on the rack. Pose the task: *How many more to make 17?*, *12 plus what equals 17?*, *12 + ? = 17.*

Taking away

E.g. 17 take away 5, 12 remove 9, 14 less 7. Present the minuend only on the rack. Pose the question: *What is five less?, What is 17 take away five?, 17 –5*.

Missing subtrahend

E.g. 17 – ? = 12, 12 – ? = 3, 14 – ? = 7. Present the minuend only on the rack. Pose the question: *How many less to make 12?, 17 take away what is 12?, 17 – ?= 12*.

Finding a difference

Any subtractive task can be interpreted as a problem of finding a difference. Difference questions can also be posed explicitly. Present one of the numbers on the rack and ask *What is the difference between 12 and 17?*

Partitions

Any subtractive task can be interpreted as a problem of finding a partition. Partition questions can also be posed explicitly. Present a number on the rack and ask *What are two numbers that add to make X?, Split X into two parts*, or *What are all the sums making X?*

Students cannot persist in solving the myriad of problems as isolated tasks. Instead, they need to structure the numbers to locate each problem in their developing network of number relations. For example, 5 + 2 = ?, 12 + ? = 17, 17–15 = ?, can all be solved by structuring 7 as 5-and-2. Initially the arithmetic rack provides a setting in which students can structure the task numbers to solve the problems. The shift to more formal written tasks creates opportunities for increasing flexibility in interpreting tasks. For example, 17–2 can be interpreted as '17 take away 2', whereas 17–15 is easier when interpreted as 'what's the difference between 15 and 17?', or '7 partitions into 5 and what?'

Progressing from the Arithmetic Rack to Mental and Written Tasks

Instruction in phases 2 and 3 progresses from using the arithmetic rack to mental strategies. The main steps in the progression are:

1. Present both addends on the rack (only possible in phase 2, with addends up to 10). Students can manipulate beads to help solve the task.
2. Present the first addend or the minuend on the rack, and pose the task verbally or in writing. Students can manipulate beads to help solve the task.

Photo 4.3 Notating strategies in the context of the bead rack

3. Flash (show briefly) the first addend or the minuend on the rack, and pose the task verbally or in writing. Students attempt the task mentally. After answering, the rack is unscreened, and students use the rack to check or explain their answer.
4. Pose the task verbally or in writing, without the rack. Students attempt the task mentally. The rack can be called on occasionally for students to check or explain their answer.

Photo 4.4   Organizing expression cards

A mix of inquiry mode and rehearsal mode activities will establish students' mastery of all combinations and partitions for numbers 1 to 20 – see the section of Instructional Activities. As with any automatized skills, even after these skills are mastered, regular review helps. All students, right through ages 7 to 11 years, can benefit from an occasional run through the combinations, ten-frame cards and the expression cards for sums to 20.

ASSESSMENT TASK GROUPS

List of Assessment Task Groups

A4.1: Combinations up to 10, with Ten-frames
A4.2: Doubles
A4.3: Combinations with 10
A4.4: Partitions of 10
A4.5: Partitions of Numbers in the Range 1 to 20
A4.6: Addition and Subtraction with a Rack (addends ≤ 10)
A4.7: Addition and Subtraction with a Rack (one addend > 10)
A4.8: Bare Number Addition and Subtraction (range ≤ 10)
A4.9: Bare Number Addition and Subtraction (addends ≤ 10)
A4.10: Bare Number Addition and Subtraction (one addend > 10)

TASK GROUP A4.1: Combinations up to 10, with Ten-frames

Materials: Red-and-green ten-frame cards.

What to do and say: Flash a ten-frame card. How many red? … *How many green?* … *How many altogether?* … *And how many more to make ten?* Similarly with other cards.

Notes:

- These tasks neatly assess most aspects of structuring numbers 1 to 10.
- Students may have more success with these tasks in the ten-frame setting, than with the verbal Assessment Tasks below.

TASK GROUP A4.2: Doubles

Materials: None.

What to do and say: Ask doubles verbally. *What is five plus five? … three plus three? …* Similarly with any of 1 + 1, 2 + 2 … 9 + 9, 10 + 10.

Notes:

- Use language familiar to the student: *five plus five, double five, five and five.*
- Typically, double seven, eight and nine are the most difficult.
- Students who are not facile with a double typically will use a counting-on strategy. In this case, ask *Can you do it without counting?*

TASK GROUP A4.3: Combinations with 10

Materials: None.

What to do and say: Pose combinations with 10 verbally. *What is 10 plus four?* Similarly: 10 plus eight, 10 plus two. Also: seven plus 10, five plus 10, one plus 10.

Notes:

- Of interest is whether the student responds immediately – 'fourteen' for the first task, for example – or uses counting on.
- Students are more likely to respond immediately on the first set than on the second set.
- Knowledge of combinations with five is also particularly useful, so it can be worth assessing: 5 and 3, 5 and 4, 5 and 2, 1 and 5 and so on.

TASK GROUP A4.4: Partitions of 10

Materials: None.

What to do and say: *I'll say a number, and you say how many more to make 10. Five.* (Answer: five.) *Nine.* (Answer: one.) Continue with other numbers: 7, 2, 4 …

Notes:

- Typically, the complements of nine, eight and five are easier for students, whereas the complements of four and three are the most difficult.

- Students who are not facile with these partitions of 10 typically will use a counting-on strategy. To solve the task in the case of four, the student will count from five to 10 and use their fingers to keep track of the number of counts (six). Alternatively, a student may raise four fingers, and try to figure out how many fingers remain down.

TASK GROUP A4.5: Partitions of Numbers in the Range 1 to 20

Materials: None.

What to do and say: *Can you tell me two numbers that add up to seven? … Can you tell me another two?* Similarly, ask for partitions of other numbers, both less than 10 (partitions of 6, 5, 9) and greater than 10 (partitions of 12, 19, 15).

Notes:

- Students who are not facile in structuring numbers may take a long time to think up a partition. For example, in partitioning 19 a student may think for a long time to answer '18 and 1', or may say '15' and then take time trying to work out the complement by counting by ones. Students who are facile will quickly answer 18 and 1, or 10 and 9, and can find other partitions such as 15 and 4 without counting.

TASK GROUP A4.6: Addition and Subtraction with a Rack (addends ≤ 10)

Materials: Arithmetic rack (alternatively, double ten-frame cards, or empty double-ten frame and counters), screen, task cards written in horizontal format.

What to do and say: Pose additive tasks with both addends in the range 1–10, and corresponding subtractive tasks, such as: $6 + 5$, $9 + 6$, $8 + 7$; $6 + \_\_ = 13$, $7 + \_\_ = 14$, $9 + \_\_ = 17$; $11 - 4$, $15 - 5$, $16 - 7$. Present the first addend or minuend on the rack, as follows.

Make 6 on the rack. Flash the rack. *What number did you see?* Display task card: $6 + 5$. *Can you work this out? … How did you do it?*

Make 6 on the rack. Flash the rack. *What number did you see?* Display task card: 6 + __ = 13. *Can you work this out? … How did you do it?*

Make 11 on the rack. Flash the rack. *What number did you see?* Display task card: 11 – 4. *Can you work this out? … How did you do it?*

Notes:

- These tasks correspond to tasks in instructional phase 2, that is, tasks with both addends in the range 1–10. Subtractive tasks in the same range are also posed.
- Five-wise, ten-wise and pair-wise patterns can be used.
- Listen carefully to the student's explanation, and temper expectations that a particular strategy will be used.
- Of interest is whether the student uses counting on or a strategy that is arithmetically more sophisticated. If the student is obviously limited to counting strategies then these tasks are unnecessary.
- These additions and subtractions can be readily derived from basic double, five and ten combinations.
- Some students memorize these combinations on the additions table.

TASK GROUP A4.7: Addition and Subtraction with a Rack (one addend > 10)

Materials: Arithmetic rack (alternatively, double ten-frame cards, or empty double-ten frame and counters), screen, task cards written in horizontal format.

What to do and say: Pose additive tasks in the range 1 to 20 with one addend greater than 10, and corresponding subtractive tasks, such as: 13 + 3, 11 + 8, 15 + __ = 20, 4 + __ = 18, 20 – 3, 17 – 15. Present with the first addend or minuend on the rack, as in Task Group A4.6.

Notes:

- These tasks correspond to tasks in instructional phase 3, that is, additive tasks with one addend greater than 10, and subtractive tasks in the same range.
- The notes for Task Group A4.6 *Addition and subtraction with a rack (addends ≤ 10)* are also relevant to this Task Group.
- These tasks are more challenging than the previous group. They lie outside the range of the standard table of basic facts for addition, and are unlikely to be memorized.
- Using counting, 17 – 15 might be solved by making 15 counts back from 17, or by the more sophisticated strategies of counting from 17 back to 15 or from 15 up to 17.
- In a non-counting solution, a student knows that 7 is a combination of 5 and 2, and can reason from this that 17 is 2 more than 15. Such a solution is indicative of facile knowledge of number structure in the range 1 – 20.

TASK GROUP A4.8: Bare Number Addition and Subtraction (range ≤ 10)

Materials: Task cards written in horizontal format.

What to do and say: Pose tasks limited to the range 1 to 10, such as $4 + 3$, $3 + 6$, $8 - 5$ and $9 - 7$. For each task, display a card. *Read this please. Can you work this out?* Observe closely and, if necessary, enquire about how the student thought through the task.

Notes:

- These tasks are limited to the range 1 to 10 and therefore belong to the domain 'Structuring the Numbers 1 to 10'. Students typically establish facility with these tasks before those in the following Task Groups. Answers to these tasks may well be memorized.

TASK GROUP A4.9: Bare Number Addition and Subtraction (addends ≤ 10)

Materials: Task cards written in horizontal format.

What to do and say: Pose tasks where both addends are in the range 1 to 10, such as $7 + 5$, $9 + 4$, $6 + 7$; $6 + \_\_ = 11$, $8 + \_\_ = 16$, $9 + \_\_ = 15$; $12 - 4$, $14 - 5$, $17 - 9$. For each task, display a card. *Read this please. Can you work this out?* If necessary, enquire about how the student thought through the task.

Notes:

- These tasks correspond to tasks in instructional phase 2, that is, tasks with both addends in the range 1–10. Subtractive tasks in the same range are also posed.
- The notes for Task Group A4.6 *Addition and subtraction with a rack (addends ≤ 10)* are also relevant to this Task Group.
- Students may succeed with the tasks in the setting of the rack, before they succeed with the corresponding bare number tasks.

TASK GROUP A4.10: Bare Number Addition and Subtraction (one addend > 10)

Materials: Task cards written in horizontal format.

What to do and say: Pose tasks with one addend greater than 10, and corresponding subtractive tasks, such as: $14 + 4$, $6 + 13$, $12 + \_\_ = 20$, $11 + \_\_ = 17$, $20 - 5$, $16 - 13$. For each task, display a card. *Read this please. Can you work this out?* If necessary, enquire about how the student thought through the task.

Notes:

- These tasks correspond to tasks in instructional phase 3, that is, additive tasks with one addend greater than 10, and corresponding subtractive tasks.
- The notes for Task Group A4.7 *Addition and subtraction with a rack (one addend > 10)* are also relevant to this Task Group.
- Students may succeed with the tasks in the setting of the rack, before they succeed with the equivalent bare number tasks.

 # INSTRUCTIONAL ACTIVITIES

List of Instructional Activities

IA4.1: Keeping Score with Tally Marks
IA4.2: Ten-frame Flashes
IA4.3: Go Fish with Mini Ten-frames
IA4.4: I Wish I Had on the Bead Rack
IA4.5: The Double-decker Bus with the Bead Rack
IA4.6: 9 Plus Game
IA4.7: 20 Minus Game
IA4.8: Making Six
IA4.9: Crackers the Parrot
IA4.10: Expression Card Families
IA4.11: Bulls-eye Dice

ACTIVITY IA4.1: Keeping Score with Tally Marks

Intended learning: To learn to count using five.

Instructional mode: Shorter, reproductive practice for any context.

Materials: Means of recording tally marks.

Description: When playing any classroom scoring game, record tally marks on the board to track the score. The game context need not be a mathematics game. When counting a tally, count out loud to reveal how adults use tally marks. *Team A has 5, 10, 15, 17, and Team B has 5, 10, 14.* Prompt classroom use of the tally marks to encourage non-count-by-ones strategies. *What is the score? How do you know without counting? How many more does team A need to have 20? … to win the game? … to tie the game?*

Responses, variations and extensions:

- Tally marks are a useful means of tracking a growing tally, reinforcing notions of grouping and privileging five. Use of tally marks in class can be effective in promoting initial non-count-by-ones strategies.
- Initially students may count-on or count from one each time to determine a new sum. If this persists, prompt with *Is there a quicker way to determine the sum?*
- Young students frequently neglect to make the crossed line for each fifth tally. Rather they may have a series of fourteen hashes. This is an ideal opportunity to discuss the benefit of grouping to facilitate easier counting of larger sets.
- A prerequisite for the successful use of this activity is facility with the forward number word sequence for counting by fives on the multiple.

ACTIVITY IA4.2: Ten-frame Flashes

Intended learning: To learn combinations and partitions of numbers in the range 1 to 10.

Instructional mode: Shorter, productive practice for individuals or groups.

Materials: Five-wise ten-frame cards 1–10.

Description: Briefly flash a standard five-wise pattern for seven. Ask *What did you see? How do you know?* If needed, prompt with *How many dots on the top row? How many on the bottom? How many dots altogether? How many more to fill the ten-frame?* Continue with other ten-frame patterns.

Responses, variations and extensions:

- The length of the flash should be such that students get a good look at the pattern but do not have enough time to count the dots by ones.
- Begin with the standard five-wise ten-frame patterns. As students develop facility with the five-plus facts, proceed to pair-wise ten-frames to work on doubles and near doubles to ten.
- Strategic use of colour may provide additional scaffolding. For example, if students have difficulty 'seeing' the empty spaces in the ten-frame, another colour of dot may be used to complete the ten rather than leaving empty spaces. Some students may need to begin with five-frames to combine and partition up to five.
- For students unable to visualize the pattern or who are not attending to the structure of the frame, an empty ten-frame and counters can be used to provide scaffolding toward visualizing the patterns. The students' task is to use the blank frame and counters to recreate a flashed pattern. Students may need a second quick look at the pattern to check their arrangement of counters.
- Notating student thinking next to the ten-frame may facilitate student discussion of strategies (see Figure 4.4). This raises awareness that a number may be partitioned in multiple ways.

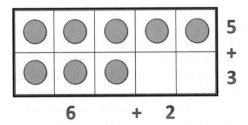

Figure 4.4 A ten-frame with students' partitions notated

- The activity may be extended to structuring number to 20 through the flashing of double ten-frames. Begin with the ten-plus facts, that is use one full frame and a partial second frame.
- The flashing procedure may be done with other dot patterns such as domino patterns.

ACTIVITY IA4.3: Go Fish with Mini Ten-frames

Intended learning: To learn partitions of 10.

Instructional mode: Longer, reproductive practice for pairs or small groups.

Materials: Best with sets of mini ten-frame cards showing 0–10 dots. Each group needs at least six sets of the eleven cards.

Description: Play Go Fish, aiming to match pairs of cards which sum to ten. Deal seven mini ten-frame cards to each player. Place the rest of the cards face down in a draw pile. A player begins a turn by asking another player for a card to match one she already has. For example, if Sally has a six in her hand, she could ask another player 'Ben, do you have a four?' If Ben has the requested card, he must hand the card over. Sally then places the matched pair of cards face up in front of her, and says a number sentence for the cards, such as 'Six and four make ten' or 'Six plus four equals ten'. She then continues her turn with a new request. If Ben does not have the requested card, he responds 'Go fish'. Sally then draws one card from the draw pile. If she draws the requested card, she plays the match, and continues her turn with a new request. If she does not draw the requested card, her turn ends. Play proceeds clockwise. The round ends when one player plays the last card from his or her hand. The winner is the player who made the most combinations of ten.

Responses, variations and extensions:

- Initially students may need to count the dots, count the empty squares or count on to 10 in order to determine the needed number of dots.

- The game can be played with playing cards and later with numeral cards. Using these cards provides progressively less scaffolding.
- A variation is that students may use more than two cards to make a combination of ten.
- Extend by partitioning other totals. When making combinations less than ten, remove cards with more dots that the desired total. For example, when playing Go Fish for 7s, remove all ten-frames with 8, 9 or 10 dots.
- Use sets of numeral cards 0–20 to work on combinations to 20.
- A solitaire game may be played by placing all cards face down in an array and playing concentration or memory to find the combinations of ten. The number of sets of ten-frame cards may be fewer for this variation.

ACTIVITY IA4.4: I Wish I Had on the Bead Rack

Intended learning: To learn combinations and partitions in the range 1 to 20, privileging five and ten.

Instructional mode: Shorter, reproductive practice for individuals, groups or whole class.

Materials: An arithmetic rack for each student and one for the teacher.

Description: Begin by familiarizing students with building numbers on the rack. *Using your bead rack, build the number I say on your rack. I wish I had 9.* Choose a few students to explain how they built 9. Create their pattern on your bead rack so all students can see. Summarize their comments drawing attention to use of colours and rows of beads. *So you made five red beads and four white beads all on the top row? So you had four beads on the top and five beads on the bottom? Did anyone do it a different way?* Continue with building a few other numbers: 10, 5, 6, 15, 16, 20. Discuss different quick moves on the bead rack: 'one-push' and 'two-push' moves, 'tilt-all, in-play' and 'tilt-all, out-of-play'.

After a familiarization period, increase the pace of the activity so that students have just enough time to create the pattern before calling a new pattern. Repeat 5, 10, 15 and 20 several times in the course of the activity to draw attention to these numbers and encourage one- or two-push building of numbers. *I wish I had 10. I have 10; I wish I had 9. I have 9; I wish I had 10. I have 10; I wish I had 11. I have 11; I wish I had 10. I have 10; I wish I had 9. I have 9; I wish I had 5. I have 5; I wish I had 10. I have 10; I wish I had 20. I have 20; I wish I had 15. I have 15; I wish I had 10.* After a quick succession of several patterns, pause to compare different patterns and ask, *Did anyone build that pattern in just one push?*

Responses, variations and extensions:

- Initially students may count-on each time to create the named number. If this persists, teachers should prompt with *Can you make the number in fewer pushes?*
- The first time students do this activity, 5, 10, 15 and 20 should dominate the sequence, to facilitate these numbers being used as anchors or standard patterns. Non-anchor numbers should be one more or one less than an anchor number. Call an anchor number after calling each non-anchor number.

- As students become facile with one-push moves, the anchor numbers should not be called as often and other non-anchor numbers should be introduced. Attention should be given to related patterns. *I wish I had 12. I have 12; I wish I had 7. How did you do that move?* Hopefully at least one student would have removed one push of 5. *I have 7; I wish I had 9. I have 9; I wish I had 16. How did you do that move?*
- A variation of this game that addresses structuring to ten is to play with a ten-bead rack or a blank ten-frame and counters.
- Teachers can quickly assess students' levels of structuring by watching the number of pushes needed to build a number. For example, frequently moving beads one at a time indicates a lower level of structuring.

ACTIVITY IA4.5: The Double-decker Bus with the Bead Rack

Intended learning: To learn non-count-by-one strategies in the range 1 to 20.

Instructional mode: Longer, productive practice for individuals, groups or whole class.

Materials: An arithmetic rack for each student and one for the teacher.

Description: Establish the story context of a double-decker bus driving around the classroom. At one stop, five passengers get on; at the next, two get off, and so on. Then pose tasks imagined within the bus story. *There were nine people sitting on the bus. Use your rack to show me what that might have looked like. The bus stopped at a stop and seven more people got on the bus. How many people are on the bus now? How did you figure that out?* A student might explain: 'At first I had nine on the top deck and seven on the bottom deck. I just moved one person from the bottom to the top deck so that there would be ten. That left six on the bottom deck. That means there are sixteen altogether on the bus'. Use the teacher rack to demonstrate the student's strategy. *Did anyone figure it out a different way? Which strategy was quicker?*

Responses, variations and extensions:

- The double-decker bus has proven a great story context for developing addition and subtraction with the arithmetic rack. Activities with the context can be developed over many weeks of lessons. Other possible contexts include children sitting on bunk beds at a sleep-over, or arranging books on two shelves.
- The arithmetic rack works best as a setting for addition and subtraction tasks once students have facility with building numbers on the rack with a few pushes only.

Photo 4.5 Making doubles on the arithmetic rack

- Initially students may count-on each time to find the sum or difference. If this persists, prompt with *Can you determine the answer without counting by ones?* If appropriate for the problem: *Is there any way colour can help you?*
- As students develop facility in using non-count-by-ones strategies, begin naming the student strategies. *Oh, I see, you used the near double. With eight on the top row and seven on the bottom, you saw the two sevens and one more* [slide the one slightly apart to highlight the double seven pattern] *to make fifteen.*
- Strategies to highlight include doubles, near doubles, 10-plus, 5-plus and compensation.
- Teachers and students may notate their strategy on an empty number line or with a series of equations, to keep a record of the strategies. This can facilitate meaningful closure discussions at the end of the activity as students review the strategies that emerged during the activity.

ACTIVITY IA4.6: 9 Plus Game

Intended learning: To solve addition problems involving nine.

Instructional mode: Shorter, reproductive practice for pairs or small groups.

Materials: 9 Plus Game Board, 4–9 Spinner, paper clip, pencil and counters of a different colour for each player.

Description: A player begins a turn by spinning the 4 to 9 spinner and adding the number spun to nine. The player says a matching number sentence, and places a counter on the resulting number on the game board. If the number is repeated on the game board, the player covers only one space per turn. If the number is not available, the player may spin again to create another addition problem. Players take turns until one player has three counters in a row.

Responses, variations and extensions:

- The best time to introduce this game is after strategies for compensation and adding through ten have emerged in classroom discussion.
- Initially students may count-on each time to determine the sum. If this persists, teachers should prompt with *Can you determine the sum without counting by ones?*
- Variations to extend the strategy are the 8 Plus Game and 19 Plus Game.

ACTIVITY IA4.7: 20 Minus Game

Intended learning: To learn the partitions of 20 using the partitions of 10.

Instructional mode: Shorter, reproductive practice, for pairs or small groups.

Materials: 20 Minus Game Board, 0–9 Spinners, paper clip, pencil and counters of a different colour for each player.

Description: This game is played in a similar manner to the 9 Plus game, IA4.6. A turn involves spinning the 0 to 9 spinner and subtracting the spun number from 20, then saying a matching number sentence and covering the resulting number on the board.

Responses, variations and extensions:

- This game is best introduced after students are facile with partitions of ten.
- Initially students may count down from 20 each time to determine the difference. If this persists, prompt with *Can you think of a partition of ten that might help you solve this subtraction problem?* Or *Can you think of an addition fact that might help you solve this subtraction problem?*
- A variation to extend the strategy is the Decuple Minus Game.

ACTIVITY IA4.8: Making Six

Intended learning: To learn combinations and partitions of numbers in the range 1 to 10.

Instructional mode: Longer, productive practice for individuals or groups.

Materials: Best with sets of numeral cards 1–6. Each group needs at least six sets, preferably ten sets, or many extra 1 and 2 cards.

Description: Show examples of sets of cards totaling 6: 3 and 3; 4, 1 and 1. Invite students to make up other combinations totalling 6. After some exploratory time, invite each group to share a different number combination, and record them. Manage discussion clarifying what is different. At some point, issue the challenge *Can we find all the different ways of making up a total of six?*

Responses, variations and extensions:

- The basic challenge can be posed without using numeral cards. However, some students have much more success engaging with the task when presented with the cards.
- Students could also show combinations with different colours of linking cubes, or Cuisenaire rods.
- Students may be used to combining only two numbers. Once they realize they can combine more than two numbers, most can find many combinations.
- Students may not find ways to be certain of having all combinations, or of justifying their list. The attempt is a valuable challenge in mathematical reasoning. Alternatively, students can just try to find as many as they can.
- Keeping the recording of the combinations organized can support students' problem-solving. For example, the 11 partitions of six could be recorded in columns:

6	51	42	33	222	111111
		411	321	2211	
			3111	21111	

- Extend by partitioning other totals. Finding all five partitions of 4 is easy. Finding all 42 partitions of 10 requires a well-organized approach.

ACTIVITY IA4.9: Crackers the Parrot

Intended learning: To make combinations and partitions involving five.

Instructional mode: Shorter, productive practice, for whole class and individuals.

Materials: Parrot puppet.

Description: Hold up the parrot. *This is Crackers. He can only say 'five'.* The parrot croaks 'five'. *We want to help Crackers look clever. Can you ask him a problem that gives the answer 5?* As students pose problems – 4 + 1, 3 + 2, 6 – 1, 10 – 5 and so on – Crackers answers 'five'. For 9 – 3, Crackers shakes his head – he is good at arithmetic. The teacher can follow up the wrong suggestion with an arithmetic rack. *If we have nine beads, we can see five beads there. How many do we need to take away – without counting?* Following the whole class session, each student writes down a half-page of problems answering five.

Photo 4.6 Crackers the parrot puppet

Responses, variations and extensions:

- Look to less advanced students early on, so they have the opportunity to offer the problems in the range 1 to 10.
- Some students may think of more advanced problems, such as 100 – 95. These need not be explained. The students see that Crackers does answer 'five', and can try to build on the idea: 80 – 75, 200 – 195, 1000 – 995 …
- Students may be using fingers, counting by ones, or using more facile strategies. The whole class session is a good opportunity to observe students' strategies, but not to intervene – rather, the momentum of making up good problems should be maintained.
- In a different lesson, Crackers only says 10, 20 or 15.
- For older students, the context might be a target with a target number. The task is to generate as many ways to reach the target number as possible. For example, if the target is 12, possible expressions might be: 6 + 6, 4 × 3, 3 + 3 + 3 + 3, a dozen, 2 × 6.

Acknowledgement: Treffers (2001).

ACTIVITY IA4.10: Expression Card Families

Intended learning: To learn relationships between addition tasks in the range 1 to 20.

Instructional mode: Longer, productive practice for individuals or groups.

Materials: A set of addition expression cards for each student or group. A set could be all 25 additions with addends in the range 1–5, or all 55 additions with totals in the range 1–10, or all 121 additions with addends in the range 0–10.

Description: As an introduction, give one expression card to each student in the class, so that much of a set is distributed through the room. *Mark, what is your expression?* 'Three plus five'. *What is your answer?* 'Eight'. *Does anyone else have an answer of eight? Could you all come and stand with Mark – you are the family of eight. Does anyone have an answer of nine? Could the nine family all gather here in the corner? … Could each of the other families gather together please?* Once gathered in families, each family can read out their expression. Return the expression cards. Next, work in groups or individually. Each group is given a set of expression cards, and is asked to organize them into families on the desk.

Responses, variations and extensions:

- In assigning each card to a family, students will be practising basic addition tasks.
- Once the cards are organized into families, the class can look for relationships: turn-arounds like 3 + 5 and 5 + 3 are in the same family, 6 + 2 is in the same family as 7 + 1, … and in the family after 5 + 2.
- Each family can be further organized: the family of eight can be ordered as 8 + 0, 7 + 1, 6 + 2 …
- Give each student an additions table grid to colour-code each family. Alternatively, each student writes out the neatly organized families.
- *How many expressions make 1? … make 2? … make 3? …*
- *Which families are you most familiar with? Which families have the tasks that require more thinking?*
- A valuable variation is to make families not by equal sum, but by similar computation strategy. *How can you find 3 + 4? As a near-double? Does anyone else have a near-double expression? Let's make a near-doubles family …* Other families might be: doubles, +1, make 10, 5-plus. These families are not as clear-cut as the equal sum families. Some expressions might belong in more than one family. A table of additions with strategy families colour-coded can be a rich discussion point.

ACTIVITY IA4.11: Bulls-eye Dice

Intended learning: To coordinate combinations and partitions in the range 1 to 20.

Instructional mode: Longer, reproductive practice for pairs or groups.

Materials: Four standard 6-sided dice for each pair, or four giant dice for the whole class version. An extra die for the Super Bulls-eye variation.

Description: Students play against each other in the group, taking turns. A player begins a turn by rolling four dice. The player then chooses some of the numbers to add together, to make a total as close as possible to the bulls-eye of 10. The turn gets a score according to how close the total is to the bulls-eye: 8 and 12 score 2, 9 and 11 score 1, 10 scores 0. The player records the

	Number sentence	Total	Score	
Dice: 6 4 3 2	6+4	10	0	(a)
Dice: 5 3 3 1	5+3+3	11	1	

	Number sentence	Total	Score	
Dice: 6 4 3 2	6+4+3−2	11	1	(b)
Dice: 5 3 3 1	5+3+3−1	10	0	

	Number sentence	Total	Score	
Dice: 6 4 3 2 & 5	6+4+3+2−5	10	0	(c)
Dice: 5 3 3 1 & 1	5+3+1+1	10	0	

Figure 4.5   Example scoring tables for (a) Bulls-eye Dice, (b) Bulls-eye Combination and (c) Super Bulls-eye

turn in a table with three columns (see Figure 4.5a). Players play six rounds, and the winner is the player with the lowest total score.

Bulls-eye Combination. In this variation, a player *has to use* all four dice, and can add *or subtract* each number to make their total, as illustrated in Figure 4.5b.

Super Bulls-eye. As with *Bulls-eye Combination*, a player rolls four dice, and needs to add *or subtract* each number to make their total. However they also roll a *bonus die*. The bonus die can be ignored, be used to replace one of the original dice, or be included as a fifth number, as illustrated in Figure 4.5c.

Responses, variations and extensions:

- Basic *Bulls-eye Dice* is easy to explain and play. About 70% of rolls can hit the bulls-eye. It is good for developing facility with combinations to 10.
- Play *Bulls-eye Combination* after basic Bulls-eye. It is more complicated, and requires more arithmetical reasoning to consider possible additions and subtractions. Having dice to arrange helps students think through the different combinations. Only about 35% of rolls can hit the bulls-eye, making a nice change from basic Bulls-eye, worth thinking hard for.
- If there is sufficient interest, introduce *Super Bulls-eye*. The bonus die creates many more possible combinations. About 90% of rolls can hit the bulls-eye, but you have to think hard.
- Any variation can be played in teams of two as well.
- *Bulls-eye Combination* can be played in a whole-class race variation. Four huge classroom dice are rolled, and the numbers are announced. All students have 20 seconds to write down their best combination with the four numbers, before the dice are rolled again. After six rounds, students swap sheets, check each other's answers, and calculate each other's scores.
- Motivated by the whole-class race variation, students can discuss thinking strategies for finding good combinations. A rich variety of combination and partition knowledge and relational thinking can emerge.

5

Conceptual Place Value

DOMAIN OVERVIEW

In Chapter 6, 'Addition and Subtraction to 100', we analyse the foundational arithmetic knowledge used in facile mental strategies for multi-digit addition and subtraction. We note that most strategies involve incrementing and decrementing numbers by tens, both on the decuple (50 and 10 more is 60) and off the decuple (47 and 10 more is 57). Furthermore, mental strategies usually involve switching between incrementing or decrementing by tens, and incrementing or decrementing by ones. Thus, being able to flexibly increment and decrement by ones and tens, and later also by hundreds, is critical knowledge for developing facile mental computation. We refer to this critical knowledge as *conceptual place value* (CPV) (Anghileri, 2006; Ellemor-Collins and Wright, 2009a; Fuson et al., 1997; Thompson and Bramald, 2002).

As well as supporting facile mental computation, CPV is important arithmetic knowledge in its own right. As students become proficient at incrementing and decrementing by ones, tens and hundreds, they:

- develop a sense of the relative sizes of numbers
- learn ways of relating multi-digit numbers to each other
- decimalize their approach to multi-digit numbers, habitually organizing numbers in terms of the base-ten units of ones, tens, hundreds, and so on.

Such base-ten thinking is critical for numeracy. Later, students learn conventional place value. Ones, tens and hundreds become formal units each of which corresponds to the value of a place in written numerals. The view taken in this book is that students can and should learn conceptual place value first. The base-ten thinking, with proficient incrementing and decrementing by 1s, 10s and 100s, establishes a conceptual basis for the formal learning of conventional place value (Beishuizen and Anghileri, 1998; Freudenthal, 1983; Menne, 2001; Wright et al., 2006c).

Learning Conceptual Place Value

Consider the following four examples of what students do, before they have facility in CPV.

Ian is shown four dots, which he identifies as 'four'. A ten-dot strip is placed beside them. *Ten more?* Ian counts to himself '4 –5, 6 … 14' in conjunction with pointing to each dot on the strip. He has not yet learned to use ten as a handy unit for counting.

Josie has learned to increment by ten, but a task involving incrementing by both tens and ones presents a new challenge. She is told there are 48 dots under a screen. Two ten-dot strips and a strip of three dots are placed alongside the screen. *How many dots altogether?* Josie answers '63'. To check her answer, she points to the screen saying '48', then to the two ten-strips saying '50, 60', and to the strip of three, saying '63'. Although she has learned to count using ten, she cannot coordinate the tens and the ones.

Kurt has learned to increment by ten in a setting of base-ten materials, but a bare number task presents a different challenge. He is asked *What is ten less than 306?* He counts to himself, back by ones '306, 305, 304 ... 296', keeping track of ten counts with twitching fingers. Without the base-ten materials, he does not use ten as a special unit. To solve the task by jumping back ten requires knowing the decade before the 300s is the 290s, and coordinating changes to the tens and the hundreds but not the ones.

Lexi has learned to increment by tens and ones, but now she is asked to find an unknown increment. *Starting at 72, how many more to make 100?* She begins to count on by ones '72, 73, 74 ...', but struggles to find a way to keep track of her count. A facile solution to this task involves finding 2 tens and an 8, or 3 tens less 2. It appears that, although Lexi can think of known numbers as made of tens and ones, she does not think of an unknown number as made of tens and ones.

When we observe students who are not yet facile in CPV, we realize the special uses of ten involved in facile thinking. During mental computation, we take such tens thinking for granted, and we aim for our students to be able to take tens thinking for granted too. But as teachers, we do not take the tens thinking for granted: rather, we appreciate that it demands a significant development in mathematical sophistication. CPV instruction challenges students to develop sophisticated tens thinking, including incrementing and decrementing by tens, coordinating tens and ones and progressing from a setting of base-ten materials to bare numbers (Cobb and Wheatley, 1988; Ellemor-Collins and Wright, 2007; Fuson et al., 1997; Gravemeijer and Stephan, 2002; Tabor, 2008; Treffers and Buys, 2001).

Assessment of Conceptual Place Value

Pose tasks of ten more, ten less, one hundred more, one hundred less.

Pose increments and decrements on the decuple, and off the decuple, and across hurdles such as hundred numbers and 1000.

Pose the tasks with and without a setting of base-ten materials.

Instruction in Conceptual Place Value

Preliminary Instruction

Before instruction in CPV, students need familiarity with grouping in tens and counting in tens. These preliminary practices are typically addressed in early number instruction. Instruction could include a task to count a heap of beads: students come to realize the advantages of first grouping the beads in tens. Another task involves four bundles of ten sticks and three loose sticks, and students are asked *how many sticks altogether?* Students learn to count '10, 20, 30, 40 ... 43', rather than count by ones.

Basic CPV Instruction

A basic CPV task involves a sequence incrementing or decrementing by tens (see Box 5.1a). Initially, pose tasks with base-ten materials. Build a starting number with the materials, then repeatedly increment the material by a ten. The students' task is to say how many there are after each increment.

BOX 5.1 (A) A BASIC CPV SEQUENCE, USING BUNDLING STICKS, (B) A MORE COMPLEX CPV SEQUENCE

(a)

Teacher	Student
XXXXX ‖‖ XX *How many sticks?*	Seventy-four.
XXXXX ‖‖ XX**X**	Eighty-four.
XXXXX ‖‖ XXX**X**	Ninety-four.
XXXXX ‖‖ XXXX**X**	Ni- ... A hundred and ni-, and four.
One hundred and...?	One hundred and four.
XXXXX **X** ‖‖ XXXXX	Two hun ... One hundred and fourteen.
XXXXX XX ‖‖ XXXXX	One hundred and twenty-four.

(b)

Teacher	Student
XXXXX XX ‖‖ XXXXX *How many sticks?*	One hundred and twenty-four.
One hundred more? ☐ XXXXX XX ‖‖ XXXXX	... Two hundred and twenty-four.
What if I take a stick? ☐ XXXXX XX ‖‖┼ XXXXX	Two hundred and twenty-three.
Take two tens? ☐ XXXXX X̶X̶ ‖‖ XXXXX	Two hundred and ... two hundred and three.
Take another ten? ☐ XXXXX ‖‖ XXXX̶X̶	... One hundred ... and ninety-three.
Take one hundred? ⊟ XXXXX ‖‖ XXXX	... Ninety-three.

☐ = bundle of 100, X = bundle of 10, | = 1 stick.

- Aim the sequence at the hurdles that present challenges for the students: incrementing off the decuple, across 100, across 110, and so on.
- Decrement as well as increment.
- Lay out the material neatly to support the students with mentally organizing the numbers.
- Listen carefully to their responses.

The students are problem solving. They are likely to draw on a sense of the whole number, and its meaning in terms of quantity or its location in the number sequence. They may also use verbal sequences. For example, in Box 5.1a, when finding ten more than 104, the student begins to say 'two hundred and ...' – perhaps cued by recall of a verbal sequence such as '100, 200 ...'. The base-ten material provides a reference for checking their answers. For example, at the same line of Box 5.1, the student looks at the material and then corrects herself.

From these initial CPV tasks, instruction can be developed along three dimensions.

A. Extend the range of numbers.
B. Make the increments and decrements more complex.
C. Distance the setting.

These three dimensions are described in the three sections below. In instruction, the teacher does not pursue them separately. Rather, the teacher extends tasks a little along dimension A, then a little along B, then a little along C, then retreats on C while extending further along B again, and so on. For example, begin with incrementing by ten in the range to 100, then extend to 200 (A), then introduce increments of multiple tens (B), then screen the materials (C), then unscreen the materials while introducing increments of ones as well as tens (B). In this way, the teacher can incrementally raise the level of tasks, challenging students to progressively mathematize their base-ten thinking.

Dimension A: Extending the Range of Numbers

Begin in the range 0 to 100, then extend to 200. Introduce hundreds materials, and extend the range to 1000. Extend across 1000 and 1100 – these hurdles may require attentive practice. Later, extend to 2000 and beyond.

Dimension B: Making the Increments and Decrements More Complex

Box 5.1b is an example of a more complex sequence. Below are four ways to make the increments and decrements more complex.

- Make increments and decrements of multiple tens or hundreds.
  What is two tens more? What is three hundreds less?

- Switch from increments and decrements of tens, to increments and decrements of ones or hundreds. Switch the unit flexibly several times over the course of a sequence.
  What is ten more … one hundred more … ten more … two more?
- Make increments and decrements of combinations of ones, tens and hundreds.
  What is twenty-one more? Take away one hundred and one ten?
- Later, tasks can involve determining unknown increments and decrements.
  There is 87 – how many more to make 100?

Dimension C: Distancing the Setting

Incrementally distance the setting from the students. At the same time, introduce more formal notation. This encourages students to rely increasingly on visualization, mental organization and symbolization. Four phases are described below.

1. Materials are **visible**.

    The students may even build the starting number themselves.

2. Materials are **screened**, but increments and decrements are **shown** briefly. After each answer, the screen can be lifted for the students to check their answers.

    - *There are one hundred and eighty-five behind here.*
      Show two new 10-dot strips, then place behind the screen. *Twenty more?*
    - Two hundred and five.
    - *Check.* Lift the screen for students to verify, then replace the screen.

3. Materials are **screened**, and increments and decrements are posed **verbally**. Answers may be written numerals, as well as spoken number words. The screen can be lifted occasionally, to check tasks with materials.

    - *We have six hundred and twenty-one. What is ten less?*
    - Six hundred and eleven. (Student writes 611.)
    - *Ten less than six hundred and eleven?*
    - Six hundred and one. (Student writes 601.)
    - *Ten less?…*

    Although in this stage, the materials are not visible, their screened presence can still support students with visualizing and organizing their problem-solving.

4. The first number is given as a **numeral**, and increments and decrements are posed **verbally**. There are no base-ten materials. Pose shorter sequences, or just single increments and decrements. Answers can be written, or notated on an empty number line (see Appendix).

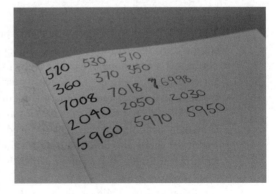

Photo 5.1   Writing 10 more and 10 less

Working with Base-ten Materials

When working with base-ten materials, be mindful that students may not see the materials the way adults expect. In particular, in their first encounters with base-ten materials, most students do not recognize that, say, four bundles of 10 sticks is 40 sticks. Furthermore, when they do first learn to read four bundles as 40, they cannot readily see how to decrement by two sticks: they may answer 'twenty' or 'two', rather than 38 sticks. It seems they cannot construct a number in tens, and then switch to constructing the same number in ones. We say that students need to learn to think of ten as simultaneously a unit and a composite: both a unit of 'one ten' and a composite of 'ten ones'. That is, they need to be able to construct numbers flexibly with tens and ones. Students will learn this sophisticated tens thinking through their work with CPV and related tasks (Cobb and Wheatley, 1988; Gravemeijer and Stephan, 2002).

Begin CPV using *groupable* materials, such as bundling sticks (see Appendix): with sticks which can be grouped into bundles of ten, and bundles which can be disaggregated into ten sticks. Later, with larger numbers, shift to *pre-grouped* materials such as dot-strips, which are neater to organize. Meanwhile, throughout CPV instruction, do not expect 'tens' to be self-evident in the materials. Rather, let the materials be a setting that supports the students during their problem-solving.

Photo 5.2 Using dot materials in conjunction with arrow cards

Distinguishing Conceptual Place Value from Conventional Place Value

The curriculum topic commonly called place value is intended to prepare students for the standard written algorithms for addition and subtraction. Instruction typically involves talking about the conventions of placing digits in columns, and demonstrating digit manipulations through manipulations of base-ten materials. We refer to this common curriculum topic as conventional place value. For many students, especially low-attainers, conventional place value approaches do not support the development of mental strategies. The formal manipulations of written symbols and materials involved in conventional place value tasks are not yet mean-ingful for them. In conceptual place value instruction, by contrast, students build on their informal arithmetical reasoning, which is based in number word sequences and quantities. The CPV instruction aims to stay in touch with the students' common sense about multi-digit numbers, and to challenge them so that through problem-solving, their common sense is

Table 5.1 Distinguishing conceptual place value from conventional place value

Conceptual place value	Conventional place value
Numbers are presented and discussed in their full value: 20 as twenty or two tens; 21 as twenty-one, or twenty and one.	Numbers may be explicitly presented or discussed in terms of digits: 20 has 2 in the tens column; 21 has 1 in the ones column.
Tasks involve increments/decrements in sequence. For example, from 611, ten less is 601, ten less is 591, one less is 590.	Typically, tasks are not presented as a sequence of increments/decrements.
Solving tasks essentially involves inquiry or problem-solving.	Solving tasks might require following a convention or rehearsing a given procedure.
Answering tasks might involve using knowledge of the number sequence.	Answers are unlikely to relate tasks to the number sequence.
Answers do not involve exchanging units. For example, students solve 195 and ten more is 205, but do not need to explain this by trading 10 tens for 1 hundred.	Answers involve explicitly exchanging or trading: 10 ones for 1 ten, 10 tens for 1 hundred.
Attention is on structuring numbers around dynamic relationships of ones, tens and hundreds.	Attention is on manipulating numbers in terms of the formal place value system.
The aim is to cultivate strong mental strategies.	The aim is to prepare students to use the standard algorithms.

advanced. Students can and should become proficient in conceptual place value, before tackling conventional place value. Attentive practice on the part of the teacher is required to make conceptual PV and conventional PV distinct in instruction. See Table 5.1 (Beishuizen and Anghileri, 1998; Cobb and Wheatley, 1988; Ellemor-Collins and Wright, 2009a; Thompson, 2003; Wright et al., 2006c).

ASSESSMENT TASK GROUPS

List of Assessment Task Groups

A5.1: Preliminary Unscreened Bundling Sticks Tasks
A5.2: Incrementing and Decrementing by Tens on the Decuple
A5.3: Incrementing and Decrementing by Tens off the Decuple

A5.4: Incrementing Flexibly by Tens and Ones
A5.5: Incrementing by Hundreds on the Centuple
A5.6: Incrementing and Decrementing by Tens across 1000
A5.7: Ten More and Ten Less
A5.8: One Hundred More and One Hundred Less

TASK GROUP A5.1: Preliminary Unscreened Bundling Sticks Tasks

Materials: Bundling sticks, including 10 bundles.

What to do and say: As a preliminary step, tell the students that there are always 10 sticks in each bundle, or confirm that they already know this. Proceed with basic incrementing and decrementing tasks, as follows. Place one bundle. *How many sticks are there?* Place a second bundle. *Now how many sticks are there (altogether)?* Continue placing bundles, up to 100 sticks. Confirm: *OK, there are 100 sticks there.* Then remove one bundle. *Now how many sticks?* Continue removing bundles, down to zero.

Notes:

- Most students are facile with the number word sequence 10, 20, 30 … 100. Once they recognize this sequence they will use it for answering the task. This is appropriate use of their number knowledge.
- However, students may switch to merely reciting the sequence, and get ahead of the actual number of bundles. If so, pause to break their rhythm, and to assert the task of numbering the sticks, rather than merely reciting a sequence.
- Students may have less facility with the backward sequence 100, 90, 80 … and so may have less facility with the decrementing task. These students might say for example, 100, 19, 18, 17 ….
- A few students may not recognize the sequence 10, 20, 30 … or know ten more than 10, ten more than 20. Instead, they will count by ones. Observe closely for finger and lip movements. This is a significant finding in assessment: instruction should immediately focus on establishing incrementing and decrementing by tens, and number word sequences by tens. Meanwhile, the students are unlikely to have success on the other Assessment Tasks below.

TASK GROUP A5.2: Incrementing and Decrementing by Tens on the Decuple

Materials: A screen of card or cloth, and bundling sticks, including 12 bundles.

What to do and say: Increment as follows. Show one bundle then place it under the screen. *How many sticks are under there?* Show a second bundle then place it under the screen. *Now how many sticks are under there (altogether)?* Continue, adding one or two bundles at a time under the screen, up to 120.

Decrement as follows. Place out 12 bundles. *How many bundles are there? … and how many sticks?* Screen the 12 bundles. Then remove one bundle and show it. *Now how many sticks under there?*

Continue, removing one or two bundles at a time, down to zero.

Notes:

- Students will typically use their knowledge of the number word sequence 10, 20, 30 ... to answer these tasks. As with Task Group A5.1, students may merely recite the sequence, losing track of the actual number of bundles under the screen.
- Some students may be facile up to 100, but falter beyond 100. Instruction should focus on the hurdle at 100 with instruction both in CPV and in number word and numeral sequences.
- Observe closely for finger or lip movements indicating counting by ones.
- Once or twice during the incrementing and decrementing, the question can be *How many sticks? ... and how many bundles?* Students

Photo 5.3   Screening bundling sticks to assess incrementing by tens off the decuple

may have difficulty with saying the number words for both the count of sticks and the count of bundles. Instruction should focus on establishing facility in switching between these counts.

TASK GROUP A5.3: Incrementing and Decrementing by Tens off the Decuple

Materials: A screen and bundling sticks, including 12 bundles.

What to do and say: Increment as follows. Place three sticks. *How many sticks are there?* Screen the three sticks. Show one bundle then place it under the screen. *Now how many sticks are under there (altogether)?* Continue, adding one or two bundles at a time under the screen, up to 123.

Decrement as follows. Place out 12 bundles and eight sticks. *How many sticks are there?* Screen the bundles and sticks. Then remove one bundle and show it. *Now how many sticks under there?* Continue, removing one or two bundles at a time, down to eight.

Notes:

- Incrementing and decrementing by tens off the decuple, rather than on the decuple, may be much more difficult for students. Observe closely for counting by ones.

- Students may be slow with initial increments or decrements, using counting by ones or otherwise thinking hard. Then they may recognize the pattern, and proceed with more facility. Instruction should focus on establishing facility from the outset.
- Students may struggle more with increments and decrements involving teen numbers: 3 to 13 to 23, 103 to 113 to 123, 28 back to 18 back to 8, 128 back to 118, back to 108. This is because students may not recognize the tens structure of teen numbers: they do not see 13 as ten and 3, in the same way they can see 43 as forty and three. Instruction should focus on developing this knowledge, by incrementing and decrementing by tens in ranges that include teen numbers.
- Students may be successful up to 100, but not beyond 100. Success up to 100 is already an important achievement. Instruction should then extend beyond 100.

TASK GROUP A5.4: Incrementing Flexibly by Tens and Ones

Materials: Two screens and a task board of dot-strips, prepared as described (see Figure 5.1). On a sheet of card about 30cm long, print or laminate six sets of dot-strips in sequence as follows: a 3-dot strip; a 10-dot strip; two 10-dot strips; a 3-dot strip; a 10-dot strip and a 1-dot strip; three 10-dot strips and a 2-dot strip.

What to do and say: Place screen A to the left of the board, and screen all dot-strips with screen B. Slide screen B to the right, thereby revealing the first 3-dot strip. *How many dots are there? (3).* Slide screen A right to screen the 3-dot strip, and slide screen B right to reveal the 10-dot strip. *How many dots now, altogether? (13).* Slide screen A right to screen the 10-dot strip, and slide screen B right to reveal the two 10-dot strips. *How many dots now, altogether? (33).* This is the task illustrated in Figure 5.1. Continue for each set of strips: slide screen A to screen the accumulating sets, slide screen B to reveal the next set, and ask *How many dots now, altogether?* The

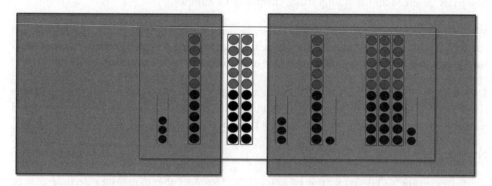

Figure 5.1 Task board with screens, for Task Group A5.4. *How many dots now, altogether? (33)*

three remaining sets are: a 3-dot strip (36); a 10-dot strip and a 1-dot strip (47); three 10-dot strips and a 2-dot strip (79).

Notes:

- The purpose of this Task Group is to assess facility with more complex increments, in particular switching units – incrementing by tens, then incrementing by ones – and mixing units – incrementing by tens and ones together.
- For these more complex tasks, it is convenient to prepare a task board with a sequence of dot-strips, rather than handling loose dot strips when administering the assessment. Practise coordinating the screens and the questions.
- This Task Group has six tasks. Students might use counting by ones during any of these tasks.
- Students might have difficulty maintaining their organization of the tens and ones. For example, the 33 + 3 task might be regarded as '63', the 47 + 11 task might be regarded as '57'.

Reference: task adapted from Cobb and Wheatley (1988).

TASK GROUP A5.5: Incrementing by Hundreds on the Centuple

Materials: A screen and 13 of the 100-dot squares.

What to do and say: As a preliminary step, check that the students know there are 100 dots in a square. Then proceed with incrementing as follows. Show a 100-dot square and place it under the screen. *How many dots are under there?* Show a second square and place it under the screen. *Now how many dots are under there (altogether)?* Continue, adding one or two squares at a time under the screen, up to 1300.

Notes:

- Typically the sequence 100, 200, … 900 is easy for students.
- Beyond 900, students may say 'ten hundred, eleven hundred…', or 'one thousand, two thousand …'. In these cases instruction should focus on incrementing by hundreds beyond 900.

TASK GROUP A5.6: Incrementing and Decrementing by Tens across 1000

Materials: A screen and base-ten dot materials.

What to do and say: Place out materials for 874: eight 100-dot squares, seven 10-dot strips, and a 4-dot strip. *How many dots are there?* Screen the materials. Show one 10-dot strip then place it under the screen. *Now how many (altogether)?* Continue, adding one or two ten-strips at a time under the screen, up to 1124.

Notes:

- To assist students to keep track of the count, keep the accumulating strips under the screen organized into 1s, 10s and 100s.
- This sequence assesses students' facility with the key hurdles at 900, 1000 and 1100.
- Assessing decrementing by tens across these hurdles could also be of interest.

TASK GROUP A5.7: Ten More and Ten Less

Materials: Numeral cards: 50, 90, 62, 273, 304, 495, 996, 1007.

What to do and say: Show the 50 card. *Read this number please … . What number is ten more than this?* Continue similarly with other cards. Then repeat with the same set of cards, but asking *What number is ten less than this?*

Notes:

- The numbers are listed roughly in order of difficulty for students, that is: on the decuple, off the decuple, in the hundreds, hurdling a centuple, hurdling 1000. It is useful to establish the current limit of students' facility with these tasks.
- Some students will count by ones for some tasks and doing so is error-prone. They may have difficulty keeping track of their count, for example counting from 304 back to 293. Or they may lack facility with the number word sequence, for example counting from 304 'back' 303, 302, 301, 330, 329 …
- Some students will not count by ones, but nevertheless will be unable to coordinate the units they are jumping. For example, for ten more than 62 they answer 73 or 71, for ten less than 304 they answer 204 or 295 or 300.

TASK GROUP A5.8: One Hundred More and One Hundred Less

Materials: Numeral cards: 50, 105, 996, 1007.

What to do and say: Show the 50 card. *Read this number please. … What number is 100 more than this?* Continue similarly with the other cards.

Then use the cards 105 and 1007 again asking *What number is 100 less than this?*

Notes:

- For some students, 100 more than 50 may be more difficult than 100 more than 105.
- 100 less than 105 can be particularly difficult for students.

INSTRUCTIONAL ACTIVITIES

List of Instructional Activities

IA5.1: Incrementing and Decrementing by Tens with Screened Bundling Sticks
IA5.2: CPV Egg Contextual Investigation
IA5.3: Read It, Build It, Check It with Arrow Cards and Base-ten Materials
IA5.4: Arrow Cards Draw Game with Base-ten Materials
IA5.5: Hopping and Leaping on the Empty Number Line
IA5.6: Crazy Grid
IA5.7: Withdrawing Money from the Automated Teller Machine

ACTIVITY IA5.1: Incrementing and Decrementing by Tens with Screened Bundling Sticks

Intended learning: To flexibly increment and decrement by tens in a quantitative context.

Instructional mode: Longer, inquiry mode for individuals or groups.

Materials: Bundling sticks – many bundles and loose sticks, screen (cloth or sheet of foam).

Description: Establish that each bundle contains ten sticks. Briefly display and then screen three bundles of sticks (see Figure 5.2). *How many bundles of sticks? How many sticks are there altogether?* Add another bundle under the screen. *How many sticks now?* Allow the child to check as needed. Continue to add bundles until there are 130 sticks. *How many sticks now?*

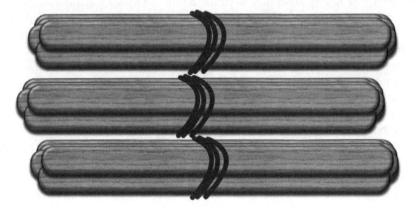

Figure 5.2   Three bundles of bundling sticks

How many bundles now? Remove a bundle. *How many sticks now?* Continue removing a bundle and asking for the total number of sticks and bundles until there are zero sticks under the screen.

Briefly display and then screen two bundles and four extra sticks. *How many sticks are there altogether?* Add another bundle under the screen. *How many sticks now?* Continue to add bundles until there are 124 sticks. *How many sticks now? How many bundles and left over sticks now?* Remove a bundle. *How many sticks now?* Continue removing a bundle and asking for the total number of sticks and bundles until there are four sticks under the screen.

Responses, variations and extensions:

- This task is designed to enable students to connect to a quantitative context, forward number word sequences (incrementing) and backward number word sequences (decrementing).
- Tracking the progressions on a 200 chart or ENL enables students to describe patterns and link quantities and numerals.
- When incrementing off the decuple, students often have difficulty with the 'teen' numbers. Beginning in the twenties will facilitate children recognizing the oral pattern of the numbers in the sequence (e.g. twenty-four, thirty-four, forty-four…).
- Bridging the century and century plus teen frequently poses a difficulty. For example, students may increment, '87, 97, 107, 207'. The bundling of ten tens into a bundle of one hundred (mega bundle) will facilitate child checking. Remove the last ten added in the sequence and ask, *How many was that?* When the student responds 107, ask, *Where is the one hundred?* When the student indicates the ten tens, add a big rubber band to form the mega bundle. Place the mega bundle back beside the seven extra. *How many was that altogether?* Add another ten. *Now how many?* If the student persists in stating 207, unscreen the collection to compare the relative size of the mega bundle (hundred) to the ten-bundle. *So do we have two mega bundles?* Remove the mega bundle and ask *How many now?* [17] Replace the mega bundle. *Now how many?*
- If necessary, the rubber bands may be removed from the bundles in order for the student to verify the number of sticks. The use of groupable base-ten materials is critically important until the student develops a mental construct of composite units and can regard tens and hundreds as units that are easily mentally composed and decomposed.
- Repeat the process with other collections (e.g. starting with five sticks) and track the increments and decrements on a 200 chart or empty number line (ENL). *What do you notice about all these numbers? How are the numbers the same? How are they different?*
- Modify the procedure by adding two bundles of ten at a time. Extend this by adding three or four bundles at a time. Record on the ENL or 200 chart.
- Once students can simultaneously conceive base-ten materials as both one ten and ten ones, use pre-grouped base-ten materials such as dot strips or base-ten blocks.
- Repeat the process by incrementing and decrementing by hundreds.
- Repeat the process by incrementing and decrementing by mixed tens and hundreds.

ACTIVITY IA5.2: CPV Egg Contextual Investigation

Intended learning: To learn to flexibly compose and decompose groups of ten.

Instructional mode: Longer, inquiry mode for individuals or groups.

Materials: Linking cubes, chart paper or record sheet and pens.

Description: This activity focuses on the base-ten system of numeration. Students propose to the egg producers' association that eggs should be packaged by the ten rather than by the dozen. (This investigation could be integrated with a task of writing a persuasive letter.)

Conduct a whole-class discussion about how eggs are packaged. In some countries, eggs are packaged by the dozens (twelves). In other countries, they are packaged by tens. Facilitate a discussion evaluating the level of customer ease in calculating the number of eggs in several cartons depending on packaging.

Have students work in pairs to create charts that show the total number of eggs in several different numbers of cartons for the two styles of packaging (see Figure 5.3). Students may use linking cubes to support their calculations of the totals if needed. Discuss the advantages and disadvantages of each type of packaging. Consider the relative ease of calculating other amounts of cartons not on the chart depending on packaging. *What is the calculation advantage of packaging the eggs in cartons of ten?*

Number of Cartons	Total Eggs in Cartons of Ten	Total Eggs in Cartons of a Dozen
1	10	12
2		
3		
4		
5		

Figures 5.3   Comparing cartons of ten with cartons of a dozen

Number of Eggs	Number of ten-egg cartons	Left over eggs
17	1	7

Figures 5.4   Packaging a number of eggs in ten-egg cartons

Once students have established that cartons of ten would be easier to calculate because it is easier to count by tens, determine the number of eggs that would be in various numbers of cartons focusing on ten-egg cartons only. Determine the number of ten-egg cartons and left over eggs that can be packaged out of various numbers of eggs (see Figure 5.4). Students can use linking cubes to check their conjectures.

Responses, variations and extensions:

- This task is designed to enable students to explore an application of units of ten. Many students lack the language to distinguish between the number of groups and the number in each group. By using the egg context, students can picture the difference between an egg and an egg carton.
- Initially students may need materials to support their thinking about the cartons of tens. Linking cubes work well for this since students can make trains of ten cubes to represent each carton.
- Careful discussion may be needed before students notice the relationship between the number of eggs and the number of cartons and leftover eggs. Lead the discussion in such a way that students notice this relationship.
- Repeat the process with hundreds by exploring the notion of egg cartons being packaged into boxes with ten cartons (100 eggs in each box).
- Repeat the process with thousands by exploring the notion of egg boxes being packaged into crates with ten boxes of eggs (1000 eggs in each crate).
- This egg context can be extended to explore additive situations. *What if we had 47 white eggs and two ten-egg cartons of brown eggs? How many eggs would we have altogether? How would we notate this on the empty number line?*
- This egg context can be extended to explore subtractive situations. *What if the farmer had 69 eggs and then sold two cartons of eggs? How many eggs would the farmer have then? What if the farmer had four cartons but 6 eggs were broken when a carton was dropped?*
- Students can use arrow cards or chips on a hundred chart to track the egg inventory.
- The context could be any item that could be packaged by tens, hundreds and thousands.

Acknowledgement: Modified from Cobb et al. (1997).

ACTIVITY IA5.3: Read It, Build It, Check It with Arrow Cards and Base-ten Materials

Intended learning: To learn the value of each place. To connect quantities and numerals. To read numerals.

Instructional mode: Longer, inquiry to rehearsal mode for individuals or groups.

Materials: One set of arrow cards for each student, up to ten 2-digit number cards, base-ten materials.

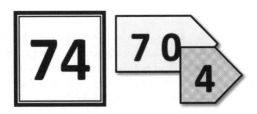

Figure 5.5 Building 74 with arrow cards

Description: Present the student with the numeral 74. *Read this number, please.* Have the student build the number using arrow cards (see Figure 5.5). Have the student compare the numeral card with the numeral formed with the arrow cards. *Are they the same number?* If not, have the student try again with the arrow cards until the numbers are the same. Have the student expand the arrow cards to read each place in order from the largest to the smallest. Point to each arrow card as the child reads the numeral on the card. Prompt the child to read the arrow cards more quickly until the child becomes aware of the 2-digit number name. Have the child build the number using base-ten materials. *Where is the 70? Where is the 4?*

Change the arrow card number and the materials so that the new number is ten more than what we have now. *What part changed?* Change the arrow cards and materials so that the new number is 20 fewer.

Continue bridging the century and beyond through both adding and subtracting collections of tens.

Responses, variations and extensions:

- This task is designed to facilitate conceptual understanding of each place in the numeral.
- This task is particularly helpful in addressing reversals (reading 52 as 25).
- Repeat the process with 3-digit numbers, bridging the century and beyond through adding and subtracting collections of tens and hundreds.
- Repeat the process with 4-digit numbers, bridging the century, millennium and beyond through adding and subtracting collections of tens, hundreds and thousands.
- Use arrow cards, base-ten materials, and the empty number line to show each change, thereby, building connections between the different settings.

ACTIVITY IA5.4: Arrow Cards Draw Game with Base-ten Materials

Intended learning: To learn the value of each place. To link quantities and numerals. To read numerals.

Instructional mode: Shorter, rehearsal mode for partners.

One set of arrow cards for each group.

on: Place all tens and ones arrow cards face down on the table. Each student draws one rd of each colour (one of each place). Students build the number with the arrow cards. dent reads his or her number and builds the number with base-ten materials. The stu- th the largest number gets all the arrow cards from both numbers. The winner is the student with the most arrow cards at the end of the game.

Responses, variations and extensions:

- This task is designed to facilitate conceptual understanding of each place in the numeral.
- This task is designed to link the quantitative and symbolic aspects of number (Thomas et al., 2010).
- Extend the activity by including the hundreds arrow cards.
- Extend the activity by including the thousands arrow cards.

ACTIVITY IA5.5: Hopping and Leaping on the Empty Number Line

Intended learning: To use the empty number line to record and compare addition and subtraction solution strategies.

Instructional mode: Longer, inquiry or rehearsal mode for individuals, small groups or whole class.

Materials: Chart paper and pen or chalkboard and chalk.

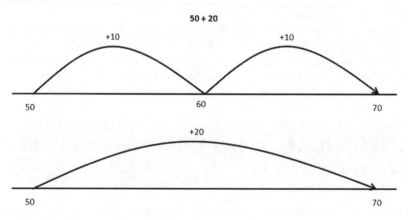

Figure 5.6   Notating 50 + 20 on the empty number line

Description: Use the empty number line (ENL – see Appendix) to notate incrementing and decrementing. Present students with a bare number problem such as 50 + 20. Record students' solutions on the ENL (see Figure 5.6). Compare different solution strategies.

Responses, variations and extensions:

- This task is designed to connect incrementing and decrementing strategies with more formal addition and subtraction notation.
- Base-ten materials may be used as a scaffold if needed.
- Eventually students should be prompted to think about the ENL without actually drawing it. In this way, they are led to anticipate solving the problem with the ENL. In this fashion, the scaffold provided by the ENL gradually fades. *If you were going to use the ENL to solve this, how would you do it?* If needed, *What would you do first? Where would that leap of 20 get you? And then?*
- Proceed through problems as follows:

  - decuple + or – decuple [50 + 20, 80 – 30]
  - decuple + or – decuple hurdling the centuple [90 + 30, 110 – 20]
  - off-decuple + or – decuple [47 + 30, 62 – 20]
  - off-decuple + or – decuple hurdling the centuple [97 + 20, 132 – 40]
  - centuple + or – centuple [700 + 200, 900 – 300]
  - off-centuple + or – decuple [139 + 40, 172 – 30]
  - off-centuple + or – decuple hurdling centuple [184 + 20, 213 – 30]
  - off-centuple + or – off-decuple [124 + 31, 165 – 23]
  - off-centuple + or – off-decuple hurdling centuple [195 + 32, 216 – 24]

ACTIVITY IA5.6: Crazy Grid

Intended learning: To add ten or multiples of ten to any number.

Instructional mode: Shorter, rehearsal mode for individuals, small groups or whole class.

Materials: Crazy grid drawn on the board or from Resource CD, base-ten materials as needed.

Description: Present a grid with one number displayed (see Figure 5.7). *One day, I was trying to print a hundred grid, and the printer went crazy. For some reason, almost none of the grid printed. Can you help me fill in the missing numbers?*

Responses, variations and extensions:

- This task is designed for students who have worked patterns on the hundred grid and are familiar with the format of the hundred grid.

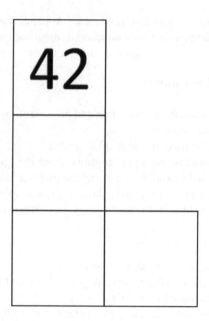

Figure 5.7 A sample crazy grid

- Examples of extensions are to begin with a number: (a) in the hundreds (257); (b) that requires hurdling the centuple (87); and (c) that is in the hundreds and requires hurdling the centuple (493).
- As students develop facility, have them insert only one specified missing number rather than all the missing numbers.

ACTIVITY IA5.7: Withdrawing Money from the Automated Teller Machine

Intended learning: To subtract decuples from a given number.

Instructional mode: Shorter, inquiry mode for whole class or small group.

Materials: ATM graphic, chart paper and pen or chalkboard and chalk, base-ten materials as needed.

Description: Introduce the context of using an ATM machine to withdraw cash from a bank account (see Figure 5.8). *Who can tell me what an Automated Teller Machine or ATM*

Figure 5.8 Automatic Teller Machine (ATM)

is? Yes, it is a machine that allows you to deposit or withdraw cash from your bank account. I went to the ATM last night to withdraw some cash. Do you know, it would only allow me to withdraw increments of £20, £50, or £100. Why do you think that was? Yes, they only stock £20, £50 and £100 notes in the machine. I thought about that. If my balance was £457 and I withdrew £20, what would my balance be? How could I figure that out? If students lack a strategy, prompt with *If I were going to make 20 using these base-ten materials, how would I do that as quickly as possible? How can we use that idea to help us with this problem?* Solve other problems of increasing complexity.

Responses, variations and extensions:

- This task is best introduced when students are facile at adding or subtracting ten from any number.
- For less facile students, the machine could have £10 notes and the initial balance could be less than £100.
- Some students may need base-ten materials to support their reasoning about the quantities.
- The ENL is an excellent tool for notating student thinking during whole-group discussions.
- School money or base-ten materials can be used to support students' reasoning.

6
Addition and Subtraction to 100

DOMAIN OVERVIEW

This domain addresses addition and subtraction in the range 1 to 100. All students can learn to solve tasks in this range using mental computation, and the benefits for their arithmetic knowledge are significant. So the aim in this domain is to develop excellent facility in mental computation. Addition and subtraction to 100 is a key component of the development of students' mental computation, alongside multiplication and division in the same range.

Students' facility with addition and subtraction becomes a foundation for much of their subsequent arithmetic learning. By adding and subtracting in the range 1 to 100, students establish their understanding of our base-ten numeration system. Students will extend their strategies in this domain to develop addition and subtraction strategies for larger numbers, negative numbers, decimal fractions and percentages. Their knowledge of addition and subtraction to 100 will also support their learning of multiplication and division – for example, four 8s found as 8 + 8 + 8 + 8, or as 16 + 16. Later, their knowledge of this domain will need to be taken absolutely for granted for measurement, data handling and symbolic algebra. Mental addition and subtraction to 100 is also one of the most useful skills in daily adult life. With the foundational importance of this domain in mind, teachers can devote considerable instructional time to the domain in the early years, and keep returning to it in subsequent years (Anghileri, 2006; Beishuizen and Anghileri, 1998; McIntosh et al., 1992; Treffers and Buys, 2001; Yackel, 2001).

This overview of the domain is organized into seven sections. In the first section we characterize facile mental computation as relational thinking, and study in detail facile students' mental strategies for addition and subtraction. In the second section we lay out the foundational arithmetic knowledge that underpins facile mental computation. The third section summarizes how to assess students' learning. The remaining sections describe the instructional approach, organized into three instructional phases. Throughout, we emphasize that facile mental computation develops by enriching arithmetic knowledge and mathematizing students' own mental strategies. It is unlikely to develop from instruction in formal place value or standardized computation strategies.

Facility with Mental Addition and Subtraction to 100

Facile students solve addition and subtraction tasks in a variety of ways. Tables 6.1 and 6.2 illustrate this variety. For four different tasks, the tables give examples of students' explanations

Table 6.1   Examples of mental strategies for addition

Label	Student strategy	Arrow notation
Addition non-regrouping: 37 + 22		
Jump	'A jump of 10 goes to 47, another jump of 10 goes to 57, and the jump of 2 goes to 59.'	$37 + 10 \rightarrow 47 + 10 \rightarrow 57 + 2 \rightarrow$ **59**
Split	'The 3 and the 2 make 50 [sic], and the 7 from there and the 2 from there is 9.'	$30 + 20 = 50, 7 + 2 = 9$ $\rightarrow 50 + 9 =$ **59**
Split-jump	'37 and 20 is, well, 30 and 20 is 50, so then 57, then 2 more is 59.'	$30 + 20 \rightarrow 50 + 7 \rightarrow 57 + 2 \rightarrow$ **59**
Addition with regrouping: 37 + 25		
Jump	'37 and 10 is 47, and 10 more is 57. Then to 60 is a jump of 3, and 2 more makes 62.'	$37 + 10 \rightarrow 47 + 10 \rightarrow 57 + 3$ $\rightarrow 60 + 2 \rightarrow$ **62**
-variation		$37 + 20 \rightarrow 57 + 5 \rightarrow$ **62**
-variation		$37 + 5 \rightarrow 42 + 20 \rightarrow 62$
Jump to the decuple	'I started at 37. I added 3 to make 40, then 10 is 50, 10 more is 60, and the last 2 is 62.'	$37 + 3 \rightarrow 40 + 10 \rightarrow 50 + 10$ $\rightarrow 60 + 2 \rightarrow$ **62**
Split	'The 30 and the 20 make 50. The 7 and the 5 make 12. 50 and 12 is 62.'	$30 + 20 = 50, 7 + 5 = 12$ $\rightarrow 50 + 12 =$ **62**
-incorrect	'... 50 and 12 is ... fifty-twelve?'	$50 + 12 \rightarrow \underline{50? \; 12} \times$
Split-jump	'30 and 20 is 50. Then the 7 makes 57. Then to add the 5 I went to 60, then to 62.'	$30 + 20 \rightarrow 50 + 7 \rightarrow 57 + 3$ $\rightarrow 60 + 2 \rightarrow$ **62**
Compensation *-variation*	'Well I knew 40 and 25 is 65. So then I took off the extra 3. And that's 62.'	$(37)40 + 25 \rightarrow 65 - 3 \rightarrow 62$ $(37)35 + 25 \rightarrow 60 + 2 \rightarrow$ **62**
Transformation	'I changed it to 40 plus 22, which is 62.'	$37^{+3} + 25^{-3} \rightarrow 40 + 22 \rightarrow$ **62**

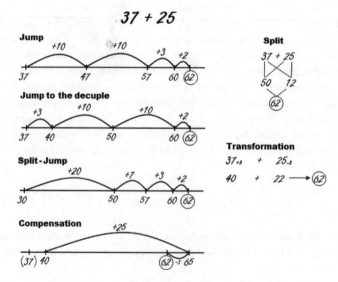

Figure 6.1   Informal notations for mental strategies for 37 + 25 from Table 6.1

Table 6.2   Examples of mental strategies for subtraction

Label	Student strategy	Arrow notation
Subtraction non-regrouping: 53−11		
Jump	'I started at 53, jumped back 10 and 1.'	$53 - 10 \rightarrow 43 - 1 \rightarrow \mathbf{42}$
Split	'50 subtract 10 is 40, and 3 subtract 1 is 2. So the answer is 42.'	$50 - 10 = 40, 3 - 1 = 2$ $\rightarrow 40 + 2 = \mathbf{42}$
Subtraction with regrouping: 53−19		
Jump	'10 less than 53 is 43, then take 3 down to 40, then there's 6 left to take off. 34.'	$53 - 10 \rightarrow 43 - 3 \rightarrow 40 - 6 \rightarrow \mathbf{34}$
Over-jump	'I subtracted 20 because that's easier, and then added 1 back on to get 34.'	$53 - 20 \rightarrow 33 + 1 \rightarrow \mathbf{34}$
Jump to the decuple	'I went back to 50 first, then I took away the 10, then I took the last 6, which made 34.'	$53 - 3 \rightarrow 50 - 10 \rightarrow 40 - 6 \rightarrow \mathbf{34}$
Split	'I did the tens, then the ones, which you can't really do, but it's like 6 less than 40.'	$50 - 10 = 40, 3 - 9 =$ 'down 6' $\rightarrow 40 - 6 = \mathbf{34}$
Split	'You can't do 3 minus 9, so I did 13 minus 9, and that means it's only 40 minus 10.'	$13 - 9 = 4, 40 - 10 = 30$ $\rightarrow 30 + 4 = \mathbf{34}$
-incorrect	'50 minus 10 is 40. 9 minus 3 is 6. So the answer is 46.'	$\underline{9 - 3} = 6, 50 - 10 = 40$ $\rightarrow 40 + 6 = \mathbf{46} \times$
Split-jump *-incorrect*	'50 minus 10 is 40, so 43 minus 9 ... is 34.'	$50 - 10 \rightarrow 40 + 3 \rightarrow 43 - 9 \rightarrow \mathbf{34}$ $50 - 10 \rightarrow 40 \underline{- 3} \rightarrow 37 - 9 \rightarrow \mathbf{28} \times$
Compensation	'You put the 3 aside, do the subtraction, and then you put the 3 back on.'	$(53)50 - 19 \rightarrow 31 + 3 \rightarrow \mathbf{34}$
Transformation	'Instead of 53 take 19 I did 54 take 20.'	$53^{+1} - 19^{+1} \rightarrow 54 - 20 \rightarrow \mathbf{34}$

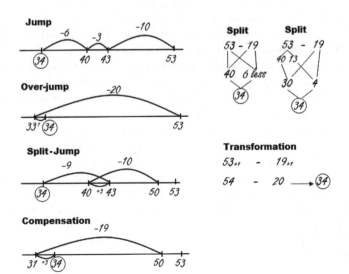

Figure 6.2   Informal notations for mental strategies for 53 − 19 from Table 6.2

of their strategies. For each explanation, a notation and a label are given. Notations for variations to these strategies and for three common incorrect strategies are also given. The *regrouping tasks* – 37 + 25 and 53 – 19 – are tasks where, as a facile student might construe it, the ones parts cross over a ten in some way. Regrouping tasks are usually the more challenging tasks, as they require coordinating ones and tens together. The *non-regrouping* tasks – 57 + 22 and 53 – 12 – are usually easier to calculate (e.g. Denvir and Brown, 1986). Figures 6.1 and 6.2 give more informal notations for select strategies from Tables 6.1 and 6.2 respectively. In this overview we will frequently refer to these tables and figures.

Note that all the strategies in Tables 6.1 and 6.2 are non-counting strategies. Strategies based on counting by ones become clearly inadequate with numbers in the range 1 to 100: they are laborious, slow and prone to error (Gray, 1991; Wright, 2001). Familiarity with the strategies in these tables is very helpful for teaching. Teachers need to use these strategies themselves, and to try to observe what strategies students are using. Teachers need ways to notate students' strategies, and ways to talk about the arithmetical thinking that is involved. Below we characterize the arithmetical thinking involved in facile mental addition and subtraction, before examining seven mental strategies in detail.

Mental Computation as Relational Thinking

In Chapter 4, for the range 1 to 20, we characterized facile mental computation as an activity of relational thinking, drawing on strong knowledge of number bonds and the part–whole construction of number. In the range 1 to 100, we similarly characterize facile mental computation as an activity of relational thinking. As an illustration of the relational thinking involved, observe Latoya, a facile calculator, solving addition tasks on three different occasions. She uses different mental computation strategies, depending on what relationships she notices in a particular task. When posed the task 37 + 25 (from Table 6.1), she thinks of 25 as 20 and 5, begins to add 20 to 37, and ends up using a jump strategy: $37 + 20 \rightarrow 57 + 3 \rightarrow 60 + 2 \rightarrow \mathbf{62}$. When posed the task 37 + 27, she immediately thinks of 7 + 7 = 14, and solves the task using a split strategy: 7 + 7 = 14, 30 + 20 = 50, 50 + 14 = **64**. When posed the task 37 + 29, she notices 29 is close to 30, and solves the task using an over-jump strategy: $37 + 30 \rightarrow 67 - 1 \rightarrow \mathbf{66}$. It is tempting to imagine that when Latoya attempts a task, she goes to her toolbox of strategies, selects an appropriate strategy, and then applies it. But on closer inspection, we see that the thinking involved in facile computation is usually not like this toolbox metaphor. There is no moment of consciously choosing a strategy. Rather, when Latoya looks at a task, she begins to notice certain relationships in the numbers, and even as she notices these, the calculation is already beginning. Then, through further arithmetical reasoning about those relationships, she brings the calculation to a conclusion. For example, when she notices 29 is close to 30, she is already beginning to add 30, and then reasons arithmetically that she needs to subtract the extra 1. It is only after solving the task that she can reflect on her thinking and say 'I used an over-jump strategy'. Thus, facile computation is not stepping back and selecting from a toolbox, so much as noticing number relationships and reasoning about relationships (Foxman and Beishuizen, 2002; Heirdsfield, 2001; Klein et al., 1998; Menne, 2001; Stephan et al., 2003; Threlfall, 2002).

This characterization of mental computation shapes our approach to instruction. In our assessment of students' mental strategies, we try to observe what relationships they are noticing and how they are reasoning. Our approach to instruction does not involve teaching students to select and use strategies, as one might teach students to select procedures. Rather, our approach involves cultivating students' awareness of number relationships, and their facility with additive reasoning. We discuss this further below, in the sections on assessment and instruction.

Labelling Strategies

Over many years, teachers and researchers have observed and categorized students' mental strategies. Several kinds of strategies commonly arise. It is useful to give labels for different strategies, in order to discuss students' thinking, and to draw attention to the number relationships used. Many different labels have been devised (Foxman and Beishuizen, 2002; Fuson et al., 1997; Heirdsfield, 2001; Tabor, 2008; Threlfall, 2002; Thompson and Smith, 1999). In this book we focus on seven widely used labels. These are listed in Table 6.3, and used to label the strategies compiled in Tables 6.1 and 6.2. We recommend that teachers use these labels in both their discussions with colleagues about strategies they observe students using, and their discussions with students in the classroom. In classroom work, more home-grown labels such as 'jump too far' and 'Naomi's strategy' can also emerge and be used productively. This is discussed further in the section on instruction below. In our approach, strategies are not taught as standard procedures and the use of labels is not intended to lead to standardization of procedures (Bobis, 2007; Threlfall, 2002).

Seven Mental Strategies

Seven mental strategies are summarized in Table 6.3. They are discussed in detail below, with reference to the examples in Tables 6.1 and 6.2.

Table 6.3   Summary of seven mental strategies

Jump	Begin from one number, jump tens then jump ones (or ones then tens).
Over-jump	Begin from one number, overshoot the jump, then compensate.
Jump to the decuple	Begin from one number, jump to the nearest decuple, jump tens, then jump remaining ones.
Split	Split tens and ones, add/subtract them separately, then recombine.
Split-jump	Split tens and ones, add/subtract tens, add first ones, jump second ones.
Compensation	Change one or both numbers, add/subtract, then compensate.
Transformation	Change both numbers while preserving the result, then add/subtract.

Note: For examples of these strategies, see Tables 6.1 and 6.2.

Jump

Jump is a very straightforward strategy. The same strategy works for all non-regrouping and regrouping tasks, and for addition and subtraction. Students who attempt to use jump rarely make procedural errors. Jump strategies are quite adaptable, for example to over-jump or jump to the decuple. A regular jump strategy involves jumping by tens off the decuple ($53 - 10 \rightarrow 43$) and jumping ones across a decuple ($43 - 9$).

Over-jump

To add or subtract 19, 18 or 17, students frequently jump 20, then back 1, 2 or 3. For some students, this becomes as routine as jumping 23 by jumping 20 and then 3. Over-jump arises for regrouping tasks, typically those jumping by a 2-digit number with 7, 8 or 9 in the ones place. Over-jump involves jumping by tens off the decuple ($53 - 20 \rightarrow 33$), but not jumping ones across a decuple. For example in solving $53 - 19$, the jump strategy involves $43 - 9$, whereas over-jump involves only $33 + 1$. Over-jump is a form of compensation strategy, because it involves rounding one number to a decuple and then compensating.

Jump to the Decuple

Jumping to the decuple can arise for any regrouping task. It involves partitioning the ones to jump to the decuple and does not involve jumping by tens off the decuple. For example $37 + 25$ involves firstly adding 3 to 37 and then adding 22 to 40. Habitual use of jump-to-the-decuple rather than jump, may indicate that the student is not facile with jumping off the decuple and instruction should address this. Jump to the decuple is particularly common for calculations involving complementary addition – see below.

Split

Working with the tens and ones separately is a powerful means of calculating with 2-digit numbers. It is exciting when students first realize they can do this, and many students mainly use various forms of the split strategy. For non-regrouping tasks, the split strategy is very straightforward. However, students with little or no knowledge of 2-digit numbers as quantities or points on a number line, can nevertheless obtain correct answers using a split strategy by adding (or subtracting) the digits in each column. Students such as these are likely to have significant difficulty with regrouping tasks. For addition tasks with regrouping, the split strategy is still reasonably straightforward. However, some students cannot recombine the subtotals of tens and ones. As shown in Table 6.1 for $37 + 25$, they calculate the subtotals of 50 and 12, and answer 'fifty-twelve', 'five hundred and twelve', or 'I don't know'. For subtraction tasks with regrouping, students can have major difficulties with the split strategy. For $53 - 19$ for example, some students can't solve the sub-task of $3 - 9$. This is the 'larger from smaller' issue. Some students can regard the difference of 6 as 'down 6' or '6 less', others regroup the tens and solve $13 - 9$, and others use split-jump, as discussed below. In contrast, some students merely solve $9 - 3$, and obtain an incorrect answer, as shown in Table 6.2. This error is often labelled the 'smaller from larger' error, or the 'buggy split' (Tabor, 2008).

Split-jump

Some students initially use split, separating off the tens of both numbers, and then use jump, appending the ones sequentially. This is labelled a split-jump strategy. For subtraction tasks with regrouping, split-jump transcends the 'larger from smaller' error that can occur using a pure split approach. Many students who habitually use split for addition tasks also use split-jump for subtraction with regrouping. However, subtraction with split-jump often involves errors such as the one shown in Table 6.2 for 53 – 19. Note that determining whether a student's strategy is jump or split-jump is sometimes difficult. In classroom teaching, this distinction is not critical. However, in diagnosis, determining whether a student habitually uses split-jump rather than jump is useful. As with habitual jumping-to-the-decuple, habitual split-jumping suggests the student is uncertain with jumping off the decuple and instruction should address this.

Compensation

Sometimes a student notices a way to adjust one number to make an easier addition or subtraction, then does the calculation, and finally compensates for the initial adjustment. Compensation strategies often involve rounding a number to the nearest decuple, as in the compensation example for 37 + 25: $40 + 25 \rightarrow 65 - 3 \rightarrow \mathbf{62}$ and for 53 – 19: $50 - 19 \rightarrow 31 + 3 \rightarrow \mathbf{34}$ (see Tables 6.1 and 6.2). Compensation may also arise from adjusting the numbers to align with a doubles fact or other known fact, as in calculating 25 + 27 thus: $25 + 25 \rightarrow 50 + 2 \rightarrow \mathbf{52}$. As well, compensation can involve adjusting a number to make the ones match in some way, as in calculating 37 + 25 thus: $35 + 25 \rightarrow 60 + 2 \rightarrow \mathbf{62}$ (see Table 6.1), or calculating 53 – 26 thus: $56 - 26 \rightarrow 30 - 3 \rightarrow \mathbf{27}$. Finally, compensation can involve changing both numbers, and compensating for the changes at the end, as in solving 37 + 28 thus: $40 + 30 \rightarrow 70 - 3 - 2 \rightarrow \mathbf{65}$.

Transformation

Sometimes a student notices a way to transform both numbers to simplify an addition or subtraction while not altering the result. A label like *transformation* or 'change both numbers' or 'change the question' highlights that a task can be changed while preserving the result. For addition tasks, students often conceive of a transformation strategy as subtracting a number from A and adding it to B. Some students find this an appealing approach. A transformation strategy typically involves the same number relationship that is used in other strategies, such as jump to the decuple or over-jump, however the procedure seems to be conceived of differently. Compare these strategies for 37 + 25 and 53 – 19, shown in Table 6.4. Note the difference between transformation for addition and transformation for subtraction. In an addition task, if x is added to one addend, then to preserve the result, x is subtracted from the other addend. In a subtraction task, if x is added to the minuend, then to preserve the result, x is *added* to the subtrahend, too.

Table 6.4 Comparing transformation with other strategies

Jump to decuple	$37 + 3 \rightarrow 40 + 20 \rightarrow 60 + 2 \rightarrow \mathbf{62}$	**Over-jump**	$53 - 20 \rightarrow 33 + 1 \rightarrow \mathbf{34}$
Transformation	$37^{+3} + 25^{-3} \rightarrow 40 + 22 \rightarrow \mathbf{62}$	**Transformation**	$53^{+1} - 19^{+1} \rightarrow 54 - 20 \rightarrow \mathbf{34}$

Jump and Split as the Main Mental Strategies

Jump and split are recognized as the two main mental strategies. Over-jump and jump to the decuple can be thought of as variations of jump. Split-jump is like a combination of split and jump. Jump or split can become a student's regular general strategy, solving any given task with the same strategy. Strategies like compensation and transformation are more task-specific, requiring insight about the numbers to change. Task-specific strategies often involve relatively sophisticated arithmetical reasoning.

Jump and split can be seen as arising out of different approaches to computation. Jump keeps the first addend or the minuend whole, and appends the second addend or subtrahend in parts. The strategy can be notated straightforwardly as a sequence of jumps on a line (see Figures 6.1 and 6.2). For this reason, jump is described as a sequential or linear approach to computation. On the other hand, split partitions both addends (addition), or both the minuend and the subtrahend (subtraction), and combines the parts separately before recombining them into a total. Split cannot be clearly notated on a line. Instead, separate collections of tens and ones can be shown and separate sums can be written (see Figures 6.1 and 6.2). For this reason, split is described as a collections-based or partitioning approach to computation (Cobb and Wheatley, 1988; Klein et al., 1998; Thompson and Smith, 1999; Wright et al., 2006c; Yackel, 2001).

Complementary Addition

Consider the task 53 − 39. Rather than solve this by thinking 'take 39 away from 53', many students will think '39 and how many more make 53?' or 'what's the gap between 39 and 53?' This strategy is called *complementary addition* or 'adding up to subtract' and is used especially when the difference between the minuend and subtrahend is relatively small. As well, this strategy is likely to arise when a missing addend task is posed explicitly, such as 39 + □ = 53. Complementary addition involves the strategies described above for direct addition and subtraction, although the answer emerges from the calculation in a different way, as shown in the examples in Table 6.5. In a class of students facile at mental computation, calculating 53 − 39 might involve using any of these complementary addition strategies, as well as any direct strategy for subtraction, equivalent to those listed for 53 − 19 in Table 6.2. This amounts to at least 13 strategies for solving the task.

Table 6.5 Complementary addition strategies for 53 − 39 or 39 + □ = 53

Jump	$39 + 10 \rightarrow 49 + 1 \rightarrow 50 + 3 \rightarrow 53$. Answer: $10 + 1 + 3 = \mathbf{14}$.
Over-jump	$39 + 20 \rightarrow 59 - 6 \rightarrow 53$. Answer: $20 - 6 = \mathbf{14}$.
Jump to the decuple	$39 + 1 \rightarrow 40 + 10 \rightarrow 50 + 3 \rightarrow 53$. Answer: $1 + 10 + 3 = \mathbf{14}$.
Compensation	$40 + 13 \rightarrow 53$. Answer: $13 + 1 = \mathbf{14}$.
Transformation	$39^{+1} + ? = 53^{+1} \rightarrow 40 + ? = 54$. Answer: $\mathbf{14}$.

Split and split-jump are used rarely for complementary addition because splitting each number into tens and ones seems to be unhelpful. In contrast, jump to the decuple is used frequently for complementary addition. For tasks involving a decuple, such as 50 − 39, jump to the decuple is very common: 39 + 1 → 40 + 10 → 50, answer: 1 + 10 = **11**. Because it is commonly used for mentally calculating change in shopping transactions, this strategy is referred to as shopkeeper addition.

Foundational Knowledge for Mental Addition and Subtraction to 100

Above, we characterized facile mental computation as relational thinking. The relational thinking relies on strong foundational knowledge of ways to relate numbers, in particular, ways to combine and partition numbers to form other numbers. We can analyse the arithmetic knowledge that students rely on in facile mental strategies for addition and subtraction to 100. Three aspects of arithmetic knowledge constitute the main foundational knowledge of the mental strategies described above: structuring numbers 1 to 20; conceptual place value; and an aspect called higher decade addition and subtraction, described below (Menne, 2001; Treffers, 1991; Treffers and Buys, 2001; Wright et al., 2006c, 2007).

- **Structuring numbers 1 to 20**
  This domain, described in Chapter 4, involves mental strategies for combining and partitioning numbers in the range 1 to 20. The sub-domain of structuring numbers 1 to 10 is particularly important.
- **Conceptual place value (CPV)**
  This domain, described in Chapter 5, involves mental strategies for incrementing and decrementing by tens, and for coordinating tens and ones.
- **Higher decade addition and subtraction**
  This aspect of arithmetic knowledge comprises adding 1-digit numbers to 2-digit numbers, and subtracting 1-digit numbers from 2-digit numbers. Knowledge of higher decade addition and subtraction derives from structuring numbers 1 to 20. We address instruction in this aspect within the broad instructional approach to addition and subtraction to 100 in the current chapter.

Observing these foundations in students' mental strategies can be difficult, because much of the thinking involved in mental strategies is almost instantaneous and taken for granted. To help our observations, we can imagine analysing strategies in slow motion, as it were. Table 6.6 offers an example analysis, laying out arithmetical steps the mind effectively notices and solves doing a jump strategy. Each step can be linked to the three foundations.

Table 6.7 details aspects of the three foundations used in mental computation. Each example in the table is a step in the strategies compiled in Tables 6.1 and 6.2. A student needs to be facile with much of this knowledge, in order to add and subtract in the range 1 to 100. A student who requires significant time to recall or to compute any of these steps will struggle to succeed

Table 6.6 Arithmetical steps and foundational knowledge involved in a jump strategy for 37 + 25

Strategy step	Aspect of knowledge	Foundation
Add 25 as + 10 + 10 + 5	Increment by tens and ones	CPV
37 + 10→ □; 47 + 10→ □	Increment by ten	CPV
57 + □ → next decuple	Jump forward to the decuple and partition 10	Higher decade A&S Structuring numbers
5 less 3 leaves □	Partition in range 1 to 10	Structuring numbers
60 + 2→ □	Jump forward from a decuple	Higher decade A&S

Table 6.7 Three foundations for mental addition and subtraction to 100

Aspect of arithmetic knowledge	Example steps in strategies
Structuring numbers 1 to 20	
Partitions of 10	7 and □ is 10; 10 less 6 is □
Combining in the range 1 to 10	7 + 2 = □; 1 + 3 = □
Partitioning in the range 1 to 10	3 and □ is 5; 3 and □ is 9
Combining in the range 1 to 20	7 + 5 = □
Partitioning in the range 1 to 20	13 − 9 = □; 19 and □→is 20
Conceptual place value (CPV)	
Incrementing/decrementing by tens on the decuple	30 + 20 → □; 50 − 10 = □
Incrementing/decrementing by tens off the decuple	37 + 10 → □; 53 − 20→□
Incrementing/decrementing by tens and ones	40 + 22 → □; 53 → □ + 13
Higher decade addition and subtraction	
Jump within a decade	57 + 2→ □; 43−1→ □; 25^{-3} → □
Jump forward from a decuple	60 + 2→ □; 50 + 7→ □
Jump back to the decuple	53 − □ → 50; 43− □→ 40
Jump forward to the decuple	57 + □ → 60; 37 + □→ 40
Jump back from a decuple	40 − 6 → □
Jump across a decuple	57 + 5 → □; 43 − 9 → □

with a whole calculation. We don't advocate step-wise instruction in these many aspects of arithmetic knowledge. However teachers' rich and detailed awareness of these many aspects is an important basis for providing instruction in mental computation.

Significantly, mental strategies do require decimalizing computation – that is, organizing numbers using 1s, 10s and 100s – for example, re-organizing 47 as 40 and 7, and knowing 47 and 10 is 57. However, they do not require knowing that in the numeral 47 the digit 4 is in the tens place, and represents 4 tens. Conventional place value knowledge of this kind is important for understanding formal written algorithms for addition and subtraction, but is not necessary for mastering mental computation. Thus, we can distinguish knowledge of conceptual place value, which is involved in mental computation, from conventional place value, which is not. This distinction is discussed in Chapter 5 (Ellemor-Collins and Wright, 2009b; Freudenthal, 1983; Thompson, 2003).

Assessment of Addition and Subtraction to 100

Pose 2-digit addition and subtraction tasks. Facile students could be extended with 3-digit tasks.

Pose tasks in a setting of base-ten materials, and tasks with bare numbers in horizontal format. Students' strategies and levels of success in these two settings might differ significantly. Observe the extent to which students' strategies refer to or otherwise are linked to the settings and how the settings might enable keeping track of the calculation.

Use a selection of tasks involving different number relationships. Regrouping tasks are more challenging and more revealing: students can solve non-regrouping tasks using a split strategy without knowledge of how to coordinate tens and ones.

When students solve tasks, observe or inquire about their strategies. Of particular interest is their relational thinking and reasoning. What number relationships are they noticing: close numbers, rounding to a decuple, doubles, partitions of 10? What is their facility with additive reasoning, such as: treating numbers in tens and ones parts, coordinating tens and ones, subtracting the correct parts, compensating?

Watch closely for use of counting-by-ones. This can indicate a need for instruction aimed at developing facility with structuring numbers 1 to 20 and higher decade addition and subtraction. Watch closely for students who seem unable to jump by tens off-the-decuple or to coordinate tens and ones. This can indicate a need for instruction aimed at developing facility with conceptual place value.

Assessment of Foundational Knowledge

As described above, facile addition and subtraction to 100 is founded on knowledge of structuring numbers to 20, conceptual place value, and higher decade addition and subtraction. It is useful to assess knowledge of these three foundations directly. Assessment of structuring numbers and of CPV is addressed in Chapters 4 and 5 respectively.

To assess higher decade addition and subtraction, pose tasks from the six types (see Table 6.7):

- jump within a decade, jump forward from a decuple and jump back to a decuple
- jump forward to the decuple, jump back from a decuple and jump across a decuple

The last three involve more extensive knowledge of combining and partitioning numbers than the first three. Facility with these tasks is closely associated with facility with structuring numbers 1 to 20.

Outline of Instruction in Addition and Subtraction to 100

For many students, additive tasks with multi-digit numbers are initially quite challenging. *A school has 72 children, 25 go on an excursion. How many remain at school?* Some students try counting back by ones, but errors in the backward number word sequence are common and keeping track of 25 counts is likely to be quite difficult. How do students progress? There is much to learn. When we understand what facile mental computation consists of, then what students need in order to progress in this domain becomes clearer. Since facile mental computation relies on strong knowledge of number relations, students need to spend considerable time learning the foundations: structuring numbers 1 to 20; CPV; and higher decade addition and subtraction. Since facile mental computation consists of relational thinking rather than procedural thinking, students need to solve additive tasks as much as possible through their own reasoning and number sense. Since facile mental computation ultimately involves new mathematical sophistication, students need to reflect on their thinking, with teachers supporting the progressive mathematization of students' strategies.

Instruction involves supporting students with each of these strands of development: learning foundational arithmetic knowledge; devising strategies to solve addition and subtraction tasks; and progressively mathematizing their thinking. The strands are pursued alongside each other, however the instructional emphasis tends to shift over time. Thus we outline the instructional approach in three broad overlapping phases.

- **Instruction phase 1: Developing foundational knowledge.**
  Emphasize developing facility in the three foundations of addition and subtraction to 100: structuring numbers 1 to 20; CPV; and higher decade addition and subtraction.
- **Instruction phase 2: Consolidating early strategies.**
  When students are progressing with the foundations, they are ready to try solving 2-digit addition and subtraction tasks. Look for the emergence of non-counting strategies such as jump or split. Students need to consolidate these, and learn to notate them.
- **Instruction phase 3: Refining strategies and extending tasks.**
  When students have consolidated using and notating non-counting strategies, shift the emphasis to comparing different strategies, and considering efficiency and elegance. Expand the variety of tasks. Introduce more formal notation, such as arrow notation and conventional number sentences. Aim towards more flexible and formal thinking.

These phases may extend over several years. Students solve tasks that are, in an arithmetical sense, progressively more complex *37 and two tens … 37 and 21 … 37 and 25 … 37 and what makes 62?* They solve tasks that are progressively less context-dependent, from settings involving manipulation of base-ten materials, to settings with screened materials, to bare number tasks. They use progressively more sophisticated strategies: jump by single tens, curtailed jump, compensation. Over two to four years of purposeful and focused instruction, almost all students can develop facile mental computation. The three instructional phases are described in the following three sections (Carpenter et al., 1998; Tabor, 2008; Treffers and Buys, 2001; Wright et al., 2007; Yackel, 2001).

Instruction Phase 1: Developing Foundational Knowledge

Initially the emphasis needs to be on students developing their knowledge of the three foundations of addition and subtraction to 100, as described in the section on foundational knowledge above:

- Structuring numbers 1 to 20
- Conceptual place value
- Higher decade addition and subtraction.

Aim to develop students' facility in each of these aspects; then they will be well resourced to grapple with 2-digit tasks and devise their own effective mental strategies. Instruction in structuring numbers 1 to 20 is addressed in Chapter 4. Instruction in CPV is addressed in Chapter 5. Instruction in higher decade addition and subtraction is described below. The section of Instructional Activities in this chapter also includes activities specifically addressing this aspect.

Higher Decade Addition and Subtraction

Higher decade addition and subtraction is about solving tasks involving a 1-digit number added to or subtracted from a 2-digit number. Students need to become facile with non-counting strategies for these tasks. All the strategies build from knowledge of structuring numbers 1 to 20. Many students need explicit instruction to link their knowledge of adding and subtracting 1-digit numbers in the range 1 to 20, to adding and subtracting 1-digit numbers in the higher decades (Menne, 2001; Wright et al., 2006b, 2006c). We distinguish six types of higher decade addition and subtraction tasks:

Type A. Jump within a decade
Type B. Jump forward from a decuple

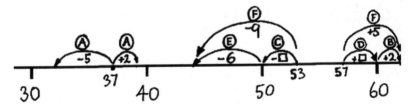

Figure 6.3   Six types of tasks for higher decade addition and subtraction

Type C. Jump back to the decuple

Type D. Jump forward to the decuple

Type E. Jump back from a decuple

Type F. Jump across a decuple

Examples for each type are listed in Table 6.7 and notated on a number line in Figure 6.3. These six types are closely related. Types B, C, D and E all involve jumping to and from the decuple. Jump forward from a decuple (B) and jump back to the decuple (C) are simple cases of jump within a decade (A). Jump forward to the decuple (D) and jump back from the decuple (E) are more challenging; they involve using partitions of 10. Jump back to the decuple (C) and jump forward to the decuple (D) are presented as unknown jumps: *From 53, how far back to 50? From 57, what is the jump to the next decuple?* This is the form in which these tasks are typically used as steps in jump strategies. For these tasks, students also need to be able to locate the next decuple: *from 57, what is the next decuple forward?* Alternative classroom terms for decuple include: decade number, tens number, or round number.

Jumps across a decuple (F) are the most challenging. They are often solved using a via-the-decuple strategy. For example, 57 + 5 is calculated by thinking 57 + ☐ = 60, partitioning 5 into 3 and ☐, then solving 60 + 2 = ☐. Thus solving F using adding via-the-decuple involves jump forward to the decuple (D) then jump forward from the decuple (B), as shown in Figure 6.3. Similarly, solving F using subtracting via-the-decuple involves jump back to the decuple (B) then jump back from the decuple (D). Jumps across a decuple (F) can be solved in other ways too. For example, 57 + 5 is solved by thinking '6 + 6 = 12, so 7 + 5 = 12, so 57 + 5 = 62' and 43 − 9 is solved by thinking '43 − 10 → 33 + 1 → 34'.

For instruction in higher decade addition and subtraction, pose tasks using a setting of ten-frame cards. To build a 2-digit number, use full 10-dot cards alongside the ten-frame cards for numbers 1 to 9: for example, 37 can be shown using three 10-dot cards and a 7-dot card. Present initial tasks with the cards in view. Then shift to screening the cards, and revealing them for students to check their answers. Alongside the screened tasks, introduce number sentence notation. Finally, transition to posing bare number tasks. Box 6.1 describes examples of how to present each task type with the ten-frame setting.

For initial instruction, restrict Instructional Activities to particular task types, to support students organizing that particular form of reasoning. For example, for one session work exclusively on jumping forward to the decuple (D). As student knowledge consolidates, pose linked types. For example, jumping forward to the decuple (D) can be linked with jumping back from a decuple (E): 57 + ☐ = 60, and 60 − 3 = ☐. Jumping forward to the decuple (D) can also be linked with jumping forward from a decuple (B) to suggest adding via-the-decuple: 57 + ☐ = 60, 60 + 2 = ☐, 57 + 5 = ☐. As another instructional approach, pose groups of tasks where students can make links between addition and subtraction in the range 1 to 20, and in the higher decades. For example:

Photo 6.1 Jump down from the decuple with 10-dot ten-frames

Type A. Jump within a decade:	8 – 5	18 – 5	28 – 5	68 – 5
Type B. Jump forward from a decuple:	10 + 2	20 + 2	30 + 2	60 + 2
Type D. Jump forward to the decuple:	7 + □ = 10	17 + □ = 20	27 + □ = 30	57 + □ = 60
Type F. Jump across a decuple:	7 + 5	17 + 5	27 + 5	57 + 5
Type F. Jump across a decuple:	13 – 9	23 – 9	33 – 9	53 – 9

BOX 6.1   PRESENTING HIGHER DECADE ADDITION AND SUBTRACTION TASKS WITH THE TEN-FRAME SETTING

A. Jump within a decade. e.g. 37 – 5 → □

Place cards for 37. *How many dots?* Screen the cards.
Cover 5 dots. *I have covered 5 dots. How many dots are there now?*

B. Jump forward from a decuple. e.g. 60 + 2 → □

Place cards for 60. *How many tens? How many dots?* Screen the cards.
Show a 2-dot card, then place it under the screen. *How many dots now?*

C. Jump back to the decuple. e.g. 53 – □→50

Place cards for 53. *How many dots?* Screen the cards. Cover the 3-dot card.
I have covered some. Now there are 50. Show briefly. *How many did I cover?*

D. Jump forward to the decuple. e.g. 57 + □ → 60

Place cards for 57. *How many dots?* Screen the cards.
What is the next decuple? How many more to make 60?

E. Jump back from a decuple. e.g. 50 – 6 → □

Place cards for 50. *How many tens? How many dots?* Screen the cards.
Cover 6 dots on one card. *I have covered 6 dots. How many dots are there now?*

F. Jump across a decuple. e.g. 57 + 5 → □

Place cards for 57. *How many dots?* Screen the cards.
Show a 5-dot card, then place it under the screen. *How many dots now?*

Leading into Phase 2: Extending to 2-digit Tasks

As students become facile with higher decade addition and subtraction, the tasks can be extended into 2-digit tasks. For example:

    65 – 3   65 – 13   65 – 23   57 + 5   57 + 15   57 + 25 …

Similarly, as students become facile with CPV, the tasks can be extended into 2-digit tasks. For example:

    37 and two tens …   37 and two tens and one …   37 + 21 …

Thus, students' work in higher decade addition and subtraction and in CPV culminates in overlapping with work in 2-digit addition and subtraction. This overlap is productive: students can approach tasks from several directions, and make connections that arise from their developing knowledge.

Instruction Phase 2: Consolidating Early Strategies

As students consolidate their knowledge of structuring numbers 1 to 20, CPV, and higher decade addition and subtraction, they are ready to attempt solving 2-digit addition and subtraction tasks with non-counting strategies. Tasks without regrouping will be easier, but at this point, tasks with regrouping are the main challenge for students. Pose tasks as open problems. Do not expect them to be solved yet. Rather, observe and take an interest in the attempts and solutions that arise. Students thinking hard about these tasks, and making their own breakthroughs, is most valuable. Rushing to establish answers or demonstrating more sophisticated strategies can significantly reduce the extent to which students remain in touch with their sense of the mathematics.

Settings

Pose 2-digit addition and subtraction tasks using settings of number lines and base-ten materials. However, ask students to solve the tasks without manipulating the setting. The important goal is to develop their mental computation, rather than learn to solve tasks by manipulating materials. As usual, screening the setting can be very effective. After students have answered a task, allow students to view and manipulate the setting in order to discuss their strategies and confirm their solutions.

Posing tasks within an established story context can also be purposeful. Familiar contexts include: numbers of children in different classrooms or buses; money amounts when shopping; page numbers when reading; numbers of days between calendar dates; a timeline marking different ages in a person's life; a table of students' heights; a list of animals' weights; sport scores; dice rolls; and tallies from data collecting activities. Also effective is taking time to establish an imagined story context, out of which 2-digit addition and subtraction tasks become compelling problems. For example, see Instructional Activity IA6.10 *Interstate Driving Context*. See also Fosnot and Dolk (2001b) and Stephan et al. (2003).

Photo 6.2 Solving an additive task in a setting of partly screened bundling sticks

A material setting or story context can influence how students think about additive and subtractive tasks. For example, when tasks are posed in a story about packing items in separate boxes, students are more likely to think about separating the boxes, and thus focus on grouping the tens and ones separately. Thus they are likely to use split strategies. By contrast, when tasks are posed in a story about distances driven along a highway, students are more likely to think about appending numbers in sequence. Thus they are likely to use jump strategies (Beishuizen, 1993; Stephan et al., 2003; Tabor, 2008).

Notating Strategies

When students reach their answers to a 2-digit task, try to elicit their strategies. *How did you get that answer?*, or *You began with 37 + 25. What was your thinking from there?* As a student tries to describe her thinking, notate the strategy on the board. The initial notation needs to be informal and relatively self-explanatory. For jump-like strategies, notation with an empty number line (ENL) works well. For split strategies, drop-down notation works well. Irregular strategies like transformation can be accommodated with an informal arrow notation. Figures 6.1 and 6.2 show examples of these notations. Notating students' strategies develops their awareness of their own thinking, and alerts them to the possibilities of other students' approaches. Importantly, notating provides a record of the strategies, on which students can draw in discussions about the strategies (Beishuizen, 1999; Bobis, 2007; Treffers, 1991; Wright et al., 2007).

As students become familiar with the notation, they can use it to record their own thinking. In some instructional approaches, students write notations while they are solving a task. For example, a student might mark jumps on an ENL, and then use those markings to help determine his answer. This approach can lead to students developing written computation methods, but not developing strong mental computation. We advocate that students should not use notation in this way. Rather, ask students to solve a task without writing, then invite them to pick up their pencils and record their strategies.

Establishing the correct answers to tasks is one important focus for class discussion. Initially, students may well arrive at different answers, or be uncertain of their answers. As much as possible, students should verify answers through their own collective reasoning. Have several students' strategies and answers displayed on the board. The teacher's role is to facilitate the discussion of answers. This involves inviting students to justify an answer, or explain their concerns with an answer. The records of strategies on the board constitute a reference point for the arguments (Beishuizen and Anghileri, 1998; Cobb et al., 1997; Fosnot and Dolk, 2001b; Tabor, 2008).

Labelling Strategies

A second important focus for class discussion is to recognize and label strategies. Initially it may not be appropriate to label the strategies. As teachers we immediately recognize a jump strategy but to the students, the strategy is merely the way they thought through that particular task. Only after several experiences of notating and reflecting on their strategies will a notion of regular strategies arise. At this point labelling makes good sense. Home-grown labels for strategies can arise out of the classroom discussion: the 'tens-and-ones strategy', the 'go-too-far-and-come-back' strategy, 'Mim's strategy'. These can provide an initial means for recognizing and labelling strategies. Ultimately, students should learn standard labels. *Mim's strategy is a strategy many people have used. It is usually called the jump strategy.*

Note that the labels and notations are not the curriculum, as such. At this point, the aim is not for students to be able to name or mimic a jump strategy on a written test, nor to be able to use the notation 'correctly'. After all, these are informal strategies and notations. Rather, the aim is for students to solve addition and subtraction tasks without counting by ones. The notations and labels are merely useful supports for reflecting on and improving their own mental strategies.

Learning to Jump and Learning to Split

There is evidence that many students develop split strategies for non-regrouping tasks once they learn about partitioning numbers into tens and ones. However, students often struggle with split strategies for regrouping tasks, especially subtraction tasks with regrouping. On the other hand, many students do not develop jump strategies without instruction in jumping by ten off the decuple. However, when students do use jump, they tend to make fewer errors than when they use split: jump does not present the same procedural difficulties with regrouping. In summary, split appears easy to start but hard to master, whereas jump is harder to start but easier to master. Hence, there has been some debate among teachers and curriculum developers about whether to preference jump or split strategies in teaching. The view taken in this book is, firstly, jumping by tens off the decuple is important basic arithmetic knowledge, and needs emphasis in instruction regardless of preferences about jump and split. Secondly, there is likely to be a variety of strategies arising in a classroom, and teachers need to support students' progressive mathematization from a variety of starting points (Beishuizen, 2001; Beishuizen et al., 1997; Fuson et al., 1997; Klein et al., 1998; Menne, 2001; Tabor, 2008).

Leading into Phase 3: Comparing Strategies

A further important focus for classroom discussion is to seek better strategies, that is strategies that are mathematically more sophisticated or more appropriate for a particular case. The aim of notating and labelling strategies is not to celebrate the diversity of approaches. Rather, the aim is to raise awareness about being strategic and insightful. Which strategy was easiest? Quickest? Neatest? Most efficient? Which made good use of number relationships? These questions can be raised from the beginning of students' attempts at 2-digit tasks. As students' strategies consolidate, these questions become the focus of instruction, and we move into phase 3.

Instruction Phase 3: Refining Strategies and Extending Tasks

In phase 3, when students have consolidated their early strategies for 2-digit addition and subtraction, shift the emphasis of instruction to refining their strategies and their relational thinking, as described in the following section. At the same time, extend the tasks in three directions: formalize the tasks and the notation, increase the complexity of tasks, and extend the range to larger numbers. These three directions are described in the sections below. Extending the tasks in these ways will build students' knowledge of number relationships in the range 1 to 100 and beyond, which will support the further refining of their mental strategies. All the developments in this phase can be regarded as progressive mathematization of students' additive thinking.

Refining Students' Strategies

Instruction to refine strategies involves holding classroom discussions about students' strategies. Discussions create valuable opportunities for students to reflect on their thinking and to see different strategies. Through the discussions, draw attention to shorter strategies and to the insightful use of number relationships. Introduce alternative strategies and ways to curtail steps in strategies. Encourage a preference for efficiency, flexibility and elegance (Beishuizen, 2001; Fosnot and Dolk, 2001b; Rousham, 2003; Selter, 2001; Treffers and Buys, 2001).

Instruction also involves being deliberate about the tasks posed. For example, pose only subtraction with regrouping tasks. Pose tasks in a story setting that are likely to elicit certain strategies. Pose a task and challenge students to find useful number relationships. Pose sets of tasks that invite certain number relationships. Some examples of task sets follow.

Small differences:	32 − 29	41 − 37	62 − 58	93 − 87
Just below a decuple:	36 + 29	45 + 39	64 − 18	49 + 27
Just above a decuple:	51 − 16	92 − 35	63 − 27	71 − 44
Near doubles:	50 − 25	60 − 31	80 − 38	71 − 35
Transformations:	40 + 23	39 + 24	37 + 26	38 + 25

Formalizing the Tasks and the Notation

Move from posing tasks in settings and story contexts to posing bare number tasks. Bare number tasks will have arisen at times in earlier phases. However, it is important not to underestimate the difference, from the students' perspective, between contextualized tasks and bare number tasks. So in phase 3, dedicate some instruction to establishing students' facility with bare number tasks.

As students become facile with ENL notation and drop-down notation, introduce more formal notation. An arrow notation, as used in Tables 6.1 and 6.2, is relatively intuitive for students familiar with ENL notation. Yet it is more compact and flexible, and moves closer to conventional mathematical notations. Conventional number sentences can be

Photo 6.3   Mentally solving bare number 2-digit addition tasks

Photo 6.4   Notating different strategies to facilitate discussion

used as a still more formal notation. Figure 6.4 shows four examples. Number sentences can be used to record separate calculations clearly, without indicating the thinking that occurs between successive calculations. This austerity is a feature of formal notation. Be mindful that a more formal notation needs to be used with more precision. We can write 37 + 20 → 57 + 5 → 62. But we cannot write 37 + 20 = 57 + 5 = 62, because according to the conventional way these symbols are used, this reads as '37 + 20 equals 57 + 5', which is false, and does not indicate the strategy as intended.

Formalizing is valuable for students' mathematical development. As instruction moves to bare number tasks and more formal notation, arithmetic thinking is less constrained by settings, and can become more flexible. Also, facility with formal notation prepares students for written computation, which is addressed in Chapter 8.

Jump

37 + 20 = 57

57 + 5 = 62

Jump to the decuple

37 + 3 = 40

40 + 20 = 60

60 + 2 = 62

Compensation

40 + 25 = 65

65 – 3 = 62

Split

30 + 20 = 50

7 + 5 = 12

50 + 12 = 62

Figure 6.4   Writing number sentences to notate mental strategies for 37 + 25

Increasing the Complexity of Tasks

Ensure students grapple with a wide variety of additive and subtractive tasks, including: missing addend tasks; missing subtrahend tasks; comparison tasks; and combinations and partitions. Pose sets of tasks involving a particular type of combination or partition, such as:

2-digit doubles:	$20 + 20, 30 + 30 \ldots 15 + 15, 25 + 25 \ldots 27 + 27 \ldots$
Partitions of 100:	How many more to make 100?
	$90 + \square, 80 + \square, 70 + \square \ldots 75 + \square, 65 + \square \ldots 23 + \square \ldots$
Partitions of decuples:	$60 = 10 + \square, 60 = 20 + \square \ldots 60 = 15 + \square, 60 = 25 + \square \ldots$

Some other important sets of combinations are the multiples, such as:

Multiples: $3, 3 + 3, 3 + 3 + 3 \ldots; 4, 4 + 4, 4 + 4 + 4 \ldots; 8, 8 + 8, 8 + 8 + 8 \ldots$

Knowledge of multiples in the range 1 to 100 is first developed using addition. It becomes foundational for developing multiplication and division. Instruction involving multiples is discussed in Chapter 7.

Pose tasks requiring only estimation, rather than exact answers. Ask students to find addition and subtraction tasks from their lives or their parents' lives. Invite students to make up tasks for each other. As students gain facility with addition and subtraction to 100, the field of problems they can solve expands greatly. There are no dangers lurking, so send them out to enjoy their new powers. A particularly exciting area to try is tasks involving finding patterns and generalizing:

Make up your own problems, all with an answer of 10.
What are all the pairs of numbers that sum to 60?
Which decuples have halves that are also decuples?

These are tasks of a higher order. They are not just about computation. They are also about algebraic reasoning. Algebraic reasoning is discussed further in Chapter 11.

Extending the Range of Numbers

Challenge students with tasks involving larger numbers. Some tasks involving 3- and 4-digit numbers require little extension in knowledge from 2-digit addition and subtraction. For example, a student who can solve $17 + 65$ can solve $417 + 65$, or indeed $9417 + 65$. Similarly, a student who can solve $42 - 39$ can probably solve $842 - 839$. Furthermore, students may gain considerable satisfaction in seeing ways that their 2-digit knowledge can be extended to include larger numbers. Tasks involving two 3-digit numbers can be made more challenging. Some students will enjoy trying to solve difficult 4-digit tasks. Be alert to how the particular numbers involved make a significant difference to the difficulty of the task. Also, subtraction tasks are typically more difficult than addition tasks (Selter, 2001).

As well as adding larger numbers, it is important for students to practise mentally adding up more than two numbers. Students can total short lists of 1-digit and 2-digit numbers: the total of prices on a shopping list, the total number of children in six classes, the total distance travelled over a week, and so on.

While it is essential that students learn to solve mentally any addition or subtraction task in the range to 100, solving mental tasks beyond that range does not seem essential. But it is certainly useful. Furthermore, attempting to solve such tasks can provide purposeful challenges. The demands on memory recall are greater, and so is the incentive to use insightful and elegant strategies. Also, when more numbers are involved, there are more possible number relationships to find and use. Students may discover that they tend to use different strategies in the higher ranges than they do in the range to 100.

Since the demands on recall are greater, a particularly useful technique for tasks in the higher ranges is to jot down a few subtotals during the calculation. Jotting can link with students' first attempts to learn written computation. If students want to do this, reward their cleverness: the use of writing to support computation is a major mathematical achievement. Requiring students to practise doing strictly mental computation remains valuable. Also valuable is for students to learn approaches to written computation. Instruction in written computation is discussed in Chapter 8.

 ## ASSESSMENT TASK GROUPS

List of Assessment Task Groups

Task group A6.1: Decuple After and Decuple Before a Number
Task group A6.2: Jump Forward from and Jump Back to a Decuple
Task group A6.3: Jump Forward to and Jump Back from a Decuple
Task group A6.4: Jump Across a Decuple
Task group A6.5: Addition and Subtraction of a Decuple
Task group A6.6: 2-digit Addition and Subtraction without Regrouping
Task group A6.7: 2-digit Addition and Subtraction with Regrouping
Task group A6.8: 3-digit Addition and Subtraction

TASK GROUP A6.1: Decuple After And Decuple Before a Number

Materials: None.

What to do and say: As a preliminary, establish a term for the decuples that the student can understand. *What do you call numbers like 20, 30, 70, 90?* (Perhaps tens numbers, decades, tidy numbers … ?) Use the agreed term in the following tasks and the Task Groups below. *What is the decuple after 30? What is the decuple before 30?* Similarly with 48, 73.

Notes:

- Students need to locate the nearest decuples to any number, in order to use jump strategies, and generally to know their way around the range 0 to 100.
- Most students with some knowledge of numbers to 100 are successful with this task. If a student is unsuccessful, instruction should focus on developing knowledge of the decuples.

TASK GROUP A6.2: Jump Forward from and Jump Back to a Decuple

Materials: Numeral card for 30, 46.

What to do and say: Jump forward from: Show the 30 card. *What is that number? What is 7 more (than 30)?*

Jump back to: Show the 46 card. *What is that number? What is the decuple before 46? How far back to 40?*

Notes:

- Jump back to a decuple is the inverse of jump forward from a decuple. The tasks involve similar knowledge, so we group them together.
- These tasks may be solved by counting-by-ones. The instructional aim is for students to know the answer in one jump.
- Students may think that the jump from 46 back down to 40 is five or seven.

TASK GROUP A6.3: Jump Forward to and Jump Back from a Decuple

Materials: Numeral card for 30, 46, 42.

What to do and say: Jump back from: Show the 30 card. *What is that number? … What is 2 less (than 30)? … What is 7 less (than 30)?*

Jump forward to: Show the 46 card. *What is that number? What is the decuple after 46? How far is it up to 50?* Similarly with 42.

Notes:

- Jump forward to a decuple is the inverse of jump back from a decuple. The tasks involve similar knowledge, so we group them together. These tasks are more challenging than Task Group A6.2, and require knowledge of partitions of ten.
- Often jumping a small number in the range of 1–5 – such as 30 back to 28, and 46 up to 50 – is easier than jumping a larger number in the range of 6–9 – such as 30 back to 23, and 42 up to 50 – even when the student is not using counting by ones.

TASK GROUP A6.4: Jump Across a Decuple

Materials: Numeral cards for 46 and 42.

What to do and say: Show the 46 card. *What is 8 more than 46?* Show the 42 card. *What is 7 less than 42?*

Notes:

- Observe closely for counting by ones. Students need to establish facility with jumping across a decuple without counting by ones.
- Strategies may involve jumping via the decuple – for example, jumping 46 to 50 to 54. This involves jumping forward to the decuple, partitioning 8 into 4 and 4, and jumping forward from the decuple.
- Other strategies are possible. Students may do 7 less than 42 as '40 less 7 plus 2', a compensation strategy. Students may have $12 - 7 = 5$ as a known fact, and extrapolate.

TASK GROUP A6.5: Addition and Subtraction of a Decuple

Materials: Task cards written in horizontal format.

What to do and say: Pose tasks involving adding a decuple to or subtracting a decuple from a 2-digit number, such as $52 + 30$, $76 - 40$. For each task, display a card. *Read this please. Can you solve this?*

Notes:

- These are typically the easiest 2-digit tasks for students.
- Students may succeed using jump or split strategies, or by simply combining digits without thinking about the tens and ones places. It may be difficult to distinguish what strategy a student has used.
- Try to observe whether a student has made a single jump of 30, or separate jumps of ten – 52, 62, 72, 82, or 50, 60, 70, 80, perhaps keeping track of three jumps of ten on the fingers.

TASK GROUP A6.6: 2-digit Addition and Subtraction without Regrouping

Materials: Task cards written in horizontal format.

What to do and say: Pose 2-digit addition and subtraction tasks without regrouping, such as $52 + 35$, $76 - 42$. For each task, display a card. *Read this please. Can you solve this?* If a student's strategy is not apparent, pose questions about their reasoning.

Notes:

- Students may succeed using jump or split strategies, or by simply combining digits without thinking about the tens and ones places.
- Success with these non-regrouping tasks does not necessarily indicate knowledge of how to coordinate tens and ones.

TASK GROUP A6.7: 2-digit Addition and Subtraction with Regrouping

Materials: Task cards written in horizontal format.

What to do and say: Pose a range of 2-digit addition and subtraction tasks with regrouping, such as 58 + 35, 53 + 19, 71 – 24, 76 – 68. For each task, display a card. *Read this please. Can you solve this?* If a student's strategy is not apparent, pose questions about their reasoning.

Notes:

- Students may try to use counting by ones for the whole calculation. Instruction should focus on the foundational knowledge of structuring numbers 1 to 20 and conceptual place value.
- Students may use counting-by-ones for parts of the calculation – for example, 58 + 35 as 58, 68, 78, 88, 89, 90, 91, 92, 93. Instruction should focus on structuring numbers 1 to 20, and higher decade addition and subtraction.
- Regrouping tasks require a robust coordination of tens and ones. Students' approaches to managing this coordination are of interest, irrespective of their final answers. Answers for 58 + 35 indicating an unsuccessful coordination of tens and ones include: 80 and 13, 813, 83.
- Students may have particular difficulty with subtraction. Watch for the 'smaller-from-larger' bug, answering 71 – 24 as 53, by thinking of 4 – 1 instead of 1 – 4.
- To develop coordination of tens and ones, return to conceptual place value tasks, and to 2-digit addition and subtraction tasks in a setting of screened base-ten materials.
- Students may have difficulty keeping their thinking sufficiently organized – for example, for 58 + 35 students may effectively calculate 58 + 53, or 58 + 30, or 58 + 33. Similarly, students may have difficulty recalling subtotals – for example, students split 58 + 35 and calculate 80 and 13, but are unable to remember both subtotals simultaneously in order to combine them. Such students need instruction in settings of screened organized materials, to further organize their own thinking. Encouraging jump-based strategies may help: jump appears to require less organization and memory than split.
- Students who have been taught a formal written algorithm for addition or subtraction may try to do the algorithm mentally, possibly visualizing writing on paper or writing on the desk. Watch for finger movements.
- There is a whole range of non-counting strategies that students may use (refer to Table 6.1). Each task is more amenable to some strategies than it is to others.
- A student's success using non-counting mental strategies is an achievement. Also consider the levels of efficiency and flexibility of a student's strategies.

TASK GROUP A6.8: 3-digit Addition and Subtraction

Materials: Task cards written in horizontal format.

What to do and say: Pose 3-digit addition and subtraction tasks, such as 488 + 130, 505 – 497. For each task, display a card. *Read this please. Can you solve this?* If a student's strategy is not apparent, pose questions about their reasoning.

Notes:

- 3-digit tasks can have a wide range of complexity. Be aware of the potential complexities of each task.
- Mental computation of 3-digit tasks can be taxing on organization and memory.
- While facile mental computation involving 2-digit tasks is essential mathematical knowledge, mental computation involving 3-digit tasks may not be essential. Teachers need to determine their instructional goal for students' level of computational facility with 3-digit tasks.
- 3-digit subtraction may be significantly more difficult than 3-digit addition. Some students may become facile with 3-digit addition before they are facile with 2-digit subtraction.

INSTRUCTIONAL ACTIVITIES

List of Instructional Activities

- IA6.1: 70 Plus Game
- IA6.2: Jumping Back to the Decuple with Mini Ten-frames
- IA6.3: Decuple Tag
- IA6.4: Adding to 50 Game
- IA6.5: Jumping Back from a Decuple with Mini Ten-frames
- IA6.6: 48 Plus Game
- IA6.7: 32 Minus Game
- IA6.8: Higher Decade Addition and Subtraction Patterns
- IA6.9: Screened Tasks with Two Collections of Mini Ten-frames
- IA6.10: Interstate Driving Context Notated on the Empty Number Line
- IA6.11: Add or Subtract 12
- IA6.12: How Many More to Make 100?
- IA6.13: How Many More to Make 60?

ACTIVITY IA6.1: 70 Plus Game

Intended learning: To add from a decuple without counting.

Instructional mode: Shorter, rehearsal mode for partners.

Materials: 70 Plus Game board and spinner, two types of counters, pencil and paper clip for spinner.

Description: This game is played in a manner similar to IA 4.6, the 9 Plus Game.

Responses, variations and extensions:

- Initially students may count on by ones to find each sum. However, students typically realize after a short period of playing the game that the addends are easily composed into related 2-digit numbers without counting.
- The game can be varied to other decuples, such as a 20 Plus Game, to help generalize this non-count-by-ones strategy to other decuples.
- Less facile students may need base-ten materials to support their problem-solving.

ACTIVITY IA6.2: Jumping Back to the Decuple with Mini Ten-frames

Intended learning: To name the decuple before a given 2-digit number and to find the difference between the decuple and the two-digit number.

Instructional mode: Longer, inquiry mode for individuals or small groups.

Materials: Mini ten-frames, a large screen.

Description: Briefly display a collection of six mini ten-frames and a four pattern (see Figure 6.5). Screen the collection with a large screen so that students can no longer see the mini ten-frames. *I have sixty-four dots all together on the mini ten-frames. I want to take away some dots so that I go back to the next decuple. Which decuple would that be?* [60] *How many dots will I remove? How do you know?* Remove large screen to enable students to check. Repeat with 92, 58, 47, etc.

Responses, variations and extensions:

- Initially students might count back by ones to find the subtrahend. If students continue with this strategy, present teen numbers with a full ten-frame and a partial ten-frame to create a teen number. For example, 19, 15, 17, 12.

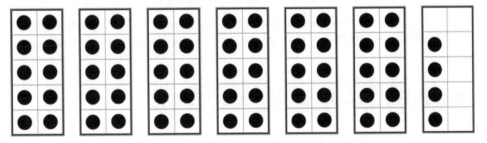

Figure 6.5 Jumping back to a decuple with ten-frames 10-dot cards for 64 – ? = 60

- If necessary, provide additional support by allowing the student to see the cards.
- Dot strips rather than ten-frames can be used.

ACTIVITY IA6.3: Decuple Tag

Intended learning: To identify the nearest decuples surrounding a number.

Instructional mode: Shorter, reproductive practice for small groups or whole class.

Materials: Chalkboard with a row of 9 trees getting progressively larger from left to right.

Description: This activity is introduced to the students by describing the context of playing the game of tag. *How many of you have ever played tag? You know the game in which someone is 'it' and that person is trying to tag the others so someone else will be 'it'. Usually when you play there are some bases that keep a person safe from being tagged. Let's say there was a game of tag in a field and all the trees in this row are bases. If I was here* [point to the space between the third and fourth tree] *trying to get to base and 'it' was bearing down on me, which base do you think I would attempt to reach? Yes, I would probably head for one of the nearest trees on either side of me, depending on where 'it' was. Let's suppose these trees have numbers painted on the trunks.* Write the decuple numbers sequentially with 10 on the smallest tree and 90 on the largest tree. Write 55 between the trees with 50 and 60. *Which two bases are the best options for 55? How about 87?* [Do not indicate where 87 would be.] *Yes, 90 is closest, but if 'it' is coming from that direction, what would be 87's next best option? Yes, 80 would be the closest base in the other direction.* Continue with other numbers; have students identify the next decuple on each side of given numbers.

Responses, variations and extensions:

- Students frequently struggle to identify the decuple numbers on either side of a given number. The tag among trees context provides a scaffold to student reasoning about the numbers.
- A variation is to have higher decuple bases (i.e. 210, 220, 230, …) or centuples as bases (200, 300, 400, …).
- This activity lays a foundation needed for adding and subtracting through ten.
- Another variation of this activity is to identify the single closest tree to each given number to introduce the notion of rounding to the nearest decuple or centuple number.

Acknowledgement: This activity is modified from a task designed by Jason Knight, Elementary Mathematics Specialist with Harford County Public Schools, Maryland, USA. Used with permission.

ACTIVITY IA6.4: Adding to 50 Game

Intended learning: To find the jump to the next decuple.

Instructional mode: Shorter, rehearsal mode for partners.

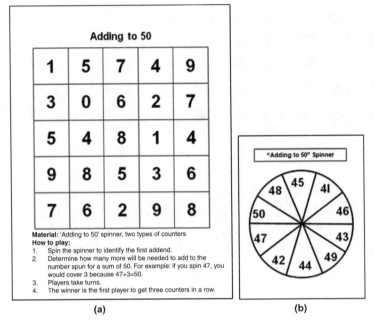

Figure 6.6   (a) Adding to 50 game board and (b) spinner

Materials: Adding to 50 Game board and spinner (see Figure 6.6), two types of counters, pencil, and paper clip for spinner.

Description: This game is played in a manner similar to IA 4.6, the 9 Plus Game. The purpose of this game is to practise higher decade addition involving adding to a decuple. Students spin the spinner to identify the first addend. They must determine the missing addend to equal a sum of 50. They must then cover the missing addend on the game board. For example, if 47 is spun, 3 would be covered on the board since 47 + 3 = 50. Students take turns until one player has three counters in a row, horizontally, vertically or diagonally.

Responses, variations and extensions:

- This game draws on students' knowledge of partitions of ten and therefore is best introduced when students are facile in structuring numbers 1 to 10.
- Some students become facile with this activity relatively quickly.
- If students count up to 50 by ones to determine the missing addend, ask them if they have a way to determine the missing addend without counting.
- Some students may benefit from having four full mini ten-frames and an empty frame on which they can build the spun number to support their thinking about the bare number tasks generated in this game.

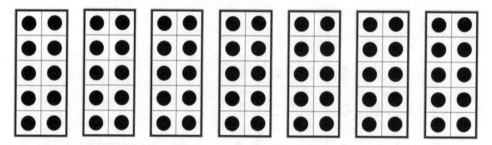

Figure 6.7 Jumping back from a decuple with ten-frames 10-dot cards for 70 − 3

ACTIVITY IA6.5: Jumping Back from a Decuple with Mini Ten-frames

Intended learning: To subtract the numbers 1–9 from a decuple without counting.

Instructional mode: Longer, inquiry mode for individuals or small groups.

Materials: Mini ten-frames, a large screen.

Description: The purpose of this activity is for students to apply knowledge of partitions of ten to subtraction from a decuple. This activity is best introduced once students have developed automaticity with partitions of ten.

Briefly display a collection of seven mini ten-frames. Screen the collection so that students can no longer see the mini ten-frames (see Figure 6.7). *How many dots do we have?* Once the student has determined the number of dots, screen three dots on the last frame. *I have covered three dots with a small card. How many dots will you be able to see if I remove this large screen? How do you know?* Remove large screen to enable students to check. Repeat with 80 − 2; 50 − 8; 40 − 6, etc.

Responses, variations and extensions:

- Initially students might count back by ones to find each difference. If students continue with this strategy, present tasks with one ten-frame only. For example, 10 − 3. This enables students to link partitioning tens with subtraction in higher decades.
- This task is typically more difficult for students than adding to a decuple.
- This activity can be done using dot strips rather than mini ten-frames.
- The activity can be extended into the hundreds.

ACTIVITY IA6.6: 48 Plus Game

Intended learning: To add nine or less across a decuple.

Instructional mode: Shorter, rehearsal mode for partners.

Materials: 48 Plus Game board, 4–9 spinner, two types of counters, pencil and paper clip for spinner.

Description: This game is played in a similar manner as IA 4.6, the 9 Plus Game. The purpose of this game is to build facility with adding a number in the range of 2 to 9 across a decuple. The game provides a venue for reproductive practice that can lead to adding through ten. This game is best introduced when students have automaticity with the partitions of ten and the partitions of numbers to nine.

Responses, variations and extensions:

- Students need facility with structuring numbers to ten in order to use more efficient strategies such as adding through the decuple.
- Initially students might count on by ones to add. If students continue with this strategy, teachers should challenge students to use what they know about partitions of ten to find more efficient ways to solve the problems.
- The ENL might facilitate students adding through the decuple to solve these tasks.
- The 67 Plus Game will help generalize this non-count-by-ones strategy to adding through other decuples.

ACTIVITY IA6.7: 32 Minus Game

Intended learning: To subtract a 1-digit number across a decuple.

Instructional mode: Shorter, rehearsal mode for partners.

Materials: 32 Minus Game board, 4–9 spinner, two types of counters, pencil and paper clip for spinner.

Description: This game is played in a manner similar to IA 4.6, the 9 Plus Game. The game provides a venue for rehearsal that can lead to subtracting through ten. This game is best introduced when students have automaticity with the partitions of ten and the partitions of numbers to nine.

Responses, variations and extensions:

- Students need facility with structuring numbers to ten in order to use more efficient strategies such as subtracting through the decuple.
- Initially students might count back by ones to subtract. If students continue with this strategy, teachers should challenge students to use what they know about partitions of ten to find more efficient ways to solve the problems.
- The ENL might facilitate students subtracting through the decuple to solve these tasks.
- The 51 Minus Game will help generalize this non-count-by-ones strategy to subtracting through other decuples.

ACTIVITY IA6.8: Higher Decade Addition and Subtraction Patterns

Intended learning: To generalize addition and subtraction across several decades without counting.

Instructional mode: Shorter, inquiry mode for individuals, small groups and whole class.

Materials: Chalkboard and chalk, or chart paper and pen.

Description: This activity involves presenting a series of related tasks designed to draw students' attention to number relationships across several decades. *What is 6 + 2?* Record the equation 6 + 2 = 8. Each of the following equations that notate student responses should be written just below 6 + 2 so that the 6 in the ones place aligns with the 6 above (see Figure 6.8). *If you know that 6 + 2 = 8, can you use that to help you work out 16 + 2? How about 26 + 2? 36 + 2?* This task is intentionally exploiting additive and subtractive patterns over several decades. It is intended that students will use the pattern rather than solve each individual task separately. Facilitate student attention to the pattern by asking, *What do you think will be the next one? Are there others?* Repeat with other patterns.

Responses, variations and extensions:

- Use variations such as the following: (a) additive patterns that do not cross the decuple (6 + 2, 16 + 2, 26 + 2, …); (b) subtractive patterns that do not cross the decuple (8 – 4, 18 – 4, 28 – 4, … or 89 – 5, 79 – 5, 69 – 5 …); (c) additive patterns that cross the decuple (8 + 5, 18 + 5, 28 + 5, …); (d) subtractive patterns that cross the decuple (12 – 4, 22 – 4, 32 – 4, …); (e) additive tasks involving decuple addends (24 + 10, 24 + 20, 24 + 30, …).

$$6 + 2 = 8$$

$$16 + 2 = 18$$

$$26 + 2 = 28$$

$$36 + 2 = 38$$

Figure 6.8   Recording a series of number sentences for higher decade additions

- If students are likely to count by ones (e.g. the string 29 + 8, 29 + 18, 29 + 28, 29 + 38 …), the teacher might supply the first equation in the string.
- It is important for students to notice patterns in order to make conjectures about generalizations. These conjectures should be an explicit topic of discussion.

ACTIVITY IA6.9: Screened Tasks with Two Collections of Mini Ten-frames

Intended learning: To add and subtract two 2-digit numbers using mental strategies of jump, split or split-jump

Instructional mode: Longer, inquiry mode for individuals or small groups.

Materials: Mini ten-frames, two screens such as pieces of cloth or foam sheets.

Description: Briefly display and then screen a collection representing 32 with mini ten-frames. *I have 32 here.* Screen the collection. *If I add 24 more here* [create a second collection of 24 and then screen], *how much will there be altogether?* [Gesture with hand to both collections.] *How do you know?* Notate student thinking using the empty number line or a series of equations so that students can compare strategies.

Responses, variations and extensions:

- Notating student strategies using the ENL or a series of equations can be very helpful in communicating strategies to other students. The split strategy should not be notated with the ENL. Rather a series of equations or drop-down notation better notates the split strategy.
- As new strategies emerge, they can be named. This facilitates students' discussions of the strategies.
- Progression through a series of tasks can elicit particular strategies. For example, the jump strategy is likely to emerge during the following progression of problems: 28 + 10, 28 + 20, 28 + 30, 28 + 34.

ACTIVITY IA6.10: Interstate Driving Context Notated on the Empty Number Line

Intended learning: To add and subtract in the range from 1 to 100 using jump strategies.

Instructional mode: Longer, inquiry mode for individuals or groups.

Materials: Chart paper and marker or blackboard and chalk.

Description: This contextual investigation is intended to draw on students' knowledge of travel to promote linear conceptions of addition and subtraction. While the context is American, similar contexts exist in other countries (see variations below). In the United States there exists an interstate highway system of limited access divided carriageways that cross multiple states. Each interstate carries a two-digit number name prefaced by a capital I for interstate (i.e. I-95 runs north–south along the eastern seaboard) and each exit is numbered. In most states, these exit numbers correspond to the number of miles from the state border (Exit 89 in Maryland is 89 miles north of the Washington, DC border). Since numbers increase as one drives north, driving south constitutes a subtractive task. Even children as young as six years can readily grapple with the context. The investigation can involve exploring several travel scenarios and is quite engaging for the students, particularly when introduced within days of a field trip involving interstate travel.

After discussing the exit numbering system and listing several exits by name and number, pose a question to the students. *If I got on the interstate at Riverside which is Exit 80 and drove nine more miles before getting off, where would I exit? How do you know? How about if I got on at White Marsh, Exit 67, and drove 20 more miles. Where would I be then?* Use the ENL to notate students' solutions. When more than one strategy emerges in the discussion, notate each solution on the ENL to facilitate student communication.

Responses, variations and extensions:

- Alternate contextual settings that use distance: In Australia, some roads have house numbers that correspond to the distance travelled from the origin of the road; in the Netherlands, some beaches have pylons marking distances in km; construct a timeline of events in an older person's life; in many cities, streets are sequentially numbered and lend themselves to calculating the number of blocks walked from, say, 42nd street to 59th street.
- When introducing this context, use an interstate and local exits (or similar context) familiar to the students. Initially include some destinations of interest to them in the scenario. This will heighten engagement. After students are used to the context, a fictitious interstate with carefully contrived exit numbers may be introduced if needed.
- Through careful selection of exit numbers and distances of travel ($54 + 10$; $54 + 20$; $54 + 30$; $54 + 32$), the jump strategy is likely to emerge in student dialogue.
- This scenario lends itself to straightforward addition ($85 + 20$) and subtraction ($74 - 26$) tasks as well as missing addend ($52 + ? = 89$) and missing subtrahend ($115 - ? = 89$) tasks.

  - *We got on the interstate at Exit 85 and drove 20 miles north. Where did we get off?* [missing sum]
  - *A car got on the interstate at Exit 74 and drove 26 miles south before running out of gas.* [See Figure 6.9 for the ENL drawn while this scenario was introduced.] *At which mile marker will the tow service find the car?* [missing difference]
  - *I got on the interstate at Exit 52 and got off at Exit 89. How far did I drive on the interstate?* [missing addend]
  - *My sister got on the interstate at Exit 115 and got off at Exit 89 when coming to see me. How far did she drive on the interstate?* [missing subtrahend]

- The ENL facilitates student discussion of solution strategies, particularly when multiple strategies are notated (see Figure 6.10).

Acknowledgement: This activity is based on the research of Tabor (2008).

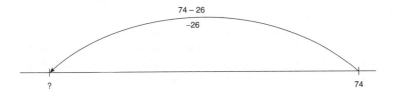

Figure 6.9   A car got on the interstate at Exit 74 and drove 26 miles south

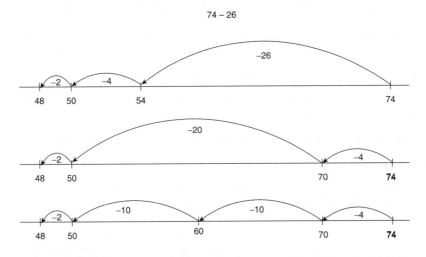

Figure 6.10   Notating different solution strategies for 74 − 26

ACTIVITY IA6.11: Add or Subtract 12

Intended learning: To use the jump method to add and subtract 12.

Instructional mode: Shorter, rehearsal mode for partners.

Materials: Add or Subtract 12 Game board and special spinner, two types of counters, pencil, and paper clip for spinner.

Description: This game is played in a manner similar to IA 4.6, the 9 Plus Game. The purpose of this game is to build facility with the jump method for adding and subtracting a ten and a few more.

Responses, variations and extensions:

* Students might initially make 12 counts (by ones) to solve the problems. If students continue with this strategy, teachers should challenge students to solve the problems in fewer counts.

- The ENL can be an effective tool to promote comparison of strategies. Encourage students to evaluate the effectiveness of the strategies. *Which strategy is easier? Why do you think that? Which strategy takes fewer jumps? Which strategy is quicker?*
- As an extension, students can be challenged to create their own game from the blank game BLM found in the Add or Subtract 12 file. They would need to identify an amount to add or subtract, create a spinner and determine all possible solutions.

ACTIVITY IA6.12: How Many More to Make 100?

Intended learning: To use knowledge of partitions of ten in order to partition 100 into two decuples.

Instructional mode: Shorter, rehearsal mode for partners.

Materials: How Many More to Make 100? Game board, decuple spinner, two types of counters, pencil and paper clip for spinner.

Description: This game is played in a manner similar to IA 4.6, the 9 Plus Game.

Responses, variations and extensions:

- Some children will initially use strategies to calculate the missing addend.
- Base-ten materials and the ENL can be used to provide a scaffold for this activity.

ACTIVITY IA6.13: How Many More to Make 60?

Intended learning: To find missing addends, emphasizing the combinations found in telling time with minutes before or after the hour.

Instructional mode: Shorter, rehearsal mode for partners.

Materials: How Many More to Make 60? Game board, two types of counters, pencil and paper clip for spinner.

Description: This game is played in a similar manner as IA 4.6, the 9 Plus Game. The purpose of this game is to build facility with the combinations of 60 that arise in telling time with respect to minutes after and minutes before the hour.

Responses, variations and extensions:

- Telling time is a context that poses difficulty for some children. Some students will initially take a significant amount of time to calculate the missing addend. For some children, time will provide an additional scaffold depending on their facility with telling time.
- Judy clocks or model clocks can be used to provide a scaffold for this activity.

7

Multiplication and Division

DOMAIN OVERVIEW

In Chapter 6 on addition and subtraction to 100 we highlighted the importance of that topic. As described in Chapter 6, addition and subtraction to 100 is not only important in its own right, as a topic in the number curriculum, but also is foundational to many subsequent topics. These include of course, multiplication and division, and also topics such as mental and written computation, and computational estimation. The topic of multiplication and division on one hand, builds on students' knowledge of addition and subtraction, and in a similar vein to addition and subtraction, is fundamental for subsequent topics such as mental and written computation, and computational estimation. As well, multiplication and division provide foundational knowledge for topics such as fractions, ratio and proportion, and percentage, all of which are core and essential areas of mathematics learning typically addressed in the primary or elementary grades.

This overview has four sections. The first describes multiplication and division from a perspective of formal arithmetic, including the interrelatedness of the four operations (addition, subtraction, multiplication and division) and principles underlying the operations. The second section addresses students' learning of multiplication and division, including exemplars of students' solution strategies, four aspects of the development of students' knowledge, and the learning of the basic facts. The third section sets out key aspects of assessment, and the fourth section describes instruction in multiplication and division over a progression of six phases.

Multiplication and Division in Formal Arithmetic

Formal Relations between Addition, Subtraction, Multiplication and Division

Chapter 4 focuses on children becoming facile with addition and subtraction in the range 1 to 20. Chapter 6 extends this focus to addition and subtraction to 100. Addition and subtraction constitute two of the four basic operations of arithmetic. As well, the operation of subtraction can be thought of as arising from the operation of addition. By this we mean that, for example, the meaning of the expression 12–9 can be explained in terms of addition: What number when added to 9 gives 12? Thus an important idea is that addition and subtraction are not merely two different operations that can be performed on a pair of whole numbers. Rather, the operations of addition and subtraction are fundamentally interrelated.

Inverse Operations

The interrelatedness of addition and subtraction is usually explained by saying that addition and subtraction are inverse operations, that is, each is the inverse of the other. Thus if we start with a number, say 14, add 6 and then subtract 6 from the result, we obtain the number we started with (14). Alternatively, we could begin with 14, subtract 6 and then add 6 to the result, and again we get the number we started with (14). Thus we have three key ideas about addition and subtraction: (a) subtraction arises from addition; (b) addition and subtraction are interrelated; and (c) addition and subtraction are inverses of each other.

The Four Basic Operations

When multiplication and division are considered along with addition and subtraction we have what are referred to as the four basic operations of arithmetic. In a formal mathematical sense, just as subtraction can be said to arise from addition, so can multiplication be said to arise from addition. And since division arises from multiplication it follows that addition is in a sense, the source of the other three basic operations.

Multiplication from Addition

The interrelatedness of addition and multiplication can be explained as follows. An initial description of addition is to say that it involves combining two numbers to obtain a third number: $5 + 3 = 8$, $21 + 9 = 30$, and so on. This description can be extended by saying that addition can also involve combining three $(7 + 8 + 2)$, four $(33 + 24 + 8 + 51)$ or any number of numbers. Of course, addition of more than two numbers involves a sequence of additions of two numbers. Thus, for example, addition of the following six numbers – 6, 3, 5, 2, 8 ,4 – can be regarded as the following five additions $6 + 3$, $9 + 5$, $14 + 2$, $16 + 8$, and finally $24 + 4$. A principle (characteristic) of the operation of addition is that the sum of those six addends is independent of the order in which the five addition operations are completed. This principle is known as associativity. The particular case of a sequence of addition operations where the addends are all the same number, for example $7 + 7 + 7 + 7 + 7$, gives rise to multiplication: $7 + 7 + 7 + 7 + 7 = 7 \times 5$. In words this equation asserts that the meaning or definition of 7 multiplied by 5 is the answer obtained when five sevens are added together. For this reason, as stated above, multiplication is said to arise from addition. More precisely, multiplication is described as repeated addition that is, repeated addition of the same number.

Division from Multiplication

Just as the operation of subtraction arises from addition (see above), the operation of division arises from multiplication. Thus division arises when we consider $\square \times 6 = 24$. Because $4 \times 6 = 24$ we say that $24 \div 6 = 4$. As well, if a number (e.g. 12) is multiplied by another number (3), and the result (36) is divided by the same number (3), we obtain the number we started with (12). Similarly, if 12 is divided by 3 and the result (4) is multiplied by 3, then we obtain the number we started with. For this reason we say multiplication and division are inverses of each other.

Division from Subtraction

Just as the operation of multiplication is regarded as repeated addition of the same number (see above), the operation of division can be regarded as repeated subtraction of the same number. Thus 35 ÷ 5 can be solved by repeatedly subtracting 5 from 35, and counting seven 5s in all.

The Interrelatedness of the Four Basic Operations

Listed below are the key ideas about the four operations of addition, subtraction, multiplication and division. Some of these ideas could be regarded as redundant – if subtraction arises from addition then it follows that addition and subtraction are interrelated. Nevertheless, it can be useful to list all of these ideas together:

(a) subtraction arises from addition
(b) addition and subtraction are interrelated
(c) addition and subtraction are inverses of each other
(d) multiplication arises from addition
(e) addition and multiplication are interrelated
(f) multiplication is repeated addition of the same number
(g) division arises from multiplication
(h) multiplication and division are interrelated
(i) multiplication and division are inverses of each other
(j) division is repeated subtraction of the same number.

As well as describing in a formal sense, how multiplication arises from addition we can also describe how, as children develop facility with basic arithmetic, their multiplicative thinking arises from their additive thinking. This is discussed later in this chapter.

A Formal Explanation of the Operation of Division

Earlier in this chapter we explained how division arises from multiplication and how division can be regarded as the inverse of multiplication. Imagine for a moment that one's task is to give an explanation or definition of division from a perspective of formal mathematics. One might use algebraic notation and explain that the answer to $a \div b$ is the number c that satisfies (makes true) the equation $b \times c = a$. One might give some arithmetical examples: 28 ÷ 4 is equal to the number that when multiplied by 4 gives 28. Alternatively, one might ask what number satisfies the equation $4 \times \square = 28$. This explanation can be enhanced by saying that 'a' in $a \div b$ could be any whole number or indeed, any of the various kinds of numbers that are important in formal mathematics (rational numbers, real numbers, etc.). An example is that 'a' could be a rational number, that is, a fraction such as ¾ or a decimal such as 2.8. In a similar vein, one might state that 'b' might be a whole number or one of those other kinds of numbers.

The Divisor must be Non-zero

Of course one must add that there is one specific but very important limitation on the value that 'b' might take and that is that 'b' must not be zero. This can be exemplified by saying it is impossible to find a number that makes the following equation true: $0 \times \square = 28$. Thus the operation of division works fine so long as we don't attempt to divide by zero. A further point is that, when two whole numbers are multiplied the answer is always another whole number, but division involving two whole numbers does not always give a whole number, for example $21 \div 5 = 4.2$ and 4.2 is a rational number (fraction) but not a whole number.

An Informal and Practical Explanation of the Operation of Division

In contrast to the formal explanation or definition discussed above, one might be interested in providing for students, an informal and practical explanation of division, that is, using a setting (instructional materials) or a context (everyday situation or story). Multiplication can be described as involving repeated equal groups. So, in order to explain division, we might look to a simple activity that results in a collection being organized into equal groups. Thus, in attempting to explain the meaning of $15 \div 3$, we get 15 red counters and think about organizing the counters into equal groups.

Two Interpretations of 15 ÷ 3

At this point, one might have the dawning awareness that there are two distinct ways to go about this: (a) we interpret the '3' as the number of counters in each group; or (b) we interpret the '3' as the number of groups. These two interpretations are shown in Figures 7.1 and 7.2. Students' initial thinking about the operation of division is likely to draw on an informal notion of division rather than a formal notion (see above). Thus from a pedagogical perspective, being explicitly aware of these two interpretations is quite important. The first of these is labelled grouping or quotitive division and the second is sharing or partitive division. The terms 'grouping' and 'sharing' in this context are informal, practical labels and the terms 'quotitive' and 'partitive' are formal mathematical terms.

15 ÷ 3

Figure 7.1 $15 \div 3$ – Division in a grouping or quotitive sense

15 ÷ 3

Figure 7.2 $15 \div 3$ – Division in a sharing or partitive sense

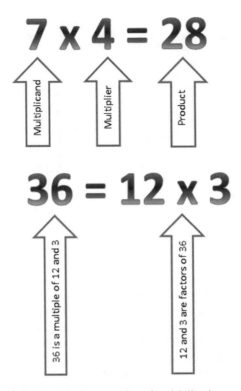

Figure 7.3   Key labels associated with the operation of multiplication

Important Terms for Talking about Multiplication and Division

Associated with the arithmetical operations of multiplication and division are some key labels for the numbers involved. From a pedagogical perspective, these labels are quite useful. In the cases of addition and subtraction respectively, key labels include *addend* and *sum*; and *minuend*, *subtrahend* and *difference*. In the case of multiplication, key labels include: *multiplicand, multiplier, product, factor* and *multiple* (see Figure 7.3). In the case of division, key labels include: *dividend, divisor, quotient* and *remainder* (see Figure 7.4).

Multiplicand and Multiplier

As indicated in Figure 7.3, in this book we adopt the following convention: 7 × 4 is interpreted with 7 as the multiplicand and 4 as the multiplier. This is consistent with reading 7 × 4 as 'seven multiplied by 4' or 'four 7s'. Also, it is consistent with the other three operations (+, −, ÷) in that the second number (e.g. the 5 in 30 ÷ 5) is regarded as operating on the first number. Thus in 7 + 4, 7 − 4, 7 × 4 or 7 ÷ 4, 7 can be referred to as the *operand* and 4 can be referred to as the *operator*.

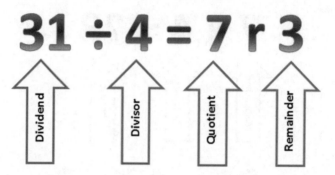

Figure 7.4 Key labels associated with the operation of division

Commutative, Associative and Distributive Principles

Commutative Principle

The commutative principle refers to the principle that when two numbers are multiplied the product is independent of which of the two factors is the multiplier and which is the multiplicand. For example $7 \times 4 = 4 \times 7$. Another way to think of this is, if we add 7 four times or add 4 seven times the result is the same. Many students seem to develop an intuitive notion of the commutative principle before they are facile with 1-digit multiplication and therefore they will sometimes commute a product to be calculated, when it results in a calculation which is easier for them, such as commuting 4×8 into 8×4. The commutative principle of multiplication is often expressed as follows:

$$6 \times 9 = 9 \times 6 \qquad\qquad a \times b = b \times a$$

Addition is also commutative. Subtraction and division are not commutative.

Associative Principle

The associative principle refers to the principle that when three factors are multiplied together, the product is independent of the order in which the two multiplication operations are done. Consider for example, $7 \times 5 \times 3$. If we multiply 7×5 obtaining 35, and then multiply 35×3 we obtain 105. Alternatively, if we multiply 5×3 obtaining 15, and then multiply 7×15 we also obtain 105. The associative principle of multiplication is often expressed as follows:

$$(7 \times 5) \times 3 = 7 \times (5 \times 3) \qquad\qquad (a \times b) \times c = a \times (b \times c)$$

Addition is also associative. Subtraction and division are not associative. As can be seen, the commutative principle refers to changing the order of the two factors to be multiplied, whereas the associative principle refers to changing the order in which two operations of multiplication are performed. Because multiplication is both commutative and associative, the value of an expression such as $2 \times 8 \times 3 \times 5$ is independent of how the four factors are multiplied together:

| $2 \times 8 \times 3 \times 5$ as: | $5 \times 2 = 10, 8 \times 3 = 24, 10 \times 24 = 240$ |
| $2 \times 8 \times 3 \times 5$ as: | $5 \times 8 = 40, 40 \times 2 = 80, 80 \times 3 = 240$ |

Distributive Principle

Distinctive and remarkable is that, unlike the commutative and associative principles, which refer to single operations (addition and multiplication), the distributive principle refers to how pairs of operations combine. Thus, the distributive principle enables us to see how addition and subtraction interact with multiplication and division. A common explanation of the distributive principle involves arithmetical or algebraic equations such as the following:

$$(8 + 5) \times 7 = (8 \times 7) + (5 \times 7) \qquad (a + b) \times c = (a \times c) + (b \times c)$$

In the arithmetical equation, the left hand side can be calculated as 13×7, that is 91; and the right hand side as $56 + 35$, that is 91. Needless to say, this result is not reliant on the particular numbers – 8, 5 and 7. Rather it is true for any three numbers and this in a sense is what is expressed in the algebraic equation. In words, the result just described typically is explained as: multiplication distributes over addition or multiplication can be distributed over addition. But this is only part of the story. There are four main forms of the distributive principle and we see another distinctive feature of the distributive principle in that, unlike commutativity and associativity, it is relevant to subtraction and division as well as addition and multiplication:

Multiplication distributes over addition:	$(8 + 5) \times 7 = 8 \times 7 + 5 \times 7$
Multiplication distributes over subtraction:	$(8 - 5) \times 7 = 8 \times 7 - 5 \times 7$
Division distributes over addition:	$(18 + 15) \div 3 = 18 \div 3 + 15 \div 3$
Division distributes over subtraction:	$(18 - 15) \div 3 = 18 \div 3 - 15 \div 3$

In its first form above (multiplication distributing over addition), the distributive principle asserts that when two numbers are multiplied, either the multiplicand or the multiplier, that is either factor, can be partitioned additively into two numbers, and each of the resulting numbers multiplied. Partitioning one of the factors into more than two numbers works fine too. Further, by virtue of the distributive principle, when a multi-digit number is multiplied (for example 257×3), we can perform the multiplication by multiplying each of 200, 50 and 7 separately by 3, and adding the three products $600 + 150 + 21$. Thus the distributive principle is inherent and implicit in well-established procedures for multiplying, and similarly for dividing.

Learning Multiplication and Division

This section focuses on progressions in students' learning of multiplication and division. First, we describe exemplars of students' solutions of additive and multiplicative tasks. Then follows a discussion of learning progressions in four interrelated aspects of multiplicative knowledge. We conclude with a discussion of the learning of the basic facts for multiplication.

A Range of Strategies for Additive and Multiplicative Tasks

Students' earliest strategies for solving arithmetic tasks typically involve: (a) counting from one; (b) counting by ones; and (c) a reliance on materials such as counters. Over time students make remarkable progressions. They learn to reason abstractly with numbers and no longer rely on counting by ones. We now describe how four students solved additive and multiplicative tasks. The students' solutions illustrate progressions in the learning of multiplication and division.

Wendy's Solution of Task 1 – Additive Task

Wendy could solve additive tasks involving two screened collections of counters but she typically counted from one when doing so. For example, when presented with the additive task of 9 + 4, she looked at the screen covering the first collection while saying the number words from one to nine, she then looked at the screen covering the second collection, saying hesitantly 'ten, eleven, twelve, thirteen!'.

Wendy's Solution of Task 2 – Multiplicative Task

Wendy was presented with a multiplicative task of 3 × 7, involving repeated equal groups. This task involved seven cards, each with three dots. The cards were placed face-down in a row, and the row of cards was screened. Her teacher unscreened the row momentarily and said 'there are seven cards and each card has three dots. How many dots altogether?'. Because Wendy could not solve this task her teacher removed the screen covering the seven cards leaving all of the cards face-down. Wendy pointed at the first card saying 'one, two, three' and then at the second card saying 'four, five, six' but was unable to continue. Her teacher then turned all seven cards face-up. Wendy slowly counted all of the dots from one and answered 'twenty-one!'.

Xavier's Solution of Task 1 – Additive Task

Xavier routinely counted on and counted back to solve additive and subtractive tasks in settings involving screened collections of counters. For example, when presented with the additive task of 9 + 4, Xavier looked at the screen covering the first collection saying 'nine' and then at the screen covering the second collection, saying 'ten, eleven, twelve, thirteen!'.

Xavier's Solution of Task 2 – Multiplicative Task

Xavier was presented with the multiplicative task of 3 × 7, involving repeated equal groups. Xavier attempted to count by threes but he apparently lost track of the number of cards. His teacher then removed the screen to reveal the seven cards, face-down. Xavier looked at the cards and said 'three, six, nine, twelve, fifteen [pause], sixteen, seventeen, eighteen [pause], nineteen, twenty, twenty-one!'.

Xavier's Solution of Task 3 – Division Task

Xavier was presented with a division task of 20 ÷ 4 involving a screened 4 × 5 array (4 columns and 5 rows). His teacher momentarily unscreened the first row saying, 'this row has four dots and there are 20 dots altogether. How many rows are there?'. Xavier said 'one, two, three, four' in coordination with four pointing actions. He then said 'five, six, seven, eight' in coordination with four more pointing actions but he could not continue.

Yoshi's Solution of Task 1 – Additive Task

When Yoshi was asked to solve the additive task 9 + 4 (with two screened collections) he said 'one more is 10 and three more make 13!'.

Yoshi's Solution of Task 2 – Multiplicative Task

When presented with the multiplicative task of 3 x 7 involving screened repeated groups of three (all 7 cards were screened), Yoshi said, 'three, six, nine, twelve, fifteen, eighteen, twenty-one!'. Thus he counted by threes, keeping track of his count and stopping when he had made seven counts.

Yoshi's Solution of Task 3 – Division Task

When presented with the division task of 20 ÷ 4 involving a screened array, Yoshi said 'one, two, three, four [pause]; five, six, seven, eight [pause], nine, ten, eleven, twelve [pause], thirteen, fourteen, fifteen, sixteen [pause], seventeen, eighteen, nineteen, twenty [pause], five!'. In explaining his solution he said, 'I counted fours'. His solution involved counting by ones to 20, and simultaneously counting each set of four counts.

Yoshi's Solution of Task 4 – Advanced Multiplicative Task

Yoshi was presented with a bare number multiplicative task (a task involving numbers only). His teacher presented a card on which 8 × 6 was written. Yoshi's solution attempt involved doubling eight. He then added eight onto 16 by adding through 20 but after reaching 24 he could not continue.

Zekara's Solution of Task 2 – Multiplicative Task

When presented with the multiplicative task of 3 × 7 involving screened repeated groups of three Zekara said, 'I know six threes are 18, and three more is 21!'.

Zekara's Solution of Task 3 – Division Task

When presented with the division task of 20 ÷ 4 involving a screened array, Zekara said, 'I know that four fives are 20, so the answer is five!'.

Zekara's s Solution of Task 4 – Advanced Multiplication Task

When presented with the bare number multiplicative task of 8 × 6 Zekara said, 'I know that three eights are 24, so six eights must be 48!'.

Four Aspects of the Development of Mathematical Knowledge

In the solution strategies described above, a progression is evident in the extent to which mathematization of students' multiplicative knowledge has occurred. We distinguish four interrelated aspects of the development of multiplicative knowledge: (a) increasing sophistication in unitizing numbers; (b) distancing of the setting, from reliance on materials to facility with bare number; (c) increasing knowledge of multiples and sequences of multiples; and (d) increasing use of non-counting strategies (Siemon et al., 2006). These aspects are discussed further below.

(a) Sophistication of Unitizing Numbers

From close observation of students' additive and multiplicative reasoning, researchers have developed two theoretical constructs to account for students' arithmetical cognition: *numerical composite* and *abstract composite unit* (Steffe and Cobb, 1988). We find these constructs helpful in observing and documenting students' facility with additive and multiplicative reasoning, and with planning and implementing instructional programmes. In terms of these constructs: (a) Wendy does not have the construct of numerical composite; (b) Xavier has the construct of numerical composite but not the construct of abstract composite unit; (c) Yoshi has the constructs of numerical composite and abstract composite unit; and (d) Zekara has both constructs and also can coordinate two abstract units.

Numerical Composite

Students who have constructed a numerical composite typically will count on to solve an additive task such as nine and four more – presented for example with two covered collections of counters. When Xavier said 'nine [pause], ten, eleven, twelve, thirteen!', 'nine' stood for having counted the first collection, and Xavier's notion of nine is referred to as a numerical composite. Thus Xavier could focus abstractly on the nine ones in the sense of a composite. This is contrasted with Wendy's solution, which is indicative of the pre-numerical student, who will typically count from one to nine before continuing to count beyond nine. For Wendy, numbers do not stand for composites of ones.

Abstract Composite Unit

Students who have constructed an abstract composite unit, typically will solve the task of nine and four more by reasoning with the two parts – nine and four – as well as the unknown whole. Thus Yoshi's strategy of adding through ten is indicative of the construct of abstract composite unit. Yoshi could regard four as either a composite or a unit as required. Also, when Yoshi solved the division task of 20 ÷ 4, he simultaneously regarded 'four' as four ones (i.e. in his count by ones from one to 20) and one four (i.e. in his keeping track of the number of times he made four counts). This flexibility in regarding numbers in two different ways (composites and units) is what distinguishes the notion of abstract composite unit from that of the numerical composite (Steffe and Cobb, 1988). The mental act of regarding 'nine' as a unit is referred to as a 'unitizing' operation (Fosnot and Dolk, 2001a). The progression from numerical composite to abstract composite unit is critical for the development of additive reasoning beyond counting on and back by ones to solve additive tasks. As well, the progression is critical for the development of multiplicative reasoning (Steffe, 1988; Sullivan et al., 2001).

Composite Unit of Composite Units

This construct involves conceptualizing a group of equal groups as a composite unit of composite units. Zekara's solutions typify this construct. When solving 8 × 6, she was aware of the sets of three groups of eight as composite units of composite units (3 units of 8, and a second 3 units of 8). 'For a situation to be established as multiplicative, it is necessary at least to coordinate two composite units in such a way that one of the composite units is distributed over elements of the other composite unit' (Steffe, 1994: 19). This construct can be described as knowing multiplication and division as operations (Wright et al., 2006a: 125).

(b) Distancing of the Setting

In the solution strategies described above, a clear progression from reliance on settings to reasoning abstractly is evident. Wendy's additive strategy of counting from one involves reasoning about collections of counters and she solved the 3×7 task only when the groups of three dots were unscreened. When Xavier solved the additive task he was less reliant than Wendy on the first screened collection because he did not count from one to nine. When solving the 3×7 task Xavier needed to see the cards face-down. In contrast to Wendy, he did not need to see the groups of three. When Yoshi solved the additive task he reasoned with the numbers (9, 1 and 3) abstractly. Apparently he did not focus on the numbers as collections of counters. His solutions to the 3×7 and $20 \div 4$ tasks were to some extent reliant on the settings of groups of three dots and the array respectively. Nevertheless, when solving 3×7, unlike Xavier he did not need to see the cards face-down. When Zekara solved the 3×7 and $20 \div 4$ tasks, she seemed to reason with the numbers and not attend to the specifics of the settings of equal groups and an array. Her solution of the 8×6 task indicates that, in contrast to Yoshi, she can reason multiplicatively in settings involving numbers only (bare number tasks).

(c) Knowledge of Multiples and Sequences of Multiples

Wendy solved the 3×7 task by counting each three by ones. When Xavier solved this task he counted in threes to 15 whereas Yoshi counted in threes to 21. Both Xavier and Yoshi knew the sequence by threes although Yoshi seems to be more facile with the sequence than Xavier. In contrast to Yoshi and Xavier, Zekara uses knowledge of the basic facts of multiplication such as 3×6, 5×4 and 8×3. Thus she is able to jump straight to a multiple, rather than count forwards through a sequence of multiples (3, 6, 9, 12 …). This knowledge separates having to use repeated addition or counting in multiples, from strategies that appear as reasoning multiplicatively with good facility. Further, Zekara, not only knows three eights but also uses it to solve six eights.

A student's knowledge of multiples typically varies markedly depending on the multiplier concerned. For example, a student's knowledge of sequences and multiples might comprise the following:

- know the sequences by 2s and by 5s
- knows doubles and 5 times for some numbers (e.g. 6×2, 8×2, 4×5, 6×5)
- knows the sequence by 3s to 15, and the sequence by 4s to 12 and can continue the sequences by adding on 3 or 4 using non-counting strategies
- does not know any multiples of 3 or 4, other than by 2 and by 5
- for 6, 7, 8, or 9 as the multiplier, does not know multiples or sequences of multiples.

For this student, the tasks 5×4, 3×4 and 7×4 will each have different strategies. 5×4 might be a known fact, 3×4 might involve skip-counting by 3s and 7×4 might be found by repeatedly adding 7, using non-counting addition strategies. Thus, in both assessment and instruction, when presenting multiplicative tasks to students the selection of numbers is very significant.

(d) Development of Non-counting Strategies

Wendy's strategies involved not only counting by ones but also counting from one. Xavier's strategy for addition involved counting on by ones. For 3×7, Xavier counted in threes to 15 and then counted by ones from 16 to 21. In contrast to Wendy and Xavier, Yoshi's strategy for addition involved adding through 10 rather than counting by ones. Yoshi solved 3×7 without counting by ones. Although he counted from one to 20 to solve the $20 \div 4$ task, he simultaneously counted the sets of four counts. Finally, Zekara did not count by ones on any of the tasks.

The development of the construct of abstract composite unit supports the cognitive shift from counting by ones, but it is not sufficient. When solving the $20 \div 4$ array task, Yoshi counted by ones and thus apparently did not know or could not use the sequence by fours (4, 8, 12, 16, 20). Thus students also require knowledge of sequences of multiples. Even with knowledge of sequences, the keeping track of the number of units (multiples) requires counting by ones. Only when the student has the construct of units of units, and knowledge of some multiplication facts, can counting by ones be abandoned.

Moving Beyond Skip Counting and Repeated Addition

Apart from skip counting, students might for example, solve 6×9 by first calculating 6×3 and 6×6, and then adding 36 and 18. Of course this last step (36 + 18) is squarely in the domain of Addition and Subtraction to 100 (Chapter 6) and might involve a jump strategy such as 36 + 20, 56 – 2, 54! This is one of many instances where solving a multiplication basic facts task involves in part using a process involving addition or subtraction in the range 1 to 100, and this serves as another illustration that children's multiplicative reasoning in the range 1 to 100 can rely heavily on, not only skip counting but also their facility with addition and subtraction in the range 1 to 100. This is what is meant by saying that pedagogically, in the range 1 to 100 and beyond, students' multiplicative reasoning is strongly linked to their additive reasoning (Anghileri, 1989; Heege, 1985; Mulligan and Mitchelmore, 1997; Sherin and Fuson, 2005).

A Learning Path for Multiplication and Division

The descriptions of solutions by Xavier, Yoshi and Zekara provided earlier are indicative of a learning path for multiplication and division to 100. Xavier solved the 3×7 task involving repeated equal groups. In doing so, 3 was a numerical composite that he could count seven times while keeping track of all of his counts. But Xavier could not solve the $20 \div 4$ task involving an array. Yoshi solved the 3×7 task but in doing so, he needed to skip count, and he solved the $20 \div 4$ task but needed to count to 20 by ones because he did not know the sequence of multiples of 4. Zekara had moved well beyond reliance on skip counting and repeated addition and had developed a high level of facility with multiplicative reasoning. Her strategies seemed to embody tacit knowledge of the distributive principle. In a following section we outline an approach to instruction for multiplication and division that can progress students broadly along this learning path, that is, from repeated counting on and back by ones or use of skip counting and repeated addition, to facile multiplicative reasoning in the range 1 to 100 and beyond.

Learning the Basic Facts for Multiplication

In broad terms, an initial focus for multiplication and division is multiplication in the range one to 100 (2 × 3, 7 × 8, 14 × 4, 4 × 21), and more specifically, multiplication involving two 1-digit factors. This sub-domain is often referred to as learning the basic facts for multiplication and was also known as the times tables. In many curricula, developing students' facility with this sub-domain is regarded as a major goal of instruction, and it is a topic that traditionally 'has taken up a considerable amount of time in primary school' (Anghileri, 2006: 94). Indeed at times, students' facility with this sub-domain is regarded as synonymous with success in learning basic arithmetic.

Since learning the basic facts has traditionally been a task of memorization or habituation, so successful memorization of the basic facts for multiplication is commonly viewed as a major hallmark of progress in arithmetic. Interestingly, memorization of the basic facts for addition or subtraction does not seem to be accorded the same status. Related to this is that, in the case of the addition and subtraction basic facts, students who have not memorized the facts, nevertheless can obtain answers by using strategies involving counting by ones. By contrast, in the case of the multiplication and division basic facts, strategies involving counting by ones are grossly inadequate.

A consequence is that the need for students to memorize facts might appear to be much more important for multiplication than for addition and subtraction – at least while counting by ones or memorization are the only alternatives considered. Research recommends a view different from these assumptions. In the case of addition and subtraction, as argued in Chapter 4, there *is* a pressing need to move students on from using counting by ones, to non-counting strategies, and ultimately to automatization of the basic facts. In the case of multiplication and division, students should *not* be pressed to memorize initially; rather, they need extensive opportunities to develop multiplicative non-counting strategies before developing automaticity.

Assessment of Multiplication and Division

In this section we provide an overview of important topics in the assessment of students' multiplication and division knowledge.

(a) Facility with Sequences of Multiples

Assessing students' facility with number word sequences of multiples is described in the chapter on number words and numerals (Chapter 3) and is relevant to the domain of multiplication and division as well. This refers to the ability to say with facility, at least the first 10 number words in the sequence, with initial focus on the sequences by 2s (2, 4, 6 … 20), by 5s (5, 10, 15 … 50) and by 3s (3, 6, 9 … 30).

(b) Facility with Multiplicative Tasks Involving Repeated Equal Groups

Assessment of early knowledge in the domain of multiplication and division should focus on copying sets of repeated equal groups, building sets of repeated equal groups and counting the

Photo 7.1 Solving a task involving screened equal groups

Photo 7.2 Solving a task involving a partly screened array

items in a set of repeated equal groups. As well, assessment should focus on distributing (sharing) items into a specified number of groups and into groups of a specified size.

(c) Facility with Multiplicative Tasks Involving Arrays

Multiplication and division tasks can be posed using the setting of rectangular arrays. An example of a multiplication task is to momentarily display the uppermost row of a 5 × 4 array (5 columns and 4 rows), tell the student that there are four rows in all, and ask the student how many dots in all. An example of a division task is to momentarily display the uppermost row only of a 3 × 6 array (3 columns and 6 rows), tell the student that there are 18 dots in all, and ask the student how many rows in all.

(d) Facility with Basic Facts for Multiplication

Students' facility with basic facts for multiplication can be assessed by presenting bare number tasks either verbally or using multiplication expression cards. Ask the student to answer quickly if possible, rather than taking time to work out the task. Students typically have least difficulty with the two times and then the five times basic facts. Thus the two times can be posed first, in random order. If the student is successful, then in a similar vein, pose the 5 times and 3 times and again if the student is successful pose the 4 times. Similarly, progress to the 9 times and 6 times. Finally, pose the 7 and 8 times which are likely to be the most difficult.

(e) Determining the Number of Squares in a Rectangular Grid

This task is aimed at students' facility to conceptualize a rectangular grid and can provide interesting insights into students' knowledge of and reasoning with grids. Present the student with

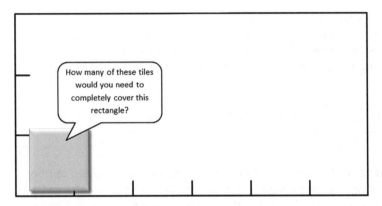

Figure 7.5   Task involving the number of squares on a rectangular grid

the diagram shown in Figure 7.5 and a unit square. Ask the student how many squares will be needed to completely cover the rectangle and also ask the student to draw what the squares would look like (Battista et al., 1998).

(f) Assessing Multiplication and Division Beyond the Basic Facts

This can involve 2-digit products with one factor in the range 1 to 10 (14×4, 23×2, 16×4, etc.) and 3-digit products with one factor in the range 1 to 10 (32×6, 51×4, 93×3, 85×2). Initially, focus mainly on tasks with rather easy calculation of the sum of the two partial products.

(g) Assessing Inverse Relationship and Commutative and Distributive Principles

Later in this chapter we set out Assessment Task Groups relevant to multiplication and division, including tasks relevant to these topics (see Task Groups A7.10, A7.11 and A7.12). The tasks are designed to gauge students' preliminary or intuitive awareness of these principles. Assessing students' facility with these tasks is important but success on these tasks does not necessarily indicate a deep or generalized knowledge of the principle. Typically, the level of sophistication of students' knowledge of these increases slowly over time. Tasks focusing on the distributive principle are likely to be more difficult because they can involve calculating and adding partial products.

Instruction in Multiplication and Division

We describe instruction in multiplication and division in terms of the following six phases:

1. Building on students' emergent strategies for multiplying and dividing
2. Instruction on sequences of multiples

3. Structuring numbers multiplicatively
4. Developing multiplicative strategies for 1-digit factors
5. Habituation of basic facts for multiplication and division
6. Extending multiplication and division to multi-digit factors and beyond 100.

Phase 1. Building on Students' Emergent Strategies for Multiplying and Dividing

Instruction to develop early knowledge of multiplication and division can begin even before students are routinely counting on or counting back to solve additive and subtractive tasks (Clark and Kamii, 1996; Kouba, 1989). This can involve materials such as counters. Students build repeated equal groups and count how many counters in all, and partition (share) a collection into a specified number of groups (Confrey, 1994; Mulligan, 1998; Pepper and Hunting, 1998; Steffe, 1992). Instructional activities and specific teaching procedures are already available (see Wright et al., 2006b, 2006c). Instruction of this kind can support students' progression to counting on and counting back to solve additive and subtractive tasks. When students are counting on and counting back, developing numerically rather than perceptually based strategies becomes the focus of multiplicative instruction.

Phase 2. Instruction on Sequences of Multiples

This phase refers to what is commonly described as counting by 2s, 5s, 3s and so on. The activity of saying a sequence such as 2, 4, 6, 8 and so on, without reference to quantity, that is, without counting items, is important as a basis for multiplicative reasoning. Because this instructional topic is about sequences of number words it is addressed in Chapter 3 on number words and numerals.

Phase 3. Structuring Numbers Multiplicatively

For this phase we use a setting that we refer to as an *n-tile* (2-tile, 5-tile, 3-tile). These are illustrated in Figure 7.6. A sequence of instruction is as follows. Using a set of 2-tiles, an initial activity is for students to count the dots on the tiles by twos in coordination with moving the tiles. The tiles should be moved successively so that, on the first five a 5×2 array is formed. Also, the first five tiles are of one colour – red; the next five of another colour – blue; the next five red again, and so on. In this way each set of five tiles constitutes a ten-frame, and each set of ten dots is demarcated by colour. Proceeding beyond 20 is fine. In the case of 5-tiles, alternate two red, two blue, two red, and so on, so that, again, each set of ten dots is demarcated. Figure 7.7 shows a setting that can be used for counting by threes. In this case the 3-tiles are arranged longwise and are used in conjunction with a row of dots where the fives and tens are demarcated.

The instructional sequence involves pursuing the progressive mathematization of students' thinking, by extending the initial activity in several ways, as described in Box 7.1. The general

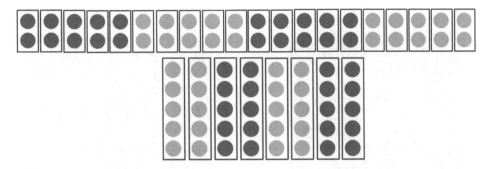

Figure 7.6   Instructional settings for learning to structure numbers multiplicatively

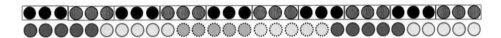

Figure 7.7   An instructional setting for structuring numbers by threes

approach to extending the activity parallels the approach described in, for example, Chapter 5 on conceptual place value. The initial focus of the activity is counting by 2s, 5s and 3s, as distinct from learning merely to say the sequence of multiples (see phase 2 above). This progresses to reasoning in situations where the number of 2s (3s, 5s) increases or perhaps decreases in jumps of more than one 2. Our instructional goal in this activity can be described as learning to structure numbers multiplicatively and we refer to this as a two-wise (three-wise, etc.) multiplicative structure.

BOX 7.1   WAYS TO EXTEND N-TILE ACTIVITIES

- Increase the range of numbers.
- Start the sequence from, say, five or eight tiles, rather than from one tile.
- Decrement as well as increment.
- Increment and decrement by more than one tile at a time.
- Use screening, unscreening and flashing of the accumulating tiles in order to progressively distance the activity from the setting (tiles).
- Build a number with tiles, for example, 25 with five 5-tiles, display briefly and then screen, and then move two more tiles under the screen and ask how many in all.
- Have students write the sequences of numbers.

Phase 4. Developing Multiplicative Strategies for 1-digit Factors

The focus of this phase is for students to develop flexible strategies for multiplying two 1-digit factors, particularly with multiplicands of 2, 5 and 3. We use a setting consisting of a 10 × 10

(a)

(b)

Photo 7.3 (a) and (b)   Posing a sequence of multiples of three using 3-tiles

array of dots, an L-shaped cover board, and a screen. These are illustrated in Figure 7.8. The cover board is a large L-shaped cut-out and is used to fix (set) a particular array. Fixing a 4 × 6 array (4 columns and 6 rows) involves covering the columns to the right of the fourth and the rows below the sixth. The screen is rectangular, differs in colour from the cover board and is used to strategically screen and unscreen rows and columns on the fixed 6 × 4 array. A sequence of instruction is as follows.

Build an array with a specific number of columns, for example three columns. Using the array, pose tasks (e.g. 3 × 4, 3 × 6) asking how many dots. Initially the screen is not used and students are encouraged to describe their strategies for determining the number of dots: *How did you work out that four lots of three is 12? I added six and six. I knew 3 threes and added one more three.* As in Phase 3, across a sequence of lessons, there is an agenda of progressively distancing from the setting and developing notation. Initially show the array and then progress to screening and flashing the array. Later progress to introducing and developing methods of recording calculations that accord with students' strategies. Results can be recorded using an ENL (empty number line – see Figure 7.9), or an arrow notation, as below.

Arrow notation $3 \times 8: 3 \times 5 \to 15, 3 \times 3 \to 9, 15 + 9 \to 24$

Recording can progress to writing all products for one multiplicand in sequence: $5 \times 1 = 5$, $5 \times 2 = 10$, $5 \times 3 = 15$, and so on. As students develop flexible mental strategies for the cases of 2, 5 and 3, progress to an emphasis on strategies that are well suited to particular multiplicands

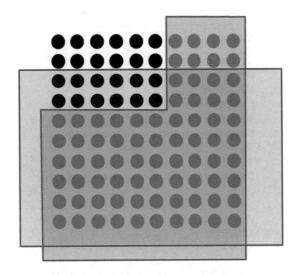

Figure 7.8   An instructional setting for multiplicative reasoning

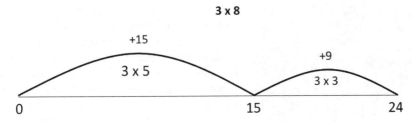

Figure 7.9   Recording 3 × 8 using an empty number line

(see Table 7.1). Strategies based on the commutative and distributive principles can also be emphasized: *To solve 3 × 9, instead of working out nine threes, I can work out three nines.* Sometimes it helps to partition one of the factors into two numbers – *I can work out 6 × 7, by adding five sixes and two sixes.*

Phase 5. Habituation of Basic Facts for Multiplication and Division

When students have developed flexible mental strategies for multiplying two 1-digit factors we advocate a systematic approach to developing automatized knowledge of the basic facts. All of the 100 basic facts are the products of two factors in the range 1–10. They can be organized in sets according to the multiplier: the 2s facts, the 3s facts, and so on. The sets can be taught in a sequence such as: 2s, 10s, 5s, 3s, 4s, 9s, 6s, 8s, 7s.

Table 7.1 Examples of a strategy for a given multiplier

Multiplier	Strategy
2	Double: 7×2 is $7 + 7$, that is 14
3	Double and add again: 9×3 is double 9 plus 9
4	Double and double again: 7×4 is $14 + 14$
	Five times minus one time: 8×4 is 40 minus 4
5	Half of 10 times: 6×5 is half of 60
6	Double three times: 4×6 is double 12
7	Use five times or six times:
	4×7 is 4×5 plus 4×2, or 4×6 plus 4
8	Double, and double, and double a third time:
	6×8 via double 6 is 12, double 12 is 24, double 24 is 48
9	Ten times minus one time: 4×9 is 40 minus 4
10	The corresponding tens number: 7×10 is 70

Photo 7.4 Developing strategies to solve related bare number tasks

The most difficult facts to habituate are likely to be 6×7, 7×6, 6×8, 8×6, 7×8, 8×7 and 7×7. When teaching a particular set, for example 4 as multiplier, first practise the facts in sequence – 1×4, 2×4, 3×4 and so on – and then in random order. Use individual expression cards to work through the set and put aside cards corresponding to the facts that the student does not know or takes significant time to figure out. The process of habituation can also involve the division basic facts. Students who have habituated the 2, 10, 5 and 3 sets are ready to work on habituation of the corresponding division basic facts. The approach to habituation of the division basic facts should parallel that of the multiplication basic facts.

Phase 6. Extending Multiplication and Division to Multi-digit Factors and Beyond 100

When students have made good progress on multiplicative reasoning with two 1-digit factors and habituating the basic facts, the instructional focus can progress to mental computation involving multiplication and division. Thus multiplication now focuses on 2-digit multiplicands, first with products in the range to 100 and then beyond. As in phase 4 above, recording methods such as the ENL and arrow notation should be used (see Figure 7.10).

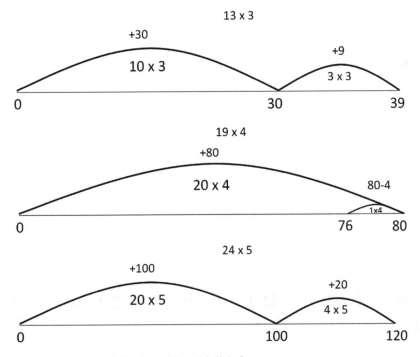

Figure 7.10   Recording multiplication with multi-digit factors

Arrow notation

13×3: 10×3 → 30, 3×3 → 9, $30 + 9$ → 39
19×4: 20×4 → 80, $80 - 4$ → 76
24×5: 20×5 → 100, 4×5 → 20, $100 + 20$ → 120

ASSESSMENT TASK GROUPS

List of Assessment Task Groups

A7.1: Multiplication with Repeated Equal Groups
A7.2: Grouping Division with Repeated Equal Groups
A7.3: Sharing Division with Repeated Equal Groups
A7.4: Multiplication with an Array
A7.5: Grouping Division with an Array
A7.6: Sharing Division with an Array

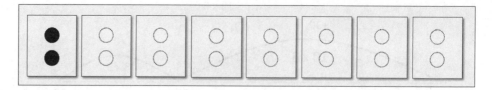

Figure 7.11 Multiplication with repeated equal groups

A7.7: Multiplication Basic Facts
A7.8: Multiplication with Bare Numbers – 2-digit × 1-digit
A7.9: Division with Bare Numbers – 2-digit Quotients
A7.10: Inverse Relationship of Multiplication and Division
A7.11: Commutative Principle
A7.12: Distributive Principle

TASK GROUP A7.1: Multiplication with Repeated Equal Groups

Materials: Eight cards, each containing two dots, a large card to screen all eight cards (see Figure 7.11).

What to do and say: Place the eight cards in a row with all but the first face-down. Screen all eight cards. Briefly display and then screen, the two dots on the face-up card. *This card has two dots.* Turn the first card face down and screen all eight cards. *Under this screen there are eight cards in all, each with two dots, like the first card. How many dots are there altogether?*

Notes:

- The purpose of this Task Group, and A7.2 and A7.3 is to assess the extent to which the student can reason multiplicatively in settings involving repeated equal groups.
- Some students count on from two by ones and lose track of the number of twos.
- In the case of students who lose track of the number of twos or are otherwise unsuccessful, remove the screen, leaving all eight cards face-down.
- In the case of students who cannot solve the task when the screen is removed, turn the first card face-up. If the student is still unsuccessful turn all cards face-up.
- Some students count by twos and use fingers to keep track of the number of twos.
- Some students use a triple count. They count the dots in each two, the number of twos, and the total number of dots. Typically, fingers on one hand are used to keep track of the number of dots in each two, and fingers on the other hand are used to keep track of the twos. At the same time they count how many dots in all, by ones.
- Some students will immediately know 2 × 8 or use a known fact such as 2 × 6, and add two twos to 12.
- Some will realize that eight twos is the same as two eights and know that multiplying a number by two is the same as doubling it.

TASK GROUP A7.2: Grouping Division with Repeated Equal Groups

Materials: Five cards, each containing four dots (in a square pattern), a large card to screen all five cards.

What to do and say: Place the five cards in a row with all but the first face-down. Screen all five cards. Briefly display and then screen the four dots on the face-up card. *This card has four dots.* Now screen all five cards. *Under this screen there are some more cards each with four dots, like the first card. There are 20 dots altogether. How many cards are there altogether?*

Notes:

- As in A7.1, students might count by ones and might use a triple count.
- Students who do not know the number word sequence of multiples of four, might use repeated addition of four, and keep track of the number of fours added.
- In the case of students who are unsuccessful turn the first card face-up.
- Some students will immediately know $20 \div 4$ or use one or more known facts such as $4 \times 2 = 8$, $8 + 8 = 16$.

TASK GROUP A7.3: Sharing Division with Repeated Equal Groups

Materials: Six cards, each containing three dots (e.g. in a triangular pattern), a large card to screen all six cards.

What to do and say: Place the six cards in a row face-down, with the screen covering all six cards. Briefly display and then screen the six cards. *There are six cards here and each card has the same number of dots on it. Altogether there are 18 dots. How many dots are there on each card?*

Notes:

- This task is likely to be more difficult than grouping division because students do not know the number of dots in each group and therefore cannot reason in terms of a repeated unit.
- In the case of students who are unsuccessful, remove the screen.
- Students might reason as follows: one dot under each card is six dots, two dots under each card is 12 dots, three dots under each card is six more than 12.
- Some students will immediately know $18 \div 6$ or use other known facts such as 6×2, $12 + 6$.

TASK GROUP A7.4: Multiplication with an Array

Materials: A 5×6 array (5 columns and 6 rows), a screen (see Figure 7.12).

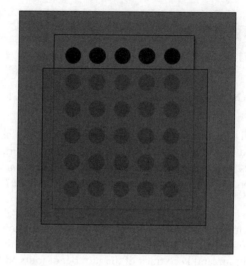

Figure 7.12 Multiplication with an array

What to do and say: Screen all but the top row of five dots. *Here is one row of the array. This row has five dots.* Now screen the whole array. *There are six rows altogether. How many dots are there altogether?*

Notes:

- The purpose of this Task Group, and A7.5 and A7.6 is to assess the extent to which the student can reason multiplicatively in settings involving a rectangular array of dots.
- Some students who can reason with repeated equal groups (see above) will be unable to reason with arrays. In such cases a preliminary activity could be used: Discuss an unscreened array (e.g. 4 × 8 or 10 × 10), referring to rows and columns, and the number of dots in each row and each column.
- In the case of students who are unsuccessful, unscreen the column on the left-hand side. If the student is still unsuccessful, unscreen all of the array.
- Some students will skip count by fives and keep track of the number of fives, and therefore stop when they have counted six fives.
- Some students will immediately know 5 × 6. Others will reason that six fives is 10 and 10 and 10, or that six fives is half of six tens.

TASK GROUP A7.5: Grouping Division with an Array

Materials: A 3 × 9 array (3 columns and 9 rows), a screen.

What to do and say: Screen all but the top row of three dots. *Here is one row of the array. This row has three dots.* Now screen the whole array. *There are 27 dots altogether. How many rows are there altogether?*

Notes:

- Less sophisticated strategies include counting by ones, a triple count, and skip counting by threes while keeping track of the threes.
- More sophisticated strategies include using known facts such as $3 \times 9 = 27$, $3 \times 10 = 30$, $3 \times 4 = 12$, $12 + 12 = 24$.
- In the case of students who are unsuccessful, unscreen the top row. When this is done students might attempt to count the dots in the unscreened row repeatedly until they reach 27, and keep track of the number of times they have counted the dots in the unscreened row.

TASK GROUP A7.6: Sharing Division with an Array

Materials: A 6×4 array (6 columns and 4 rows), a screen.

What to do and say: Place the array under the screen without displaying it. *Under this screen is an array with four rows. The array has 24 dots altogether. How many dots in each row?*

Notes:

- This task is likely to be more difficult than grouping division with an array because students do not know the number of dots in each row and therefore cannot reason in terms of a repeated unit.
- Students might reason that there are four dots in each column and then figure out how many fours make 24.
- Students might work out half of 24, and then half of 12, and then reason that there are six dots in each row.
- In the case of students who are unsuccessful, unscreen the column on the left-hand side.

TASK GROUP A7.7: Multiplication Basic Facts

Materials: Ten expression cards as follows: 1×3, 2×3, 3×3, 4×3 … 10×3.

What to do and say: *I will show you a card with a multiplication basic fact. Tell me the answer as quickly as you can.* Initially proceed through the facts in order starting from 1×3. Then mix up the cards and proceed through the facts again. Put aside cards for facts which the student answers incorrectly or does not answer in two seconds. Similarly with cards for other multipliers ($n \times 2$, $n \times 5$, etc.).

Notes:

- The purpose of this Task Group is to determine for each multiplier, the basic multiplication facts that the student has habituated.
- If the student is not successful on the first run when the facts are in order, do not persist with the second run.

- Students who answer within about two seconds typically will know the fact or use a sophisticated strategy, that is the strategy does not involve counting by ones and involves little or no skip counting.

Task Group A7.8: Multiplication with Bare Numbers – 2-digit × 1-digit

Materials: Expression cards with tasks such as 12 × 3, 24 × 2, 11 × 5, 32 × 4, 48 × 3, 71 × 2, 35 × 3, 16 × 6, paper and pencil.

What to do and say: *I am going to show you a card with a multiplication problem. Try to work out the answer. You may work it out in your head or use paper and pencil.*

Notes:

- The purpose of this Task Group is to assess students' facility with multiplication involving a 2-digit multiplicand and a 1-digit multiplier, and involving bare numbers (i.e. in the absence of any setting).
- Endeavour to determine the use of known basic facts, implicit use of commutative and distributive principles, and use of additive reasoning in the range 1 to 100 and beyond (e.g. 30 + 6, 120 + 24, 90 + 36).

TASK GROUP A7.9: Division with Bare Numbers – 2-digit Quotients

Materials: Expression cards with tasks such as: (a) 39 ÷ 3, 60 ÷ 5, 88 ÷ 2, 124 ÷ 4, 42 ÷ 3; and (b) 42 ÷ 14, 48 ÷ 12, 80 ÷ 16, 63 ÷ 21.

What to do and say: *I am going to show you a card with a division problem. Try to work out the answer. You may work it out in your head or use paper and pencil.*

Notes:

- The purpose of this Task Group is to assess students' facility with division involving a 2-digit quotient and a 1-digit divisor or dividend, and involving bare numbers (i.e. in the absence of any setting).
- Set (a) tasks such as 39 ÷ 3 are likely to invoke thinking from a perspective of sharing division – share 39 into 3 groups. Set (b) tasks such as 42 ÷ 14 are likely to invoke thinking from a perspective of grouping division – given 42, make groups of 14.
- Endeavour to determine the use of known basic facts, the use of the inverse relationship of multiplication and division, implicit use of commutative and distributive principles, and use of additive reasoning in the range 1 to 100 and beyond.

TASK GROUP A7.10: Inverse Relationship of Multiplication and Division

Materials: Cards as follows: $12 \times 7 = 84$, $84 \div 12$, $80 \div 5 = 16$.

What to do and say: Display the two cards. *Read the first card [$12 \times 7 = 84$]. Can you use that to help you solve 84 divided by 12? Can you think of another problem that you can use $12 \times 7 = 84$ to help you solve? Read this card [$80 \div 5 = 16$]. Can you think of a problem that you could solve using $80 \div 5 = 16$?*

Notes:

- The purpose of this task is to gauge the students' facility with the inverse relationship.
- The inverse relationship can be considered in two main ways: can a known multiplication be used to solve the corresponding division; and can a known division be used to solve the corresponding multiplication?
- Students might reverse the dividend and the divisor, for example in saying that $12 \times 7 = 84$ can help them to solve $7 \div 84$.
- Students might have no more than a superficial knowledge that a multiplication equation such as $6 \times 7 = 42$ can give rise to a division equation such as $42 \div 7 = 6$.
- Pose additional questions with a view to gaining insight into the depth of students' knowledge of the inverse relationship. Ask open-ended questions, and take care not to dominate the conversation or to 'put words into the student's mouth'.

TASK GROUP A7.11: Commutative Principle

Materials: Cards as follows: $14 \times 3 = 42$, 3×14, $7 \times 5 = 35$, 5×35, 35×7, 5×7.

What to do and say: Display the two cards. *Read the first card. Can you use that to help you solve 3 multiplied by 14? Display the card $7 \times 5 = 35$. Read this card. Can you use that to solve any of these problems [5×35, 35×7, 5×7]? Which ones?*

Notes:

- The purpose of this task is to gauge the student's facility with the commutative principle of multiplication.
- In similar vein to A7.10, pose additional questions with a view to gaining insight into the depth of the student's knowledge of the commutative principle.

TASK GROUP A7.12: Distributive Principle

Materials: Cards as follows: $23 \times 3 = 69$, $2 \times 3 = 6$, 25×3, 49×3, $76 \div 4$.

What to do and say: Display the first three cards. *Read the first two cards. Can you use those to help you work out 25 × 3? Read this card [49 × 3]. Can you think of an easy way to work this out? Read this card [76 ÷ 4]. Can you think of an easy way to work this out?*

Notes:

- The purpose of this task is to gauge the student's facility with the distributive principle.
- The distributive principle has four main forms in all: multiplication over addition; multiplication over subtraction; division over addition; and division over subtraction (see earlier in this chapter).
- In a similar vein to A7.10 and A7.11, pose additional questions with a view to gaining insight into the depth of the students' knowledge of the distributive principle.

 INSTRUCTIONAL ACTIVITIES

List of Instructional Activities

ACTIVITY IA7.1: Counting Items in Equal Groups

Intended learning: To use skip counting to count items in equal groups.

Instructional mode: Shorter, inquiry mode for whole group, small group or individuals.

Materials: A collection of objects or pictures of objects that come in equal groups (e.g. pairs of shoes, wheels on tricycles, fingers on one or two hands).

Description: This initial exploration allows students to develop the concept of using a group as a unit. Introduce the discussion by saying, *How many fingers are in this room?* Have one student stand. *How many fingers do you have?* Continue to have students stand one at a time and identify the new number of fingers displayed. If the notion of skip counting does not emerge prompt with, *How many fingers do most people have? Is there a way we can quickly count all these fingers?* Repeat the process with other equal groups. Initially each item in each group should be visible. Eventually, each group should be visible, but the items within each group should not be discernible. For example, fingers in the four-finger wrapped Kit Kat bars allow students to reason about the individual fingers without seeing them until they are unwrapped.

Responses, variations and extensions:

- This activity is most effective after students have experience with the forward number word sequences of 10s, 5s, 3s and 2s.
- If students count by ones prompt with *How could we count this more quickly?*

ACTIVITY IA7.2: Snack Time

Intended learning: To develop initial strategies for multiplication.

Instructional mode: Shorter, rehearsal mode for pairs.

Materials: Snack time record sheet (see Figure 7.13), 6 paper bowls, unit cubes or blocks to model snacks, one 1–6 dot cube, and one decahedron with the numerals 0–9 for each pair.

Description: This activity allows students to repeatedly create equal groups of a specified number. Introduce the activity. *You are going to be fixing the snack orders for a group of children at the zoo. We need to make sure that all of the snacks are equal. Today the snack will be grapes. Roll the dot cube to see how many servings you will need to prepare to fill the order. Roll the 0–9 decahedron to determine the number of grapes you will need for each bowl. Finally, calculate the total number of grapes*

Snack Time

Round 1					
Player 1			Player 2		
Number of Bowls	Number of Grapes Per Bowl	Total Grapes Needed	Number of Bowls	Number of Grapes Per Bowl	Total Grapes Needed

Round 2					
Player 1			Player 2		
Number of Bowls	Number of Grapes Per	Total Grapes Needed	Number of Bowls	Number of Grapes Per Bowl	Total Grapes Needed

Figure 7.13   Snack time recording sheet

you will need in order to prepare the snack. You may use the bowls and blocks to help you. Your partner's job is to make sure that you have the snack order correct. Record your snack order on your record sheet and then exchange jobs with your partner.

Responses, variations and extensions:

- This activity allows students to see the group markers (bowls) as well as the items in each group (unit cubes or blocks representing the fruit in the bowls).
- Students benefit from repeated experiences with this activity.

ACTIVITY IA7.3: Counting Dot Tiles

Intended learning: To use sequences of multiples to count equal groups.

Instructional mode: Longer, inquiry mode for individuals, pairs or whole class.

Materials: Set of dot tiles.

Description: This activity allows students to use sequences of multiples to count quickly items in equal groups. The tiles within each set have the same dot pattern. There are geometric dot patterns for 3, 4 and 5 as well as two-colour linear arrangements of dots available in groups of 2, 3, 4, 5, 6, 7, 8, 9 and 10. There are several variations of the task involving the student determining the total number of dots on all tiles or the number of tiles when the total number of dots is given.

Variations:

- **A Growing and Shrinking Line of Tiles:** The teacher displays one tile at a time and asks the students *How many dots?* The teacher adds another tile and asks again, *Now how many dots?* This procedure continues with the teacher adding another tile and asking for the new total number of dots (see Figure 7.14). Once all tiles are visible, the teacher can remove a tile and ask, *Now how many dots?* This continues until all tiles have been removed. With this task all dots are visible. A student could thus count by ones to determine the total number of dots at each step.
- **Adding to or Subtracting from Covered Tiles:** This variation functions in the same way as above except the teacher uses a screen to cover all but the last tile added to the collection. Thus, the student is encouraged to work from the previous total to determine the new total rather than counting the dots on all the tiles each time a tile is added.

Figure 7.14   Row of 3-pattern geometric dot tiles

- **Get Me:** Arrange each type of tile in a separate stack. Ask the student to use the tiles to create an arrangement of tiles to match a certain criterion. *Get me seven four-tiles. How many tiles altogether? How many dots are on each tile? How many dots are there altogether? Write an equation to match your arrangement. Using one type of tile only, make an arrangement with a total of 24 dots. Which type of tile did you use? How many tiles did you need? How did you figure it out?* Students might use repeated addition until they reach the specified product or might use division to determine the number of tiles needed. Some students may initially attempt to use a tile that is not a factor of the specified product. If needed, you might prompt the student to use a particular type of tile.

- **Unknown Number of Tiles:** A pile of one type of tiles is visible to the student in such a manner that the student knows how many dots are on each tile. Without the student seeing, the teacher arranges an unknown number of tiles under a screen. *I have 24 dots made from the 3-dot tiles. How many tiles did I use?*

- **Unknown Type of Tile:** Without the student seeing, the teacher arranges an unknown type of tile under a screen. *I have 24 dots made with 8 tiles. How many dots are on each tile?*

ACTIVITY IA7.4: Arrays on the 100-bead Rack

Intended learning: To explore arrays of various dimensions.

Instructional mode: Longer, inquiry mode for individuals, pairs or whole class.

Materials: 100-bead rack (commercially available or constructed with two colours of pony beads and pipe cleaners attached to a foam board. See Figure 7.15).

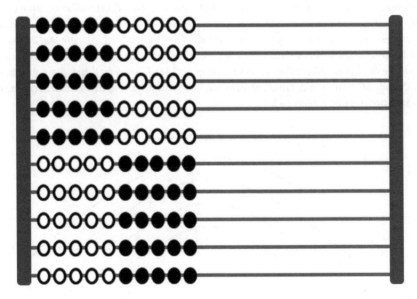

Figure 7.15   100-bead arithmetic rack

Description: This activity allows students to explore easily arrays of any dimension up to 10 × 10. It is useful to establish a convention for beads that are 'in play' and beads that are 'out of play'. For example, you might establish that the beads that are in play to form the array are the beads that are pushed to the left beginning with the top row. This is particularly important for monitoring student work in larger groups. Have the student construct an array of specified dimensions. *Use your bead rack to construct an array of four rows with three beads in each row. How many beads do you have altogether? How do you know?* Repeat this procedure to construct arrays of other dimensions.

Responses, variations and extensions:

- The bead rack can be used to count by a number in the range one to ten. For example, a student counts by sixes (6, 12, 18 …) and for each count the teacher pushes six beads on a row.
- The teacher might specify a particular product made with a given number of rows. *Make me an array with a total of 28 beads arranged on 7 equal rows.* The student must determine how many beads to put on each row.
- The teacher might specify a product made of rows of a specified number. *Use rows of 4 to make me an array with a total of 28 beads.* The student must determine how many rows are needed to construct the array. *How many rows did you need?*
- Investigate notions of commutative principle by comparing related arrays. *What do you notice about this array with six rows of four beads and this other array with four rows of six beads?*
- For arrays with at least one factor greater than five, notions of the distributive principle can be used to facilitate calculation. *This array has four rows of eight beads. How could we use the colour to help us determine the product?* $8 \times 4 = (5 + 3) \times 4 = (5 \times 4) + (3 \times 4) = 20 + 12 = 32$
- The teacher can construct a screened array for a given product and ask students for possible dimensions. *I have an array with 24 dots. What is one way I could have made my array? Are there other ways? Let's display each different array on your bead racks. Notate each different array with an expression or equation. Did we find them all? How can we know for sure that we found them all?* Possible suggestions would be an organized list or rainbow factoring (see Figure 7.16). *Could we have done 12 rows of 2? Why or why not?* [The bead rack has the constraints of a maximum of 10 rows and a maximum of ten beads on each row, but a student might suggest using more than one bead rack.]

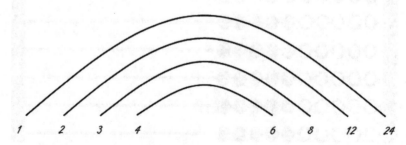

Figure 7.16 Rainbow factoring for 24

ACTIVITY IA7.5: Array Bingo

Intended learning: To develop facility with multiplication facts to 9×9.

Instructional mode: Longer, rehearsal mode for whole group or small groups.

Materials: One deck of array bingo cards per participant.

Description: Each participant selects 16 array bingo cards and places them face up in a 4 by 4 array on the desktop (see Figure 7.17). The leader announces one product at a time. If the student has an array or arrays equal to the announced product, the card(s) is turned face down. Play continues until a student has four cards in a row face down, either horizontally, vertically, or diagonally, and calls 'Array bingo!' The student must then verify each card by telling the fact represented by each card.

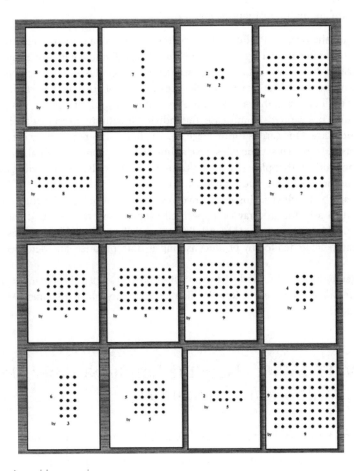

Figure 7.17 Array bingo cards

Responses, variations and extensions:

- All announced products may focus on a specific concept unbeknownst to the students. For example, the leader might choose to announce multiples of 7, prime numbers, composite numbers, etc.
- After a student achieves array bingo, discuss the products that were announced. *What did you notice about these products? Yes, all of these arrays in this game were made of only a single row of dots. Why was that?* [They were all prime numbers.]
- For students who attempt to count the dots by ones, prompt with *Can you find a quicker way to find the product without counting by ones?* Students may suggest skip counting, or going from a known quantity. For example, to determine the product of 6 and 7, a student might use the square 6×6 and count on one more group of 6.
- For less facile students, cards may be sorted to limit products to 25 dots.
- As students develop facility, cards with the bare number expressions (6×4) may be substituted for the arrays.
- Small group and partner variations include:

  ○ **Who has the Greater Product?:** Each partner turns over a card and determines the product of his or her array. There is no time limit. The individual with the greater product gets both cards. In the event of a tie (the product of each card is equal), each tying player flips over another card. The player with the greatest product on the new card, wins that turn and gets all the cards that are face-up. Play continues until one player has all the cards or until time has expired. In this case, the individual with the most cards wins the game.

  ○ **Product Race:** One card is flipped face up. The first partner to identify correctly the product gets the card. This game does have a time element. If an individual incorrectly identifies the product, that player is penalized one card. This discourages wild guesses that can imprint incorrect facts. The individual with the most cards wins.

  ○ **Go Fish for Products:** This game involves the traditional go fish rules except that the individual asks for an array of a specified product. In order to lay down a match, the individual must have two cards with the same product. The perfect squares are wild cards and can be matched to any product as long as both products are identified.

Acknowledgement: Activity modified from B. Kobett (1999), Professional Development Workshop for Grade 5 Teachers at Roye-Williams Elementary, Havre de Grace, Maryland. Used with permission.

ACTIVITY IA7.6: Using the Empty Number Line to Model Multiplicative Situations

Intended learning: To develop the concept of multiplication as repeated addition.

Instructional mode: Shorter, inquiry mode for whole group, small group, or individuals.

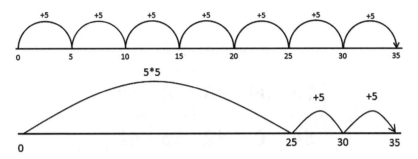

Figure 7.18   ENLs for seven groups of five

Materials: Chalkboard and chalk, whiteboard and marker, or chart paper and marker for modelling student strategies. Individual student slates (whiteboards, chalkboards, etc.) for use in solving the problem.

Description: This exploration allows students to develop the concept of using repeated addition to solve multiplicative problems. The empty number line (ENL) should be used to notate and communicate student problem-solving strategies. Begin with a context that is easily imagined by the students. *I just bought 7 packs of pencils for the classroom. Each pack has 5 pencils. How many pencils is that altogether?* Give students some time to solve the problem. Note student strategies while they are working. Carefully orchestrate the discussion by having students share their strategies in increasing complexity. For a student using repeated addition, use the ENL to notate their thinking (see Figure 7.18). Discuss advantages and potential disadvantages of the different strategies used.

Responses, variations and extensions:

- A range of different strategies might be used to solve this problem.
- Some students may need materials to support their access to the problem.
- For many students, understanding the problem is the first step to successful problem solving. Teachers may need to pay particular attention to building vocabulary related to groups (i.e. packages, packs, sets, lots, flocks, herds).
- The empty number line can be used to model division as repeated subtraction.

ACTIVITY IA7.7: The Multiples Games

Intended learning: To develop facility with a family of multiplication facts.

Instructional mode: Shorter, rehearsal mode for pairs.

Materials: 0–9 Spinner, game board, and two kinds of markers (dried beans, bingo chips, etc.).

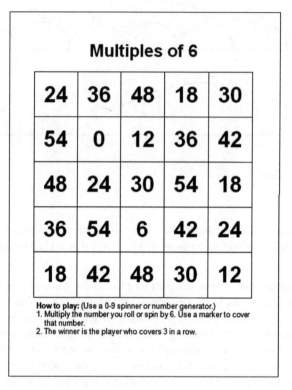

Figure 7.19 Multiples of 6 game board

Description: Each game board focuses on the multiples of one factor in the range of 2 to 10. The player spins the spinner and then multiplies the spun number by the focus factor of the game board. (See Figure 7.19 for the *multiples of 6* sample.) Players alternate spinning the spinner and covering the resulting product until one player has three markers in a row, horizontally, vertically or diagonally. If the product resulting from the spin is no longer available, the player may spin again.

Responses, variations and extensions:

- These games are most effective with students who have a concept of multiplication as repeated addition.
- Students may use materials to calculate the facts as needed.
- Students should be cautioned not to guess; rather, they should use strategies to determine the products. Inaccurate guesses can imprint the incorrect fact leading to further difficulty.
- For an extension, encourage students to select strategically the product if it is available in more than one location. Moves may either advance a player's own cause or block the opponent from achieving three in a row.

- To encourage students to use the inverse relationship, ask *What would you need to spin in order to win the game?*
- 'Perfect Squares' is a variation in which the student squares the spun number.

ACTIVITY IA7.8: The Factoring Game

Intended learning: To develop facility with a family of division facts.

Instructional mode: Shorter, rehearsal mode for pairs.

Materials: Multiples spinner, Factoring Game Board, and two kinds of markers (dried beans, bingo chips, etc.).

Description: Each spinner focuses on the multiples of one factor in the range of 2–9. The player spins the spinner and then divides the spun number by the focus factor of the spinner. (See Figure 7.20 for the *multiples of 3 spinner* sample.) Players alternate spinning the spinner and covering the resulting factor until one player has three markers in a row, horizontally, vertically or diagonally. If the factor resulting from the spin is no longer available, the player may spin again.

(a)

Factoring Game Board

1	5	7	4	9
3	0	6	2	7
5	4	8	1	4
9	8	5	3	6
7	6	2	9	8

How to play: (Use the "Multiples of 3" spinner).
1. Divide the number you spin by the factor listed above the spinner. Use a marker to cover the unknown factor (quotient).
2. Winner is the player who covers 3 in a row.
For example: if you are playing Factoring by 3 and you spin 24 on the "Multiples of 3" spinner, you would cover 8.

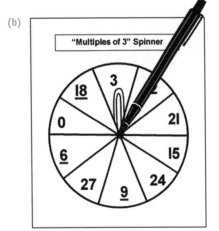

(b)

Figure 7.20   (a) Factoring game board, and (b) spinner

Responses, variations and extensions:

- These games are most effective with students who have a concept of division as repeated subtraction.
- Students may use materials to calculate the facts as needed.
- Students should be cautioned not to guess. Rather, they should use strategies to determine the factors.
- For an extension, encourage students to select strategically the factor if it is available in more than one location. Moves may either advance a player's own cause or block the opponent from achieving three in a row.
- To encourage students to use the inverse relationship, ask *What would you need to spin in order to win the game?*

8
Written Computation

DOMAIN OVERVIEW

In Chapter 2, we described the broad approach to developing mental computation and written computation. We sketched a progression in the mathematization of computation knowledge over five phases (see Figure 2.1):

1. Initial context-bound mental strategies
2. Sophisticated context-independent mental strategies, which can be notated informally
3. Informal jotting, combining mental strategies with writing
4. Semi-formal written strategies
5. Formal written algorithms.

The domains *Addition and Subtraction to 100* and *Multiplication and Division* have each addressed the first two phases of that progression, developing sophisticated mental strategies and informal notations for, respectively, additive tasks and multiplicative tasks. This domain *Written Computation* addresses the last three phases of that progression: jotting strategies, semi-formal written strategies and formal written algorithms, across the four operations of addition, subtraction, multiplication and division.

Written Computation Methods: Jotting, Semi-formal Strategies and Formal Algorithms

For calculations with larger numbers, mental computation can be unwieldy. Writing can be used to make larger calculations more efficient and reliable. We distinguish three different kinds of written computation method: informal jottings, semi-formal strategies and formal algorithms. Figure 8.1 shows an example of each kind for each of the four operations: addition, subtraction, multiplication and division (Anghileri, 2006; Fosnot and Dolk 2001a, 2001b; Thompson, 1999; Treffers et al., 2001).

Jotting

We use the term *jotting* for idiosyncratic informal writing to help solve a calculation problem. Sometimes the calculation essentially uses a mental strategy, but some intermediate results are

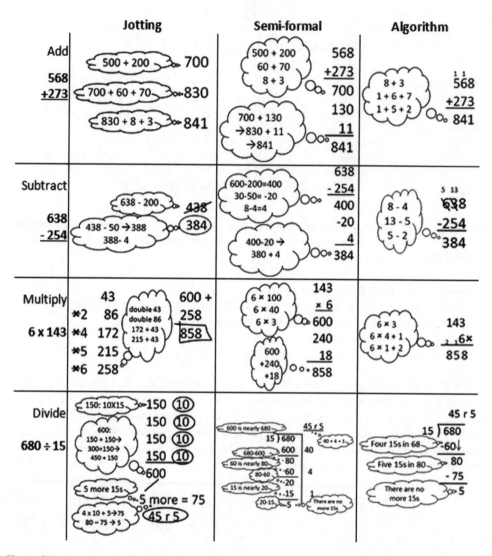

Figure 8.1 An example of a jotting, a semi-formal strategy and a formal algorithm for each of the four operations

jotted down to avoid having to remember them. Sometimes the writing is more involved, recording different trials or partial results while the student grapples with solving the task. In the jotting method for addition shown in Figure 8.1, the student was using a mental split-jump strategy, making an accumulating total. She jotted two of the intermediate totals down to help keep track. The method is largely mental, nevertheless the writing is important to the student's thinking. Without jotting those two intermediate totals down, the student may have been unable to complete the addition. In the jotting method for division shown in Figure 8.1, the writing is keeping track of several aspects of the calculation, and is clearly more central to the students' problem solving than in the case of the jotting method for addition.

(a)   (b)

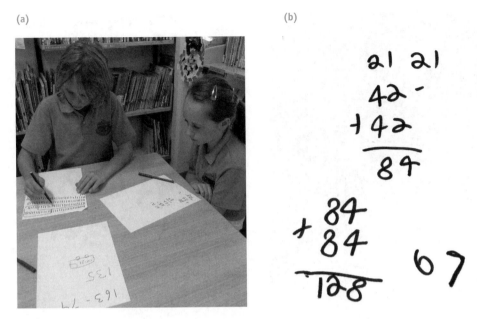

Photo 8.1 (a) and (b)   Jotting to solve a division problem

Semi-formal Written Strategies

Semi-formal written strategies are well-organized, standardized, written strategies. They can be personal inventions, but are usually taught strategies. They are also known as column calculations or alternative algorithms. The four examples of semi-formal strategies shown in Figure 8.1 are sometimes known as, respectively: column addition or the partial sums method; column subtraction or the partial differences method; column multiplication or the partial products method; and column division or the partial quotients method. A semi-formal strategy still involves doing multi-digit calculations mentally, but the writing systematically records intermediate results, and keeps them organized. In the partial sums method, for example, the addends are arranged vertically in a stack. Partial sums – that is, intermediate totals for separate sums of the 100s, the 10s, and the 1s – are each calculated mentally as whole numbers, and recorded under the line. The total of the partial sums is then calculated mentally, and the answer recorded at the bottom.

Formal Algorithms

Formal algorithms are probably the most familiar written computation methods. They are also referred to as *standard* or *traditional* algorithms, because in recent generations these have been the methods taught in schools. *Algorithm* means a step-by-step procedure for computing a standard task. In the formal algorithms, mental calculations mainly involve 1-digit numbers. The algorithm generates the answer because of the precise conventions governing how the written digits are arranged. The steps of the addition algorithm shown in Figure 8.1 can be summarized as

(a)

(b)

Photo 8.2 (a) and (b) Using semi-formal written strategies

follows. First, the addends are written vertically in a stack, and aligned in place value columns. Then each column is summed in turn, beginning with the 1s column and proceeding from right to left. Within a column, the digits are summed mentally and the total is recorded below, in the same column. If a column total is 10 or greater, the number of tens is recorded in the next column along, to be included in the sum of that column. When the left-most column has been summed, the numeral formed below the line is the final answer.

Comparing Semi-formal Strategies and Formal Algorithms

The semi-formal strategies and formal algorithms are marvellous mathematical inventions. It is worth distinguishing their characteristics and the arithmetical reasoning that they encompass (Anghileri, 2001, 2006; Plunkett, 1979; Ruthven, 1998; Thompson, 1997, 1999).

Number Sense

Semi-formal strategies are embedded in students' number sense to a greater extent than formal algorithms. A student used to the partial sums method would quickly have a sense that the answer to 568 + 273 will be about 800, whereas a student thinking only in terms of the addition algorithm might reach an incorrect answer in the 8000s with little or no awareness of error. On the other hand, the partial sums method becomes unwieldy when used to add many numbers, or to add numbers with many digits. These are the circumstances for which the algorithms were developed, and where they served so magnificently for centuries, until calculators arrived.

Reliance on Mental Computation

A semi-formal strategy relies on multi-digit mental computation. The partial sums method in Figure 8.1 is essentially a mental split strategy, that is, the hundreds, tens and ones parts of each number are added separately, and these intermediate subtotals are then added. The writing helps to organize and keep track of the calculations, while actually adding numbers together remains a mental task.

In contrast, the algorithms rely on the place value notation to keep track of the meaning of the digits. The student need not think about the separate parts of the numbers, but rather operates on parts of the notation, mentally calculating with 1-digit numbers only. Notice that, in the partial sums method, the final total is calculated mentally, and then written down as a record. In the addition algorithm, by contrast, the final total is never conceived. Instead it simply appears as a numeral out of the successive concatenation of digits under the line. That appearance is either magical or logical, depending on your understanding of the arithmetical processes underlying the algorithm.

Formality

A semi-formal strategy involves using the form – that is, the layout – of the writing to help organize the calculation. By stacking the addends, it is easy to compile the hundreds parts, the tens parts and the ones parts. By recording the subtotals, the subtotals do not need to be remembered. However, the strategy does not depend on a precise layout. For example, in the partial sums method in Figure 8.1, the partial sums are calculated in left to right order – hundreds, then tens then ones. Nevertheless, the order is inconsequential, as long as each part is summed and recorded. The placement of the written subtotals is also inconsequential, since the subtotals are added together as whole numbers (700 → 830 → 841), not by columns.

In contrast, the algorithms depend on a precise form or layout of the writing, aligning the digits in columns. They also depend on a precise procedure, working from right to left, and so on. Using an algorithm requires thinking at a formal level of layout and procedures, rather than thinking about whole numbers.

Place Value

The semi-formal strategies require reasoning with whole numbers. For example, the student calculates 500 + 200 = 700, not 5 + 2 = 7. This thinking involves what we have called conceptual place value, adding and subtracting whole hundreds, tens and ones, but it does not involve conventional place value.

In contrast, understanding the arithmetical processes underlying the algorithms does involve an understanding of conventional place value. Ones, tens and hundreds are treated as formal units. Digits stand for a number of such units. Adding digits symbolizes adding the actual numbers. The relationship of one column to the next is consistent across the columns: thus, as we carry ten ones to the tens column, so we can carry ten hundreds to the thousands column. (For a discussion of the distinction between conceptual place value and conventional place value, see Chapter 5.)

Significance of Written Computation Methods in the Curriculum

In past generations, formal algorithms were essential tools for arithmetic. In turn, they were typically invested with great importance in school curricula. In recent decades, with the arrival of calculators and computers, the usefulness of formal algorithms has waned. The importance of different computation methods in contemporary school curricula is now contested. Within the curriculum, we need to acknowledge how the different methods are useful. Arithmetic in the range 0 to 100, and indeed to 1000, is best done with facile mental strategies. Many arithmetic tasks only require an estimation or approximation, and these are typically derived from mental strategies too. More involved tasks are well served by a calculator. Hence written methods are not essential. However, they are still useful.

Jotting is a common technique for adults, to extend mental computation without a calculator. More generally, jotting down partial results is a basic technique for all types of problem-solving, so students are well served with practising jotting. Semi-formal strategies are a neat way to organize and support mental strategies. They are closely aligned with mental strategies, so students learn them readily, and often find them useful. Semi-formal strategies also serve a didactic purpose, in developing a vertically aligned notation. They are an effective precursor to learning formal algorithms. Formal algorithms, in turn, serve the didactic purpose of developing insight into conventional place value and the number system. More broadly, they offer an early experience of the power of formalization and rigour. The algorithms are significant mathematical inventions and are often assumed to be an integral part of cultural knowledge, hence many students appreciate learning them. And in some circumstances, some students prefer using an algorithm to using a calculator. However, the formal algorithms for multiplication and division are condensed and demanding methods, and are treated with a light touch in many contemporary curricula (Anghileri, 2006; Plunkett, 1979; Ruthven, 1998; Thompson, 1997; Treffers et al., 2001).

Learning Written Computation

When we observe students learning to use written methods for computation, we recognize three broad themes: familiarization, mathematization and induction.

Familiarization

Learning written methods requires in part, a familiarization with particular notations. All written computation methods involve an interplay between notation and mental calculation. Hence, learning to use the methods requires learning to connect the notations with mental calculations. This is rarely straightforward. Once we are familiar with a written method, we tend to take for granted the meaning of the notations. However, when we encounter a written method for the first time, it is evident that the meaning of the notation is not obvious. What is this line for, where did this number come from? We can have the experience of the markings swimming on the page: we don't know how to pin them down, how to read them. Learning to read the new notation is a little like learning a new language. We need some time to observe it, try it out, talk about it – that is, time to familiarize – before we can progress. To support familiarization, teachers can provide learning environments rich in written mathematics, and talk with students about their notations (Carruthers and Worthington, 2006; Munn, 1997).

Mathematization

Written methods are learnt in part by mathematization. Students can begin by using jotting while doing mental computation. Then they can reflect on which intermediate totals they record, or how to keep them orderly on the page. As they develop more insight into their strategies, and more formal ways to reason arithmetically, they are mathematizing. As they develop clearer ways of using writing to support what they are doing, with more consistent and more abbreviated ways of arranging the notations, they are mathematizing. Mathematizing in these ways can link jotting to semi-formal strategies, and link semi-formal strategies to formal algorithms (Anghileri, 2001; Treffers et al., 2001).

Induction

At the same time, learning new notation is also an experience of induction into society's ways of knowing. Teachers offer *Here is an established way to write this*, and students try to copy that established way. Students are unlikely to invent neat semi-formal strategies, let alone formal algorithms. These are the inventions of generations of mathematicians, which can be passed on to students when the students are ready.

Difficulties Learning Algorithms from Base-ten Materials

It has been common in teaching to assume that students can learn how an algorithm works by modelling the algorithm with base-ten materials. While such an activity may help some students, it can be frustratingly ineffective. Research offers two reasons why.

Firstly, students need the insight of viewing ten units of one as one unit of ten to understand how an algorithm works. This unitizing insight is fundamentally abstract, it is not somehow out there in the rubber band around the bundling sticks. For students with this insight, the materials are probably unnecessary. For students without this insight, the materials probably will not help. Secondly, a written algorithm does not involve merely recording the manipulations of materials; rather, it involves formally symbolizing arithmetical reasoning. So a student cannot simply transfer an understanding of manipulations of materials to an understanding of a written algorithm. The correspondence from one to the other is much more mathematically demanding than a mere transfer of knowledge (Cobb, 1991; Gravemeijer, 1991; Hart, 1989b).

The effective use of base-ten materials is not as a model for algorithms, rather, as a setting for tasks. When students solve tasks in a setting of base-ten materials, they can construct their own understanding of base-ten arithmetical reasoning. This is central to the instruction described in Chapters 5 and 6 on conceptual place value and addition and subtraction to 100. Students can then learn to symbolize calculations in writing, through jotting and semi-formal strategies, as described in the present chapter. Such a development of reasoning and symbolization prepares students to make sense of algorithms. In short, the best basis for learning algorithms is strong mental strategies and facility with semi-formal written computation, rather than manipulations of materials (Fosnot and Dolk, 2001b; Treffers et al., 2001). The issues of symbolization and instruction with materials are also discussed in Chapter 2.

Assessment of Written Computation

Pose multi-digit computation tasks in the range beyond 100. Assess facility with tasks in a meaningful context, and with bare number tasks. To assess a particular method, direct students to use that method. An alternative is to present a finished written computation, which may have errors in it, and ask students to assess the computation and correct any errors. Students' own assessments provide insight into their knowledge of the written computation method. Assessment can consider three aspects of written computation: students' reasoning and procedure; students' facility with the written layout; and students' facility with the mental calculations involved. Students who are making errors in a procedure but not in the mental calculations need different help from students who get the procedure correct, but make errors in the mental calculations. Determining these different profiles is important.

Jotting Methods

Students' reasoning can be hard to observe, but monitoring it is critical. What is the students' level of facility with working their way through to a solution, keeping track of all the parts necessary, and making sense of the final answer? How can the written layout be better organized? Are students hampered by lack of facility with the mental calculations involved?

Semi-formal Strategies

Are students following the procedure consistently? How can the written layout be made more regular? Again, are students hampered by lack of facility with the mental calculations?

Formal Algorithms

Are students appropriately handling each step in the algorithm procedure? Where does the written layout need to be corrected? Are students making errors in their 1-digit mental calculations? Watch for students who are not yet ready to submit to the formal rigour required to succeed with algorithms.

Outline of Instruction in Written Computation

When students have developed facility with multi-digit mental computation, they are ready to develop written computation methods. In outline, instruction proceeds to first developing jotting, then semi-formal written strategies, and finally formal algorithms. Once there are strong mental strategies, we invite students to try jotting, and possibly invent their own written methods. Over time, students become familiar with the practice of using writing to support computation. Then we can introduce semi-formal strategies, in order of simplicity: addition first, then subtraction, and later, multiplication and division. For students who are ready, the formal addition algorithm can be learned as a relatively straightforward abbreviation of a semi-formal addition strategy. The formal subtraction algorithm requires considerably more care, and should be delayed until the addition algorithm is well established. The multiplication and division algorithms are treated with a light touch in many contemporary curricula. More comprehensive instructional sequences for developing semi-formal strategies and formal algorithms are described in Fosnot and Dolk (2001a, 2001b) and Treffers et al. (2001).

Throughout instruction in written methods, keep in mind the three themes of learning highlighted above. Students need opportunities to *familiarize* with notation, and with connecting notation to mental computation. They need opportunities to *mathematize* their computation through notating and formalizing their thinking. And they need opportunities to be *inducted* into regular methods. Also keep in mind the appropriate use of base-ten materials as a setting for tasks. If a student is struggling with a task, it can help to simplify the task, or to present the task in a setting of base-ten materials, so that the student can reconnect with their mental strategies. Avoid trying to model the written method with materials.

Be aware that, when the number curriculum is dominated by algorithms, teaching time tends to be consumed by demonstrating and correcting the algorithm procedures. While algorithms do require procedural precision, an excess of time spent teaching procedures has several drawbacks. Teachers have less opportunity to support mathematizing, which needs to be their main offering. In turn, students develop a distorted view of mathematics as about procedures and rules, losing touch with mental computation, number sense and problem solving. Also, many students struggle to learn algorithms this way – they may not yet be ready for such a formal approach to computation (Anghileri, 2001; Anghileri et al., 2002; Kamii and Dominick, 1998; Thompson, 1997, 1999; Treffers et al., 2001).

Instruction in Jotting

The domain *Addition and Subtraction to 100* in Chapter 6 focuses on the development of efficient mental strategies for multi-digit addition and subtraction, such as jump, split and compensation. The development of these strategies involves strong knowledge of conceptual place value: incrementing and decrementing by 1s, 10s and 100s. When students have strong mental strategies for addition and subtraction, they can begin to use jotting to support their mental strategies.

A difficult 3-digit addition task is a good place to begin. If students are finding this easy mentally, try an addition of three numbers or of 4-digit numbers. Pose the task and allow students to solve it. Record students' different strategies, and discuss the challenge of keeping track of intermediate sums. Invite students to use jotting as a way of managing that challenge. As students trial jotting, lead the class to reflect on how they use jotting, much as they have discussed their mental strategies.

Notice that students can be remarkably disorganized in their use of jotting – some results are written, others aren't, and numbers are written all over the page. Help students try simple techniques to get more organized with writing: try starting at the top left of the page, try keeping the numbers in the order they are written, try underlining the final answer. Challenge students to record their work in a way that other students can follow what they have done. At the same time, do not be prescriptive. Jotting needs to be a personal device. Also, the didactic purpose of introducing jotting is for students to make their own sense of how writing can connect to and support calculation.

The domain *Multiplication and Division* in Chapter 7 focuses on the development of efficient mental strategies for multiplication and division in the range 1 to 100. When students have developed strong mental strategies, encourage them to try using jotting for multiplication and division tasks in the range 1 to 1000. Students draw on an impressive body of number knowledge to solve multi-digit multiplicative tasks, including: organizing a context into an array or equal groups; splitting numbers into 100s, 10s and 1s; multi-digit addition and subtraction; repeated addition and subtraction; doubling; multiplying by ten; known multiplication facts; and quickly derived facts. The calculations are typically reasonably complex, and jotting down intermediate steps and results can become very useful. At the same time, the jotting may need to be more organized.

Some students will quickly make jotting a natural extension of their mental computation strategies. They may establish regular habits of which subtotals they record, and how they arrange them on the page. In this way, students can invent their own written strategies. Such a process of formalization is certainly to be encouraged. It is a rich experience of mathematization, and will prepare them well for induction into semi-formal strategies and algorithms. At the same time, ensure that such students continue to practise purely mental computation too. Other students may find jotting to be an awkward and unfamiliar practice. Give these students time to familiarize themselves with jotting. Students learning to connect their own writing with their own mathematical thinking is a fundamental goal of school. Some of these students may remain hesitant to invent their own uses of writing, while thriving on induction into semi-formal written strategies.

Instruction in Semi-formal Written Strategies

Semi-formal written strategies may not be required learning in a mathematics syllabus, so need not be forced on students. They can be offered as a further mathematization of students' efforts to use jotting to support mental computation, and as very handy methods of computation. They also serve as a demonstration of how neat and consistent a column notation can be, and as a preparation for learning the formal algorithms. A semi-formal strategy may appeal immediately to some students. In general, however, allow students some time to observe and familiarize themselves with a semi-formal written strategy before asking them to use it themselves. When students do begin to use the written strategy, encourage a neat and orderly approach, as appropriate to the strategy. Bear in mind that a semi-formal strategy does not require the same precision in writing or procedure as a formal algorithm. Also, continue to discuss the multi-digit mental strategies students use in the calculations. Students will benefit from continued practice of mental computation and extended conceptual place value tasks.

Written Strategy for Addition

When students are familiar with using jotting for larger addition tasks – and some may have devised their own regular written strategy – we can introduce an established semi-formal written strategy, such as the partial sums method. Begin with a 3-digit addition task. Discuss various students' strategies first – they will follow new notation best when they already understand the calculation. Next, focus attention on a split strategy. Introduce the semi-formal notation as a neat way to write down the intermediate totals in the split strategy. Though it is still essentially a split strategy, the column notation is very brief, and is not self-explanatory. Induction into the use of the notation requires care that students are following the calculation that has been done mentally. When students do begin to use the written strategy, continue to discuss students' mental strategies for calculating the partial sums and the final sum. Calculating the final sum, in particular, remains a significant mental computation task. In the example in Figure 8.1, the final sum is 700 + 130 + 11. Students must be facile with these mental computations before they will experience success with written strategies.

Written Strategy for Subtraction

Begin with a 3-digit subtraction task involving regrouping, such as 638−254. As with addition, after discussion of various student strategies, focus attention on a split strategy. The key issue is: how do students manage the deficit situation 30−50 in their thinking? Many will have ways of making sense of this, using terms such as 'back 20' or '20 less'. Now introduce the semi-formal notation as a neat way to write down the intermediate subtotals in the split strategy. Share the use of the minus sign to notate the deficit situation. However, other notations can be equally effective. Keeping the notation connected to students' ways of thinking through the calculation is the priority. When students begin to use the semi-formal strategy, they may wish to use jottings around the basic column notation, before they can abbreviate to the most regular column subtraction form. Again, continue to discuss and practise mental computation as well.

Written Strategy for Multiplication

Begin with a 1-digit by 2-digit multiplication task. Discuss students' strategies. There can be many approaches, including use of repeated addition, and use of doubling, as in the jotting example in Figure 8.1. Next, focus attention on splitting approaches. Introduce semi-formal column notation for writing down the intermediate totals of a splitting approach. For students who still think in terms of repeated addition, this notation may be difficult to follow, and too difficult to use. Insisting that they use the notation is unnecessary. Allow students to use jotting and other means to link their repeated addition to the 'times' approach. Extending to multiplying a 1-digit number by a 3-digit number can be a satisfying challenge. Multiplying a 2-digit number by a 2-digit number may be less straightforward – how is this to be split into intermediate results? Students will need experience solving these tasks with their own jotting approaches, before introducing the semi-formal splitting strategy. Take time, allow students' variations, and keep discussing students' approaches to raise awareness of the potential for abbreviation. That is, maintain the blend of familiarization, mathematization and induction.

   An alternative instructional sequence involves using arrays. Present 2-digit by 2-digit tasks in the context of dot arrays. Students can construct the multiplication as a rectangular array of dots, and organize the array into easily calculated parts. Later, students can sketch an array without dots, as a rectangular diagram of the four partial products, as shown in Figure 8.2. This is referred to as an open array. The semi-formal partial products method can then be used to notate the calculation.

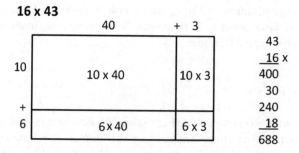

Figure 8.2   16 × 43 solved using an open array diagram and partial products method

Written Strategies for Division

Solving a division task is more convoluted than solving tasks involving any of the other three operations. Consider the task of 680 ÷ 15 shown in Figure 8.1. 680 is called the *dividend*, 15 is the *divisor*, 45 is the *quotient*, 5 is the *remainder*. To solve this task, repeated addition or subtraction of the divisor is too inefficient. All methods involve segmenting the dividend somehow – into segments of 150 or 300, for example. Success requires making fair estimates of these segments – what multiples of the divisor will fit into the dividend? Also, there needs to be some way to check the segments against the total dividend. In the jotting example, four segments of 150 make 600 – what is left to make 680? Finally, there needs to be some way of keeping track of the quotient: 150 is ten 15s, so four lots of 150 is forty 15s; the quotient so far is forty and there are still some 15s to come. No method that achieves all of this can be straightforward to understand. Development of a semi-formal strategy takes time, and may involve several steps of formalization in students' thinking and notation. A key to success is to keep students in touch with their way of thinking through the problem. Attention to three instructional issues will help.

Firstly, present tasks with contexts: for example, a realistic situation of putting a school of 680 students into groups of 15. The context helps students to distinguish the roles of the numbers involved – it is 15 students per group, not 15 groups, for example. Secondly, build strong knowledge of multiples and estimating segments. Begin any large division task by writing out a list of easy multiples of the divisor, such as doubles and multiples of 10. Figure 8.3 includes such a list for the task of 680 ÷ 15. Spend time making and using these lists, and discussing students' use of segments in their jotting solutions. Thirdly, help students to write down what they are doing. Using words in the notation, as shown in Figure 8.3, can help students stay in touch with sense making. Initial jotting methods may merely record block multiplying, as in the jotting example. A main innovation in the partial quotients method is to systematically record the subtraction of the segments.

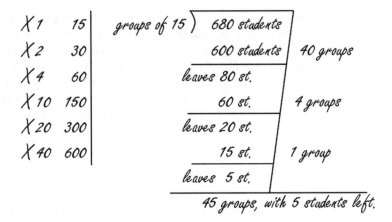

Figure 8.3   A written strategy to solve 680 ÷ 15, including a table of handy multiples of 15, and notation elaborated with words

Instruction in Formal Algorithms

When students are facile with a semi-formal method, and show aptitude for working procedurally, they can be inducted into the procedures for the formal algorithm. To induct, lead students step-by-step through the procedure. Alternatively, perform an algorithm without explanation, then challenge students to figure out the method and use it themselves, as though breaking a code or resolving a card trick.

Students can usually accept that the digit-based algorithm works, but initially they are unlikely to understand *how* it works. Knowledge of formal place value develops in part through learning the formal algorithms. Meanwhile, learning to use the algorithms involves learning to calculate with the formal thinking involved in the algorithm, rather than with number sense alone. Number sense can be used to check the reasonableness of final answers. However, while students are working through an algorithm, they need to follow precisely a formal procedure rather than be guided by number sense. So, establish a classroom practice of estimating a rough answer before using an algorithm, then checking the reasonableness of the answer obtained from the algorithm. At the same time, when using an algorithm, make the shift to formal thinking explicit. Encourage and support students to take pride in being neat, consistent and systematic in their written work. Treated with awareness, this shift to formal thinking is a major development in mathematization. Students without sufficient mental computation knowledge or formal thinking should not be pressed to use algorithms prematurely – this can hamper their development of both number sense and formal mathematics (Kamii and Dominick, 1998; Treffers, 1991). The formal algorithms for multiplication and division, as shown in the examples in Figure 8.1, are highly abbreviated methods. Instruction in these algorithms is beyond the scope of this book.

Addition Algorithm

A semi-formal strategy like partial sums is not dissimilar from the addition algorithm. The development from one to the other can be relatively smooth. One innovation is to work right to left rather than left to right. This can be practised while still using a semi-formal strategy and thinking in whole numbers: add ones first, then tens, then hundreds. The major innovation is to work with single-digit numbers rather than with tens and hundreds. Students need clear induction into what is written below the line, and how extra tens are marked in above the line. Pay particular attention to the situation when a column sum is exactly 10: '0' needs to be written below the line.

Subtraction Algorithm

The development from a semi-formal subtraction strategy to the subtraction algorithm is more protracted than for addition. Regrouping situations, that is those with a deficit minuend, require distinctive techniques in the algorithm. When students are familiar with the addition

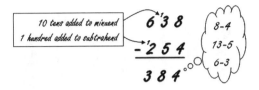

Figure 8.4   Example of the equal additions technique in a subtraction algorithm

algorithm, they can learn the basic form of the subtraction algorithm: work from right to left, calculate with single-digit numbers rather than with tens and hundreds, and record the result for each column below the line. Then they need to recognize the issue of columns with a deficit minuend – the upper number – such as 3 − 5 in the tens column in the subtraction algorithm example of Figure 8.1. Induct the students into a regular technique for handling columns with a deficit minuend. One standard technique is to regroup numbers in the minuend as shown in the example in Figure 8.1. This technique is referred to as *decomposition* or *regrouping*. An alternative technique is to mark an addition of ten units to the minuend, and an equal addition of ten units to the subtrahend – the lower number – in the next column left, as shown in Figure 8.4. This technique is referred to as *equal additions* or *constant differences*. Both these techniques require considerable practice to establish consistent written working. Both are subtle in their exploitation of formal place value and may not be properly understood by students.

ASSESSMENT TASK GROUPS

List of Assessment Task Groups

A8.1: Multi-digit Tasks in a Context: The School Excursion
A8.2: Open-ended Horizontal Bare Number Tasks
A8.3: Using a Semi-formal Strategy
A8.4: Algorithm Error Analysis

TASK GROUP A8.1: Multi-digit Tasks in a Context: The School Excursion

Materials: Writing materials, and task printed with pictures.

What to do and say: Present the following school excursion tasks. Pose the tasks orally or in print. Encourage students to write if they wish. Display the key numerical information with pictures, as shown in Figure 8.5.

Figure 8.5   The school excursion task

Anthill school and Beetletown school go on an excursion together.

(a) There are 247 Anthill students and 183 Beetletown students. How many students altogether?

(b) When they arrive, the students from each school line up to check the roll. The Anthill line is longer than the Beetletown line, because Anthill has more students than Beetletown. How many more Anthill students are there?

(c) They eat lunch in a picnic area. Some students sit at picnic tables, the rest on picnic rugs. Each table fits 8 students, and there are 34 tables for students. How many students are sitting at tables?

(d) At the end of the excursion, buses take the 247 Anthill students back to Anthill school. Each bus can take 25 students. How many buses do they need?

Notes:

• Tasks (a) and (b), the addition and subtraction tasks, are both 3-digit tasks involving regrouping. Task (c), the multiplication task, is a 1-digit by 2-digit task that does not involve regrouping. Task (d), the division task, involves a 2-digit divisor of 25, which has commonly known multiples.

• The numbers in the Task Group can be changed so that the resulting tasks are closely attuned to students' abilities.

• Some students can be more successful with tasks posed in a story context than with corresponding tasks posed in a bare number format, as per Task Group A8.2 below. Hence, posing Assessment Tasks in both context and bare number format can be informative.

TASK GROUP A8.2: Open-ended Horizontal Bare Number Tasks

Materials: A piece of paper with one horizontal bare number task (327 + 254) written at the top of the paper and otherwise blank.

What to do and say: Present the task and a pencil to the student. *Do you have a way to work this out? Feel free to write on the paper.*

Notes:

- These tasks are designed to assess students' methods for solving tasks involving multi-digit operations. These tasks are most effectively presented in an interview format in which the assessor can closely monitor student utterances and the sequence in which jottings are written. The problems are intentionally written in a horizontal format so that no one solution method will be privileged.
- Students may use mental strategies, jottings, semi-formal strategies or formal algorithms to solve these problems.
- Addition tasks could include:

  - 327 + 254 (regrouping in the ones)
  - 584 + 123 (regrouping in the tens)
  - 915 + 364 (regrouping in the hundreds)
  - 247 + 183 (regrouping in the tens and the ones, with a zero in the answer)
  - 5060 + 345 (4-digit task).

- Subtraction tasks could include:

  - 357 − 224 (no regrouping)
  - 247 − 183 (regrouping in the tens)
  - 720 − 541 (regrouping in tens and ones, involving a zero)
  - 1220 − 365 (regrouping in hundreds, tens and ones, involving a zero).

- Multiplication tasks could include:

  - 8 × 34 (no regrouping in the addition of partial sums)
  - 8 × 39 (with regrouping in the addition of partial sums)
  - 5 × 175 (1-digit × 3-digit)
  - 40 × 62 (decuple × 2-digit)
  - 13 × 56 (2-digit × 2-digit)

- Division tasks could include:

  - 365 ÷ 5 (1-digit divisor, no remainder)
  - 365 ÷ 7 (1-digit divisor, with remainder)
  - 247 ÷ 25 (less demanding 2-digit divisor, with remainder)
  - 238 ÷ 14 (more demanding 2-digit divisor, no remainder)

Subtraction Prompt

LaToya solved the subtraction problem 529 - 354 with a written method. See her work below:

$$529 = 500 + 20 + 9$$
$$- \ 354 = 300 + 50 + 4$$
$$200 - 30 + 5 = 175$$

Can you use LaToya's method to solve 728 − 143?

Figure 8.6 The prompt for a semi-formal strategy task

TASK GROUP A8.3: Using a Semi-formal Strategy

Materials: Writing materials, and written strategy prompts.

What to do and say: Present the prepared task prompt, as shown in Figure 8.6.

Notes:

- These tasks are designed to assess how readily students can make sense of and use semi-formal written strategies. Students are provided with a sample strategy and asked to use the same strategy to solve another problem. The students must determine the strategy based on the sample that is given.
- Though they may not recognize the sample strategy, students with knowledge of another semi-formal strategy for the same operation are more likely to be successful than students with no knowledge of relevant semi-formal strategies.

TASK GROUP A8.4: Algorithm Error Analysis

Materials: Writing materials, and algorithm error analysis prompts.

What to do and say: Present the prepared task prompt as shown in Figure 8.7. *Read this to me. Can you find and fix the student's error?*

Notes:

- These tasks are designed to assess students' knowledge of formal arithmetic with multi-digit numbers. Each task prompt shows, for a given arithmetic problem, an attempted written solution that includes an error commonly made by students using formal algorithms. The students' task is to find the error, correct it, and so find the correct solution.

Error Analysis Addition Prompt

Bill incorrectly solved the addition problem 674 + 235 and got the sum 8,109. Where did Bill go wrong? Please correct his work. Give some advice to Bill to help him solve addition problems correctly.

The correct sum: _____

Advice to Bill:

Figure 8.7   The prompt for an algorithm error analysis task

- If a student is unable to correct the error in the addition task, it is highly unlikely that the student will be successful with the other operations.
- Successfully finding and correcting an error indicates good depth of knowledge of an algorithm.
- Students' advice on how to correct an error can reveal the depth of their knowledge of the algorithm.

INSTRUCTIONAL ACTIVITIES

List of Instructional Activities

IA8.1: Group Monster
IA8.2: Sum of the Century
IA8.3: Decomposition with Arrow Cards
IA8.4: Palindromization
IA8.5: Catch 22
IA8.6: Shortcut 100
IA8.7: The Prodigal Sum

ACTIVITY IA8.1: Group Monster

Intended learning: To use informal mental and written strategies for addition and multiplication tasks.

Instructional mode: Longer, inquiry mode for groups.

Materials: Writing materials, measuring tapes.

Description: Begin by imagining that each group is a single monster. A group of five is a monster with five mouths, ten ears and ten googly eyes. Then, each group needs to create a list of the impressive real figures and measurements for their group monster. How many limbs, how many teeth, how many claws (i.e. in the group in total)? What is the monster's age (total the students' ages)? What is the height of the monster (total the students' heights)? How much water does the monster drink each day? Groups can determine what attributes they want to list, but they need to calculate the real figures for their group monster. To finish the activity, each group presents their monstrous figures.

Responses, variations and extensions:

- Some group monster figures can be calculated mentally – for example, the number of legs. Some calculations will be beyond mental computation – for example, the total group height. Students can use informal written strategies – jotting – for these calculations.
- Group monster figures are more impressive with larger numbers, so students can be motivated to work with larger numbers. Instead of finding the number of drinks in a day, how about calculating the total volume drunk, in millilitres? Instead of the number of arms, imagine the monster with just one arm – but how long is that arm, in centimetres?
- Some figures can be estimates – for example, how far does the monster walk each day? Still, they need to be reasonable estimates, which will involve some calculating.
- Students may want to organize their data collection in a table, with a column for each member of the group and a final column for the totals.
- The activity can be exciting for students, with imaginative opportunities for performance or story writing. At the same time, it is the real figures for the group that make the monsters impressive. Students can feel very big, knowing their group monster really is 37 years old and 579 cm tall.

ACTIVITY IA8.2: Sum of the Century

Intended learning: To use informal strategies to add a list of 1-digit and 2-digit numbers.

Instructional mode: Longer, inquiry mode for individuals or groups.

Materials: Writing materials, a single set of digit cards 1–7 for each group.

Description: Introduce the idea. *Make some numerals with your digit cards, enough to use all seven cards. For example, I have made: 17, 25, 34 and 6.* Write these numbers on the board. *Now add the numbers together. I get … 34 plus 6 is 40* [jot down 40], *plus 25 is 65* [jot down 65], *plus 17 is 75 … 80 … 82.* Write the answer 82. Students calculate their totals, and report them. Try a different arrangement of digit cards. Initiate discussion of students' computation strategies, including how they are jotting down subtotals.

Now pose the problem. *Can you make a list of numbers using the seven digit cards that have a sum of exactly 100?* Support students to find solutions through their own cooperative inquiry, and to reflect on their problem-solving strategies.

Responses, variations and extensions:

- Some students will do the calculations mentally. Some will find informal jotting helpful. Some may use column computation strategies.
- Support students to keep their written work clear and organized.
- Solutions can be found by trial and error. Insight into the problem involves paying attention to the place value of the digits. Record some solutions on the board, with each list written in vertical format. In each case, the sum of the tens is 80 and the sum of the ones is 20. By organizing the digits in tens and ones, other solutions can be readily produced, namely, any list of numbers with the tens digits as: 1 and 7; 1, 2 and 5; 1, 3 and 4; 2 and 6; or 3 and 5.

ACTIVITY IA8.3: Decomposition with Arrow Cards

Intended learning: To do semi-formal multi-digit calculations by decomposing numbers into hundreds, tens and ones parts.

Instructional mode: Inquiry or rehearsal mode for individuals.

Materials: Arrow cards. A large classroom set works well.

Description: Students begin work on a multi-digit calculation task, such as 384 + 155. Write the calculation on the board in vertical format, one number under the other. Ask a student to build each number with arrow cards, and hold the arrow card numerals beside the written numerals on the board. Then decompose each arrow card numeral into its separate cards, sticking the cards onto the board in a horizontal list, as in 300, 80, 4. Students can use the decomposed arrow card setting to help organize their calculation into hundreds, tens and ones parts, as is done in a partial sums strategy.

Responses, variations and extensions:

- Can be used with an addition, subtraction or multiplication task, when students are developing semi-formal written strategies.
- Students could use their own arrow card sets.
- After solving some tasks, students need to be challenged to solve tasks without using the arrow cards. A helpful prompt is, *If you were going to use the arrow cards, what would you do?* This encourages students to reflect on their previous activity.

ACTIVITY IA8.4: Palindromization

Intended learning: To add multi-digit numbers using semi-formal or formal written strategies.

Instructional mode: Longer, inquiry mode for individuals or groups.

```
36                    37
63+                   73+
90                    100
 9                     10
99  in one step       110  not yet
                      011+
                      121  in two steps
```

Figure 8.8   Palindromizing 36 and 37

Materials: Writing materials, a hundreds chart per group.

Description: Palindromes are words or sentences that read the same when the order of the letters is reversed, for example: level; Hannah; do geese see God? Examples of palindromic numbers include 66, 121 and 2002. Begin the activity by introducing palindromes and palindromic numbers, writing a few on the board. Then introduce the palindromization technique. Write 36 on the board. *Thirty-six isn't a palindrome. But there is a technique that can turn a number into a palindrome: reverse the digits, and add the original number.* Write 63 beneath 36, and complete writing the sum in vertical format – *36 plus 63 is 99 – we got a palindromic number. Let's try 37:* 37 requires two steps to palindromize (see Figure 8.8). Set some for the class to try: 25, 52, 84.

The activity can finish here, with students practising the palindromization technique, and hence practising column addition. Alternatively, begin a class investigation of the following question: *Does palindromization work for any number up to 100?* Support a discussion of how to organize the investigation. Students can use a hundreds chart to record which numbers need testing. Students can realize that about half the numbers don't need testing, because they are already palindromes (e.g. 22, 33) or palindromes after one easy step (e.g. 21, 36). Some students may also recognize that half the remaining numbers don't need testing because they are reversals: if 37 works, then so will 73. That accounts for all but 20 of the numbers. The results for the 20 numbers are: 1 step (29, 38, 47, 56); 2 steps (19, 28, 37, 39, 46, 48, 49, 57, 58, 67); 3 steps (59, 68); 4 steps (69, 78); 6 steps (79); 24 steps (89).

Responses, variations and extensions:

- The activity generates considerable multi-digit addition practice.
- The interest in generating a palindrome brings attention to the digits in the numerals while students are calculating. Some students who use a semi-formal written strategy, such as partial sums, may begin to use more abbreviated forms, focusing on the digits in each column.
- Watch for 79 and 97, which require a 4-digit addition with regrouping.
- Watch especially for 89 and 98. Requiring 24 steps to palindromize into the 13-digit number 8813200023188, this case requires a calculator, determination and patience. Still, a good approach is not to reveal an answer that students are willing to find for themselves.
- In pursuing the investigation, allow the students to develop their own investigative approaches. They are learning how to test a conjecture, as well as how to calculate an addition.

- Palindromization can be extended to 3-digit numbers, and beyond. The conjecture that palindromization works for *all* numbers remains an open question: mathematicians have not been able to prove it true or false. Some numbers appear to be unpalindromizable: 196 remains unpalindromized after millions of iterations (e.g. http://mathworld.wolfram. com/196-Algorithm.html).

ACTIVITY IA8.5: Catch 22

Intended learning: To use written strategies for multi-digit addition and division, and to develop insight into place value.

Instructional mode: Longer, inquiry mode for individuals or groups.

Materials: Writing materials, a set of digit cards for each group.

Description: Each group plays the role of a number machine. Lead the groups through the five-step program for their machine.

1. Select three different digits (e.g. 1, 4, 7)
2. Calculate the sum of the three digits (e.g. 1 + 4 + 7 = 12)
3. Write out the six different 2-digit numerals that can be made with the digits (e.g. 14, 17, 41, 47, 71, 74)
4. Calculate the sum of the six numbers (e.g. 14 + 17 + 41 + 47 + 71 + 74 = 264)
5. Divide the big sum from step 4, by the little sum from step 2 (e.g. 264 ÷ 12 = 22).

The machines report their output. They all report 22! Is there something wrong with the machines? Try running the program again.

The second phase of the activity is to investigate whether the program output is always 22, and why. Allow the students to develop their own investigative approaches. Writing the six numbers in column format and summing the tens and ones separately can help reveal the arithmetic pattern in the program. In the six numbers, each digit appears twice in both the ones and the tens. So the sum of the ones is 2 times the sum of the three digits, and the sum of the tens is 20 times the sum of the three digits. Therefore the sum of the six numbers is 22 times the sum of the three digits.

Responses, variations and extensions:

- An optional approach in the group machines is to make each group member responsible for a different step, like a production line.
- Running the machine program generates practice in multi-digit addition and division. After some turns being machines, students could pause to discuss their computation strategies, especially for division.
- While investigating the program, students might begin to organize their calculations into tens and ones.

- Instead of investigating whether the big sum ÷ 22 equals the little sum, students might switch to investigating the equivalent question of whether the little sum × 22 equals the big sum, showing an insightful implicit understanding that multiplication is the inverse of division.

ACTIVITY IA8.6: Shortcut 100

Intended learning: To use semi-formal written strategies for 3-digit multiplication.

Instructional mode: Longer, inquiry mode for individuals or groups.

Materials: Writing materials.

Description: Solicit two numbers just beyond 100 (e.g. 104 and 107). *I need a number a bit greater than 100. And another one.* Challenge students to multiply the two numbers together. Discuss solutions and strategies.

Next, introduce a written shortcut technique for multiplications of this form (see Figure 8.9a). Write the two numbers in vertical format. Beside each one, write the excess from 100: 104 has an excess of 4, 107 an excess of 7. Add on a diagonal: 107 + 4 = 111. The sum of the diagonal gives the first three digits of the answer. Multiply the excesses: 4 × 7 = 28. The product of the excesses gives the last two digits of the answer: the final answer is 11,128. Students practise using the shortcut for a few tasks. They also calculate the same tasks using their own method, to confirm that the shortcut works.

Finally, challenge students to explain why the shortcut works. Students can compare calculations using the shortcut with calculations using a column strategy such as the partial products method, to help analyse how these calculations work.

Responses, variations and extensions:

- The initial multiplications are a manageable challenge in multi-digit multiplication, suitable for students developing informal or semi-formal written strategies.
- Learning the shortcut is an experience of following a formal written procedure, like a formal algorithm. Some students may have difficulty with following the procedure, others may find it easy and enjoyable.

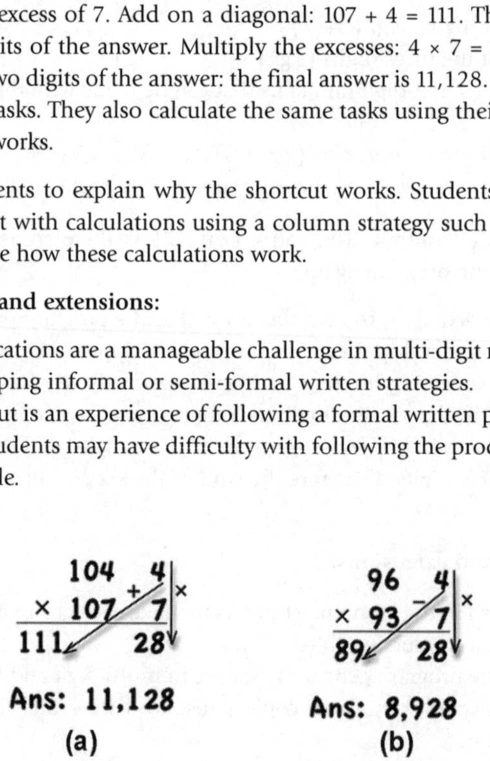

Figure 8.9 (a) Shortcut for 104 × 107 and (b) shortcut for 96 × 93

- When students try cases where the product of the excesses is a 1-digit number, they should realize that a 0 needs to be inserted in the tens place of the answer.
- Trying to explain why the shortcut works can develop insight into place value.
- An alternative productive challenge is to determine the range of cases for which the shortcut works. The shortcut works when the product of the excesses is a 1- or 2-digit number, including cases up to 101 × 199, 102 × 149, 103 × 133, ... 109 × 111.
- For students who enjoy the shortcut, there is a parallel shortcut technique for multiplying two numbers just *less* than 100. Figure 8.9b illustrates an example: the *deficits* from 100 of each number are recorded, the *difference* on the diagonal gives the first digits of the answer, and the product of the deficits gives the last two digits of the answer. Why does this work?

ACTIVITY IA8.7: The Prodigal Sum

Intended learning: To use formal algorithms for multi-digit addition and subtraction.

Instructional mode: Longer, inquiry mode for individuals or groups.

Materials: Writing materials, and a single set of digit cards 0–9 for each student.

Description: Pose the following problem using a diagram as in Figure 8.10a. *I had a 3-digit addition sum here: a 3-digit number plus another 3-digit number, and the answer was a 3-digit number. But the digits have walked off somewhere. It was a very interesting sum, because it used all the digits 1 to 9. Can you figure out what the sum was?* Students copy the blank diagram, and arrange digit cards in the diagram to find possible 3-digit numbers. A significant breakthrough is to recognize that a solution needs to involve regrouping in one column. Students should come to realize there is more than one solution. Challenge students to find more.

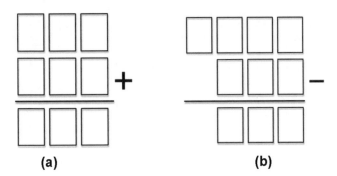

(a)   **(b)**

Figure 8.10 (a) Complete the addition using the digits 1–9 and (b) complete the subtraction using the digits 0–9

Responses, variations and extensions:

- Students will probably need to do many written additions to test the possible arrangements.
- Solving the problem involves working with the relationships between the digits in the addition. A formal addition algorithm also involves the relationships between digits, whereas a semi-formal addition strategy involves the relationships between whole tens and hundreds. Hence, testing arrangements and working towards a solution are considerably easier when using the formal addition algorithm, rather than using a semi-formal strategy.
- Demonstrating why a solution needs to involve regrouping in one column relies on a subtle analysis of patterns of odd and even digits, worthy of a separate investigation.
- A similar problem can be posed to complete the subtraction diagram shown in Figure 8.10b using all the digits 0–9.

PART III

9

Early Algebraic Reasoning

For many students and ex-students, algebra is regarded as an advanced mathematics topic that is studied in high school and involves learning rules about how to manipulate mathematical symbols. Algebra, when viewed that way, seems to be quite separate from important, less advanced mathematics topics such as arithmetical computation, fractions and decimals. However, there is considerable interest in research and curriculum development focused on linking instruction on number and arithmetic with instruction on early algebraic reasoning. Thus learning algebra can be a more productive undertaking, when supporting students' development of algebraic reasoning begins in the early years of school and is not divorced from arithmetic. In this chapter we outline what early algebraic reasoning is and describe some approaches to developing it in the primary and elementary grades.

Basis for Instruction in Early Algebraic Reasoning

In this section we first overview broad changes in the teaching of number and arithmetic and describe how this has led to the emergence of an algebraic focus. We then describe how focusing on generalizations in number and arithmetic is a form of early algebraic reasoning. Next follows an overview of the advantages of emphasizing early algebraic reasoning. Finally, we describe ways of harnessing children's innate facility for sense making, as a basis for teaching early algebraic reasoning.

Shifting Emphases in Arithmetic Teaching

Learning arithmetic is a major focus of mathematics instruction for 7–11-year-olds. In earlier generations, the focus of instruction in arithmetic was on automaticity of the so-called basic facts or tables, along with mastery of algorithms, that is, formal written methods for calculating with multi-digit numbers. In historical terms this has always been the strong focus of arithmetic instruction. Such instruction was considered essential in order to produce citizens who could understand and apply arithmetic and who could calculate with facility.

Over the last 20 years and longer, this view of arithmetic instruction has slowly declined in the face of the onset of the electronic age. This has ensured that the ability to use the formal algorithms for skilful calculation with multi-digit numbers is no longer the central focus of arithmetic instruction. Important now is the idea that students develop strong conceptual knowledge of arithmetic, which includes being able to calculate with strong facility, using a range of calculation strategies rather than simply developing mastery of the formal algorithms (e.g. see Chapter 8). Also important are using networks of number relations, understanding equality, developing insight into properties of numbers and operations, and describing patterns and functions (MacGregor and Stacey, 1999). This new emphasis in arithmetic instruction can be characterized as a reduction in the importance of standardized methods of computation and an increase in the importance of an algebraic focus in arithmetic. This has been referred to as the 'algebrafying' of elementary school mathematics (Blanton and Kaput, 2003), that is, taking a more algebraic approach to basic arithmetic.

Early Algebraic Reasoning as Generalized Arithmetic

One way to characterize algebra is to describe it as generalized arithmetic. Whereas arithmetic reasoning focuses largely on specific calculations, a focus of algebraic reasoning is the patterns that can be observed across calculations, that is, the recurring patterns of arithmetic. Mason (2008: 57) observed that when children first start school they 'have already displayed enormous powers for making sense of the worlds they inhabit', and argues 'that the central problem of teaching is to get learners to make use of those powers and to develop them, and that algebraic thinking is what happens when those powers are used in the context of number and relationships' (2008: 57).

An alternative label for patterns of arithmetic is generalizations. Thus a focus of early algebraic reasoning is making generalizations about arithmetic. The young student who observes that 10 + 4, 10 + 9, 10 + 6 and so on, are each equal to a corresponding teen number, has made a generalization. Another example is as follows: learning arithmetic involves learning to add and subtract two 1-digit numbers and later, two 2-digit numbers with facility. Thus learning to compute addition and subtraction in the range 1 to 100 with facility could rightly be regarded as a milestone in learning arithmetic (see Chapter 6). An algebraic extension of this topic could involve asking students to look for a pattern when adding two even numbers, two odd numbers or an odd and an even. Again, the term 'pattern' in this sense means very much the same as generalization. In other words, the students have been asked to find generalizations about what happens to various combinations of odd and even numbers, when added or subtracted.

Advantages of Emphasizing Early Algebraic Reasoning

An emphasis on early algebraic reasoning in arithmetic instruction has two important advantages. The first is that it will enhance the learning of arithmetic. Students whose mathematics learning includes a focus on early algebraic reasoning are likely to develop a deeper conceptual knowledge of arithmetic. As well, these students are likely to find mathematics more enjoyable and satisfying when their learning is characterized by greater conceptual knowledge than is the case with a more conventional approach to arithmetic instruction. This joy and satisfaction can be linked to students' use and development of natural powers of sense making (Mason, 2008). Second, an early focus on algebraic reasoning in arithmetic instruction is likely to provide a stronger basis for later, more formal learning of algebra – unlike a conventional approach where algebraic reasoning is not emphasized. This is important because mastering formal algebra enables access to a range of careers and endeavours. Further, as reasoned by Kaput (2008: 6), 'in response to societal needs for a deeper mathematical literacy, all students are now expected to learn algebra. This expectation is legally codified in high-stakes accountability measures that define academic success in terms of success in algebra'.

Harnessing Children's Powers

Mason (2008) provides detailed descriptions of what he refers to as children's natural powers of sense making: imagining and expressing; focusing and de-focusing; specializing and generalizing; conjecturing and convincing; and classifying and characterizing. These are natural in the sense that from the beginning of life, children's learning and development involves routinely using these capacities. Mason asserts that developing algebraic thinking requires teachers to harness these natural powers of sense making. These powers have much in common with what curricula describe as mathematical processes and the challenge in teaching arithmetic and algebraic reasoning is to develop instructional practices that routinely harness these powers in a significant way.

Examples of Instruction Linking to Early Algebraic Reasoning

In this section we discuss three examples of how number and early arithmetic can be taught from algebraic perspectives. These are: reasoning about relationships in arithmetic such as expressing links among the partitions of ten; making generalizations about the effects of changes to small quantities; and developing a deeper understanding of equality in arithmetic.

Reasoning about Arithmetic Relationships

In Chapter 4 we describe the topic of structuring numbers, first in the range 1 to 10 and then in the range 1 to 20. One important topic is for students to learn to partition numbers, particularly 5 and 10. Students learn to partition 10 via the instructional setting we call partitioned ten-frames. In Chapter 2 we discuss the general approach to instruction that we advocate, including for example, progressively distancing from the setting (instructional materials). In the case of partitioning 10, the student is asked to recite a partition – 'eight plus two equals ten' with the ten-frame visible. In the next phase, the ten-frame is flashed (briefly displayed) and again the student's task is to recite the partition. Following this, recitation of the partitions moves to a phase involving formal arithmetic in the absence of the setting. This formal arithmetic is verbal

Photo 9.1   Connecting arithmetic to algebraic thinking

and written. Verbal because the student can recite the partitions and written because the student can record the partitions. The process of recording can first involve the student either writing number sentences (e.g. 8 + 2 = 10) or selecting cards on which the number sentences are already recorded. A final phase can involve the student recording all partitions in a systematic way (e.g. 0 + 10, 1 + 9, 2 + 8 … 10 + 0). This final phase involves thinking that is qualitatively different from the arithmetical thinking in which students engage initially, when they generate the individual partitions. This is because this phase involves systematic, ordered recording and reasoning about relationships between the different partitions. Thus the students' reasoning shifts from, on one hand, relating 1 to 9 to, on the other hand, relating 1 and 9 to 2 and 8 to 3 and 7, and so on. Thus the students' reasoning shifts from forming individual partitions, that is relating numbers in a pair to each other, to forming higher level relationships among those pairs. This illustrates what is referred to as reasoning about relationships (Yackel, 1997).

The above example serves to illustrate how the general approach to instruction that we advocate – progressing from use of an instructional setting to systematic recording using number sentences – involves a progression on the part of the student from reasoning arithmetically to reasoning about relationships, that is to reasoning algebraically.

The Mathematics of Change

Tierney and Nemirovsky (1997) describe an instructional topic that involves making generalizations about changes involving adding or subtracting. This topic can involve working with numbers in the range one to 10, and is appropriate for the early years of school. As well, it can be adapted for older students.

For an initial activity, the teacher places four counters in a bag. The teacher adds two more counters and then removes one, and then adds another two. Students are encouraged to watch carefully and, after each change, to determine how many counters are in the bag. Students may use pencil and paper to record the changes. Some students will keep track mentally while others will invent ways of recording the changes. The teacher's role includes engendering observations such as the following. The net change of a sequence of changes does not depend on the order of the changes or the beginning number of counters. The net effect of adding and subtracting the same number is no change. 'It is possible to go from any number to any other number in any number of changes' (Tierney and Nemirovsky, 1997: 336). This instructional topic is ideally suited to introducing and progressively developing appropriate notation systems. Students can learn to use a sequence of simple number sentences to record changes.

We highlight several ways these activities can be extended. For example, providing missing changes, working with coins instead of counters and working with 2- or 3-digit numbers. The latter can involve using materials such as bundling sticks or base-ten dot materials and a plastic box with a lid. Tasks can also involve working backwards: do not disclose the starting number of counters, make two or three changes and tell students the final number of counters. The potential power of these mathematics of change activities is that they involve a process of building generalizations from quantitative reasoning, which is a core strand of algebraic reasoning (Kaput, 2008).

Learning About Equality

Consider students solving tasks such as the following: $6 + 9 = \Box$; $8 \times 7 = \Box$. When the students correctly answer the tasks, an observer might assume that the student reasons that the number on the right hand side, that is, the result they have written in the box, must equal the answer obtained when the expression on the left hand side is calculated. Thus, that the student has correctly answered the tasks, might be regarded as confirming that the student has a reasonably sophisticated notion of arithmetical equality. In reality, the student might interpret the equals sign as indicating: work out the answer for the expression on the left hand side and write it in the box on the right hand side. Thus the equals sign is interpreted as an instruction to perform a calculation and write the answer in an appropriate place. What seems likely is that, for many students, when they first encounter algebra, this is the notion they have of the equals sign.

One potential difficulty for students is the difference in the way the equals sign is used in the arithmetic they learn in the elementary grades, compared with its use when they learn algebra in high school. In arithmetic, students encounter number sentences such as those above, and in algebra they encounter equations such as: $a\,(b + c) = ab + ac$ and $y = x^2 - x - 6$. In both cases the equals sign indicates equality, but nevertheless, the role of the equal sign seems to differ.

Typically, number sentences such as the following $(7 + 4 = 11)$ are introduced to students in the early years. MacGregor and Stacey (1999) argued that students' developing knowledge of equality provides an important basis for their learning of algebra. Much has been written about difficulties that students encounter with the equals sign and it seems that, for many students, these difficulties persist throughout their years of mathematics learning. Falkner et al. (1999), for example, reported that sixth-graders presented with the following task: $8 + 4 = \Box + 5$, answered 12 or 17 (rather than 7). As well, they observed a range of misconceptions and difficulties when first- and second-graders were asked whether the following number sentences are true or false:

$7 = 3 + 4$	$8 + 2 = 10 + 4$	$7 + 4 = 15 - 4$	$8 = 8$

One response to students' on-going difficulties with the equals sign is to introduce much earlier to students the use of the equals sign in a variety of different number sentences with forms such as those shown above. When shown a number sentence such as $a = b + 2$, and asked which is the larger of a and b, many students will incorrectly answer b. They seem to reason that 2 has been added to b and therefore b is larger than a. Falkner and colleagues reported that as a result of an ongoing focus on equality, first- and second-graders developed a sophisticated understanding and avoided this common misconception. Carpenter et al. (2003) provide an extensive overview of a programme of instruction related to mathematical equality, and, more broadly, approaches to the integration of arithmetic and algebra in the elementary grades.

Patterns and Functions

Earlier in this chapter we described building generalizations from arithmetical reasoning as an important strand of algebraic reasoning. A second important strand is the idea of function (Kaput, 2008), which is, of course, a key notion in advanced mathematics. The idea of function is often portrayed in elementary curricula and texts as being concerned with a rule, perhaps referred to as a function machine. For example, the function machine depicted in Figure 9.1 takes a number as an input and gives a number as an output according to the rule 'multiply by 3 and then add 1'. For an input of 7, the output is 22 (i.e. $7 \times 3 + 1$). In more formal terms, a function can be thought of as a transformation. The function transforms any given input number into an output number. Another way to describe functions is that they are concerned with systematic variation, that is, how the output varies systematically with the input, and often this is depicted graphically or in a table.

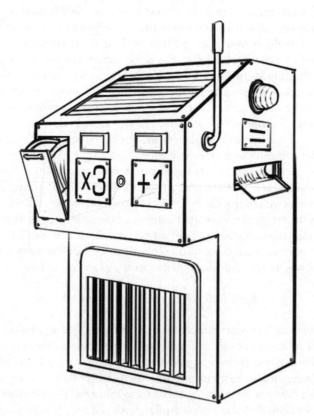

Figure 9.1 Function machine: multiply by 3 and then add 1

Repeating Pattern:

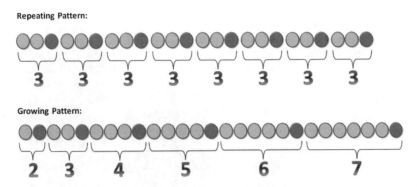

Growing Pattern:

Figure 9.2 A repeating pattern and a growing pattern

Early ideas of function arise in the context of elementary patterns. Mulligan and Mitchelmore (2009) highlight the importance in the early years, of an explicit focus on developing students' awareness of pattern and structure. As well, mathematics curricula and programmes typically associate patterning activities with developing early algebraic reasoning. Indeed, many mathematics curricula include a strand with a title along the lines of patterns and algebra. Elementary patterns, such as a linear arrangement involving red counters and blue counters, take two main forms: repeating patterns and growing patterns (see Figure 9.2). Growing patterns particularly can take geometric forms. These two forms of patterns are discussed in the following two sections.

Working with Repeating Patterns

An initial focus for students is identifying the repeating component of a repeating pattern. Warren and Cooper (2008) advise that, although this can be difficult, it is an important step in enabling students to differentiate between a repeating pattern and a growing pattern. As well, they describe how repeating patterns can be linked to repeated addition and hence multiplication and also division with remainder. In the repeating pattern above (Figure 9.2), there are three counters in the repeating component, therefore in seven components there will be 21 counters. As well, determining which counter is, for example, the 17th can be linked to dividing 17 by 3, that is, division with remainder.

Working with Growing Patterns

Consider the following problem.

> **Desks problem.** Six people sit at a rectangular desk, two on each of the long sides and one on each of short sides. Desks are adjoined linearly, end to end. How many people can sit around an arrangement of a given number of desks?

Figure 9.3 Desk and chairs problem

As shown in Figure 9.3, the problem can be presented to students in a geometric or figural form with an accompanying table of values that is to be developed by the students (Moss et al., 2008; Warren and Cooper, 2008).

From Elementary Patterns to the Idea of Function

Warren and Cooper (2008) detail an approach using growing patterns of this form, to develop students' notions of function (see also Moss et al., 2008). For example, the desk and chairs problem above gives rise to a growing pattern with the following sequence: 6, 10, 14, 18…, each term in the sequence has a corresponding step number (1st, 2nd, 3rd, 4th…) and students are directed to find values in the table corresponding to particular step numbers, for example for step number 3, the value is 14. There are two ways that students will typically solve this task. The first is known formally as a recursive approach, and informally as a growing rule, and it involves reasoning from the previous term. Thus to determine the 7th term, the student uses a rule of adding four to obtain the next term. Therefore the 5th term is 22, the 6th is 26 and the 7th is 30, and so on. The second approach is more difficult, less likely to be used by students, but ultimately the more useful in terms of linking to ideas of function. This approach is known formally as an explicit function approach, and informally as a position rule. This would involve determining that any term in the sequence is equal to four times its step number plus two ($s \times 4 + 2$). This step rule closely resembles the function rule ($7 \times 3 + 1$) referred to above. In instruction, challenge students to find values not adjacent to a known value. For example, how many people around a row of 100 desks (adjoined)? To solve such challenges, students must begin to develop a position rule.

Notating with Patterns

Warren and Cooper (2008) describe an initial development of notating corresponding to this work with patterns. First, with respect to the repeating pattern shown above, the teacher might ask how students could determine the number of counters for an unstated number of terms. Students might respond that the number of terms is multiplied by 3. Students can then be asked for ways that this could be written, such as $c = \square \times 3$ or $c = t \times 3$. In this way students' learning can progress from providing descriptions of repeating and growing patterns to using symbols to write equations that symbolize a function, that is, a relationship between two quantities.

Linear Functions

In instruction be aware of different kinds of functions. The growing number pattern that arises in the desks problem (described earlier) is an example of what is called a linear function, whereas the growing number pattern that arises in the handshake problem (see outlined below) is an example of what is called a quadratic function. In this context, a simple example of a linear function is $b = a \times 4$. If a changes from 4 to 5, b changes from 16 to 20. Thus when a increases by 1, b increases by 4, and one could say that, for each increase in a of a given size, b increases by a constant amount. In the case of the desk and chairs problem, b increases by 4 for each increase of 1 in a. A simple example of a quadratic function is $b = a \times a$: when a changes from 4 to 5, b changes from 16 to 25 but when a changes from 5 to 6, b changes from 25 to 36. In this case b does not increase by a constant amount for increases in a of a given size. Typically, finding and expressing a function is easier with linear functions than non-linear, such as the quadratic.

Building Generalizations from Arithmetic

In this section we list strategies for mathematical problem solving and provide an example of how an algebraic approach can be taken to working with open-ended mathematical problems. We then discuss and exemplify the important processes of conjecturing and generalizing, including a list of conjectures for students to investigate. Finally, we describe links between early algebraic reasoning and the themes of progressive mathematization described in Chapter 2.

Figure 9.4 The handshake problem

Problem-solving Strategies

For a good number of years, mathematics education researchers have highlighted the importance of mathematical problem solving, and of students learning to use general strategies for mathematical problem solving. These include solving a simpler or similar problem, acting out the problem, looking for a pattern, using a table or diagram, working backwards by guessing an answer, and checking. Mathematical problem solving in this sense provides an important avenue for algebraic reasoning. The much-touted handshake problem lends itself to many of the strategies for problem solving just listed.

> **The handshake problem.** *There are six people in the room and every person shakes every other person's hand once only. How many handshakes are there altogether?* (See Figure 9.4.)

This problem can be made more algebraic for students by asking them to consider different numbers of people in the room and suggesting that they look for a pattern. This could lead to the development of growing rules (see earlier in this chapter). Further, asking students to solve the problem in the case of a large number of people, say 50, can lead them to seek a generalization about the numbers of people and handshakes (Blanton and Kaput, 2003), that is, a position rule (see above).

Opportunities for Conjecturing and Generalizing

Building generalizations from arithmetic reasoning is an important strand of algebraic reasoning (Kaput, 2008). Generalizations can be made about addition and subtraction involving even or odd numbers. The following are examples of additional topics that can provide opportunities for generalizing, that is algebraic reasoning.

Table 9.1 Factors and number of factors

Number	Factors	Number of factors
1	1	1
2	1, 2	2
3	1, 3	2
4	1, 2, 4	3
5	1, 5	2
6	1, 2, 3, 6	4
7	1, 7	2
8	1, 2, 4, 8	4
9	1, 3, 9	3
10	1, 2, 5, 10	4
11	1, 11	2

Factors, Prime Numbers and Composite Numbers

Table 9.1 lists the factors of the numbers from one to 11 and the number of factors for each number. This can lead to classifying numbers as prime (two factors only) or composite (more than two factors), and this means of classifying can be applied to larger numbers. Table 9.1 can be extended to facilitate students making generalizations such as, all prime numbers greater than 2 are odd numbers and all square numbers have an odd number of factors.

Triangular and Square Numbers

Triangular numbers are obtained by adding the numbers from one up to a given number, and square numbers are obtained by adding the odd numbers from one. Figure 9.5 shows how triangular and square numbers can be demonstrated graphically. Table 9.2 shows the first five triangular numbers – 1, 3, 6, 10 and 15 – and the first five square numbers – 1, 4, 9, 16 and 25. Also indicated is how the triangular and square numbers can be obtained via multiplication. Students can extend the lists of equations and attempt to determine a growing rule and a position rule (see earlier in this chapter) for figuring out additional numbers. This can lead to tasks such as the following. Find a way to work out the sum of the numbers from 1 to 20 or the sum of the first 10 odd numbers. Check your answer by adding up the numbers.

Conjecturing and Justifying

When students undertake activities like those above, their investigations can lead to making conjectures about patterns or generalizations. The processes of conjecturing and providing a justification for one's conjecture are fundamental mathematical processes in which students should engage. 'Explicitly articulating generalizations about the behaviour of the operations, justifying them, and considering the extent or limits of the generalization – are a central aspect of early algebraic reasoning' (Schifter et al., 2009: 231).

Triangular Numbers

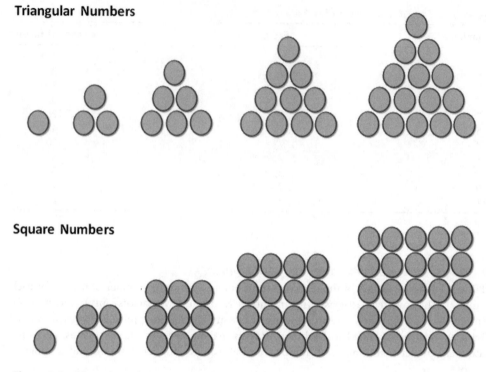

Square Numbers

Figure 9.5   Triangular and square numbers shown graphically

Table 9.2   Triangular numbers and square numbers

1	= 1	= 1 × 2 ÷ 2	1	= 1	= 1 × 1
1 + 2	= 3	= 2 × 3 ÷ 2	1 + 3	= 4	= 2 × 2
1 + 2 + 3	= 6	= 3 × 4 ÷ 2	1 + 3 + 5	= 9	= 3 × 3
1 + 2 + 3 + 4	= 10	= 4 × 5 ÷ 2	1 + 3 + 5 + 7	= 16	= 4 × 4
1 + 2 + 3 + 4 + 5	= 15	= 5 × 6 ÷ 2	1 + 3 + 5 + 7 + 9	= 25	= 5 × 5

Examples of Conjectures

The following are some examples of conjectures that students might generate from an initial investigation. After generating conjectures students can attempt to justify them. Keep in mind that some conjectures might ultimately be refuted.

- The sum of two odd numbers is an even number (e.g. 7 + 5 = 12).
- The product of two odd numbers is an odd number (e.g. 7 × 5 = 35).

- When an odd number is subtracted from an even number the answer is an odd number (e.g. $20 - 17 = 3$).
- The sum of three consecutive numbers is a multiple of three (e.g. $9 + 10 + 11 = 3 \times 10$).
- When two numbers are to be added, if I add a number to the first addend and subtract it from the second addend, the sum is unchanged (e.g. $9 + 5 = 10 + 4$).
- When two numbers are to be subtracted, if I add a number to the minuend and also to the subtrahend, the difference is unchanged (e.g. $16 - 12 = 18 - 14$).
- The square of a number is one more than the product of the number above it and the number below it (e.g. $7 \times 7 = 6 \times 8 + 1$).
- Every even number greater than two can be expressed as the sum of two prime numbers. This is the famous Goldbach's conjecture which remains unresolved.

Algebraic Reasoning and Progressive Mathematization

In Chapter 2 we characterize our approach to instruction in arithmetic in terms of progressive mathematization and the eight themes of structuring numbers, extending the range of numbers, decimalizing, unitizing, distancing materials, notating, formalizing and generalizing. Each of these themes can be considered from the perspective of progressing from arithmetical to algebraic reasoning. Thus we advocate that, in arithmetic instruction, teachers should always be aware of the potential for algebraic reasoning about arithmetic.

10

Understanding Fractions
Peter Gould

CHAPTER OVERVIEW

Coming to understand that fractions are special forms of numbers is a very challenging part of mathematics learning. Before they start school children begin to develop quite sophisticated counting techniques to determine the number word associated with quantity, as well as to find the sum or difference between two amounts. Even early work with multiplication and division makes substantial use of coordinating counting strategies. Given the power of counting strategies, it is not surprising that fractions are often introduced in a way that appears to only involve counting parts. However, fractions do not rely on counting to express their meaning as relational quantities, and a heavy emphasis on counting shaded parts of various shapes can lead to very limiting beliefs as to what fractions are.

Fractions describe a multiplicative relationship between quantities. Counting by twos, *two, four, six* … represents an additive relationship. That is, six is four more than two. A *multiplicative* relationship between two and six exists when we recognize that six is three times two, or equivalently that two is one-third of six. The difference between viewing fractions as existing in a multiplicative relationship rather than an additive relationship is central to appreciating fractions as a special type of number.

Although a fraction should be understood as a relational number, that is, a single number that represents a multiplicative relationship between two quantities, many students come to believe that a fraction corresponds to two separate counts. This is not surprising as the partitioned shapes that are commonly used to introduce fractions require little more than counting discrete things followed by recording one count over the other.

To help students develop an understanding of fractions as numbers, and in particular numbers that represent a multiplicative relationship between two quantities, we must change our reliance on pre-partitioned shapes to introduce the idea of fraction numbers. Regional models, the shaded shapes we draw for fractions, are of little assistance to students who do not treat area as a multiplicative relationship. Indeed area cannot be used as the basis of comparison of a part to the whole before students have developed an understanding of area.

Teaching in a way that supports the development of a robust fraction concept relies on developing fractions that are transparent to the multiplicative relationships they represent. Although an adult may see one part and the whole from which it comes as being in a multiplicative relationship, a student may interpret the relationship as requiring only additive counting.

The way that fraction notation is introduced also needs to be thought through carefully. Even students who can successfully memorize the algorithms associated with operating with fractions may have no understanding that the fraction notation is used as a measure of quantity. Put simply, many students do not realise that $\frac{11}{12}$ is a number that is close to 1 or a measure that is close to the whole.

This chapter provides both a rationale for why learning fractions can be so challenging for students and identifies critical areas that need to be addressed in planning instruction. The following chapter, Chapter 11, details a learning trajectory or levels of progression of students' learning to help navigate a way through these identified areas.

A Pathway to Understanding Fractions as Numbers

Students tend to work through a number of levels in developing an understanding of fractions as numbers. At the foundation of fraction knowledge is the process of partitioning. When we refer to partitioning to create representations of fractional quantities, such as *nths*, we mean that some quantity is taken as a fixed whole and divided into *n* equal parts. However, not all partitions are equally easy. For example, creating thirds, fifths and sevenths is much harder than creating halves, quarters and eighths. Fortunately, the process of verifying the multiplicative relationship between the part and the whole is more important than being able to create difficult partitions.

Having established an appreciation that the part (identified within the whole) and the fixed unit whole are related by multiplication, not addition, the next significant challenge is to understand what happens to our measure of quantity when the whole is exceeded. That is, students may come to understand fractions as representing quantity by increasing fractional parts of length until the whole is exceeded, creating a need to re-form the whole. In this way students can progress from establishing unit fractions to common fractions, by making and accumulating multiple copies of the unit fraction. When the whole has been re-formed and exceeded, the transition from improper fractions to mixed numbers can be established.

To understand fractions as numbers rather than parts of objects or collections, students need to recognize that fractions are parts of the number one, not parts of pizzas. This transition from fractions represented by a relationship involving quantities of length, area or groups of objects to fractions as numbers is a significant achievement. Finally, to be able to operate with fractions, students also need to be able to move fluently between different ways of representing the same quantity with equivalent fractions, which may involve regrouping sub-units. Establishing multiple ways of representing fractions as numbers creates a basis for operating with rational numbers.

Fractions in Context and as Relational Numbers

Most teaching programmes used to introduce fractions move from contexts such as sharing food, to presentations using area models. That is, discussions of 'half an apple' or 'a quarter of a sandwich' are closely followed by experiences of shading partitions of common shapes, such as circles and squares. These partitions of common shapes have been described as regional models of fractions.

Although regional models are used to introduce fractions, some students attend to the discrete, countable features of the area models. This can lead to the intended continuous 'parts of a whole' representation of a fraction being interpreted as countable objects. When teachers and students refer to equal parts, it is not always clear exactly what attribute is being considered. To further confound the problem, the underpinning idea of area as a quantifiable attribute is frequently not taught before students are expected to make area comparisons through the interpretation of regional models.

To be able to interpret the part–whole comparison of area intended by the regional model, students need to be familiar with the context, which for regional models includes the concept of area. As well as understanding that area is used in part-to-whole comparisons with regional models, students need to have a multiplicative sense of area rather than an additive appreciation. An additive appreciation of area typically results in counting units of area rather than multiplicatively subdividing a unit.

The emphasis in teaching fractions on counting the number of parts has meant that some students have developed concept images for fractions that are solely dependent on *the number of parts* in a model.

Partitioned Fractions

In practice, fractions exist in essentially two forms: representations of comparisons, sometimes called partitioned fractions, and mathematical objects, also known as quantity fractions. A *partitioned fraction* (Isoda et al., 2007; Yoshida, 2004) can be described as the fraction formed when partitioning objects into b equal parts and selecting a out of b parts to arrive at the partitioned fraction a/b. A partitioned fraction can be of either discrete or continuous objects but a partitioned fraction is always a fraction *of something*.

Quantity Fractions

The second type of fraction describes fractions as abstract, unit-less numbers. *Quantity fractions* refer to fractional quantities of a type of universal measurement unit, which operates in a similar way to the 'metre' being used as a standard measurement unit. Asking the question, which is larger, one-half or three-eighths, only makes sense if the question is one of quantity fractions, else you would need to know which unit is being referenced. Abstract quantity fractions reference a universal unit, a unique unit-whole, which is independent of any situation. If the mathematical objects 'one-half' and 'three-eighths' do not refer to a universal whole, we cannot compare them.

The transition from partitioned fractions to quantity fractions has not been made explicit for many students learning fractions. It is difficult for students to become aware of a unit-whole when the unit-whole is often implicit in everyday situations involving fractions. To make the transition from partitioned fractions to quantity fractions, students need to develop a sense of the size of fractions as numeric quantities. Despite the fundamental value of developing a sense of the size of fractions, it does not appear to be specifically taught or learnt. Studies in several countries (Carpenter et al., 1981; Hart, 1989a; Kerslake, 1986; Ni and Zhou, 2005; Yoshida and

Kuriyama, 1995) have confirmed that the underpinning knowledge of 'fractions as mathematical objects' (quantity fractions) is frequently absent from students' concepts.

Key Ideas in Understanding Fractions

There are a number of key ideas that help to guide the teaching of fractions towards enabling the development of a quantitative sense of fractions. These ideas include why fractions must be thought about as units linked in multiplicative relationships and what this means for fraction models and notation. When planning teaching sequences, opportunities need to be provided that enable students to move from working with fractions as parts of objects (with a focus initially on linear features), through the introduction of the need for an equal whole, to fractions as unit-less relational numbers.

Although the idea that fractional parts must refer to same-sized wholes is very important to the development of fraction knowledge, this idea is often overlooked when describing how children develop fraction knowledge. Fractions can be compared when they refer to same-sized wholes, as the equal wholes provide a basis for comparing fractions that represent quantities. In particular, recognizing and constructing equivalent fractions relies upon each fraction representing relationships with same-sized unit-wholes.

1. Fractions are Multiplicative

Suppose a student who has been taught fractions is asked to explain which fraction is larger, $\frac{9}{10}$ or $\frac{12}{13}$. The student could respond by drawing two rectangles, one made up of ten equal parts and the other composed of thirteen equal parts. If the student forms the rectangles drawn to represent each whole by *adding* on small rectangular pieces, an apparently 'correct answer' could be arrived at through an incorrect additive method. The equality of the wholes used to represent part–whole relationships is lost (see Figure 10.1).

Adding units of area will result in the whole growing, as above. Adding three parts to ten parts results in an additive part–whole relationship (three plus ten is thirteen). A multiplicative part–whole relationship relies on subdividing a fixed unit. That is, thirteen times the one part makes the whole, and the length of the whole remains unchanged no matter how many parts are formed.

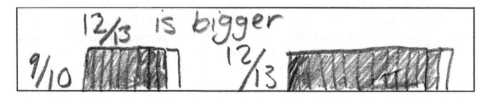

Figure 10.1   A Year 6 drawing showing an additive approach to representing larger denominators

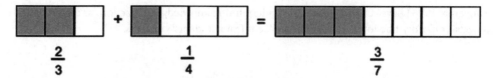

Figure 10.2 An additive interpretation of fractions due to a lack of reference to the whole

Interpreting Fraction Notation

Not all students use a drawing when determining which fraction is larger, $\frac{9}{10}$ or $\frac{12}{13}$. Some students argue that the two fractions are the same size because you could go from $\frac{9}{10}$ to $\frac{12}{13}$ by adding 3 to the top and the bottom. This error can be seen to be an additive interpretation of the fraction notation. When the fraction notation is introduced as a way of recording the result of two counts (the number of parts for the numerator and the total number of parts for the denominator) it is readily interpreted incorrectly as an additive notation.

An additive interpretation of fraction notation also contributes to many of the common errors associated with operating with the notation. Developing students' fraction notation from two counts (number of parts shaded and total number of parts) makes use of an additive interpretation, as the fixed whole is effectively ignored (see Figure 10.2). If the fixed whole is ignored in naming fractions, the logical errors associated with fraction operations are reinforced. Building a quantitative multiplicative relationship between the parts and the fixed unit-whole, and the fraction notation, is essential in creating a sense of the size of fractions as numbers.

2. Coordinating Units

Fractions are relational numbers and that relationship is multiplicative. To manage the components that contribute to the multiplicative relationship, students need to coordinate units. Coordinating units is an important activity in multiplication and in dealing with fractions. Initially students can only operate with a single level of units. They may identify the number of parts in a group or the number of groups but they cannot simultaneously coordinate both units. If students have units at only one level these units are in effect parts, rather than parts related multiplicatively to the whole.

When students can coordinate units at two levels with fractions, they recognize how to repeatedly create or iterate unit fractions, such as one-third, to form a whole. In contrast to coordinating units involved in the process of multiplication, fraction units need to be multiplicatively linked to the whole. Although it is reasonable for students to move through a process of repeated addition on the way to developing multiplication as an operation, repeated addition with fractional parts can readily exceed the whole. The **simultaneous** coordination of units at the level of the part (one-third) and at the level of the whole (three-thirds) is tethered to the notion of a fixed whole to establish a multiplicative relationship.

To construct improper fractions as quantities, students need to coordinate three levels of units (Hackenberg, 2007). The idea of the whole becomes clearer when it is exceeded, making it necessary to reform the unit-whole. A student who truly thinks of five-quarters as an improper fraction appreciates that the quantity is made up of five units, any one of which can repeatedly be produced so that four quarters recreates one whole with the fifth quarter going beyond the whole. Students who have only two levels of units may operate with fractions greater than one, but they don't produce improper fractions in this sense. Typically, if they produce five quarters they will re-label them as five fifths. Composition of partitioning, such as finding one fractional quantity of another fraction, also requires coordinating units at three levels.

Finding Out What Students Think – Units at One Level

When asked to shade different fractional parts of a circle, the Year 5 student, whose response is shown, made three equal parts to represent one-third and six equal parts to represent one-sixth. That is, the number of parts corresponding to the denominator appears as the dominant feature of this student's representation of the fraction. The unit parts are not coordinated with the number of parts constituting the whole.

In the example shown in Figure 10.3, the student appears to believe that one-third requires creating three equal parts, counting and shading the parts. For other students, fractions appear to be defined solely by the number of parts without attention to the equality of all of the parts. In Figure 10.4, the student has represented fractional quantities as the number of parts out of the total number of parts. This is not a comparison of areas but rather identifying the fraction name with the number of parts.

Students can and do form incomplete fraction concepts from activities associated with common parts-of-a-whole models. In the above examples the number of parts formed is the defining

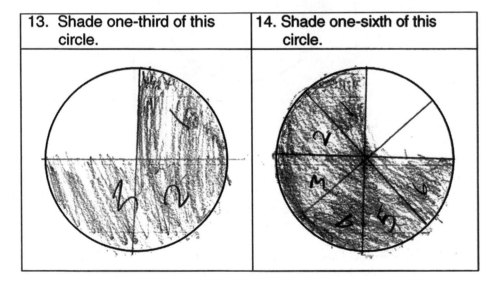

13. Shade one-third of this circle.	14. Shade one-sixth of this circle.

Figure 10.3 A Year 5 student showing one-third as 3 equal parts and one-sixth as 6 equal parts

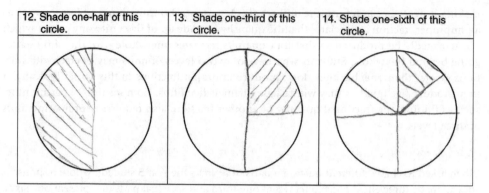

Figure 10.4   A Year 6 student's representation of fractions as a number of parts

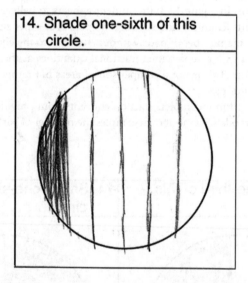

Figure 10.5   Equidistant partitioning

characteristic of the fraction representations rather than the area of the parts. A similar focus appears when students use equidistant parallel partitioning to form sub-units. The circle in Figure 10.5, shaded by a student to represent one-sixth of the circle, appears to have been subdivided by **equidistant parallel partitioning**. That is, what has been subdivided is not area but rather horizontal distance.

As using vertical parallel lines works in creating fractions of a rectangular region, some students also attempt to use them in a circular region to produce thirds, fourths or fifths (Pothier and Sawada, 1983). Most students subdivide rectangular regions using length rather than area (see e.g. Armstrong and Novillis Larson, 1995). The units that are formed by parallel partitioning are effectively only units that are operating on one level, as they do not link to the whole through area. Although one part out of six parts is shown, the parts are not treated as a relationship between areas. The area of the circle is meant to represent the whole and yet the parts appear to be formed by subdividing length.

The dominance of the vertical and horizontal directions in students' recordings when forming parts of shapes suggests that some students only attend to linear distance when dividing regional models, even circles. Linear partitioning is also associated with students using 'half-way points' for one-half. The use of linear partitioning can persist well into high school, with one study (Gould, 2008: 145) reporting approximately 10% of students in Years 4–8 using parallel partitioning to attempt to represent one-third of a circle.

Instead of seeing the fraction as a multiplicative relationship between the parts and the whole, some students see:

- parts from parallel partitions
- a number of parts (not equal parts)
- a number of equal parts (not a fraction of the whole).

In short, manifestations of students failing to establish a multiplicative relationship between parts and wholes abound. The fraction notation $\frac{a}{b}$ itself encourages a 'count' interpretation of the regional 'parts of a whole' model. Developing a multiplicative interpretation of fractions and their notation underpins why we create common subdivisions (denominators) to add or subtract fractions.

In teaching fractions, we have in the past relied heavily on representations that assume a multiplicative part–whole relationship instead of using activities designed to foster that relationship. Shading or attaching notation to pre-partitioned diagrams is typical of assuming that children have already developed this relationship.

3. Models and Notation

Perhaps the most widely used model of fractions is the area or regional model. The intent of the regional model is to represent the fraction by the relationship between a part of the area and the whole area. The regional model can also be described as a continuous model. As well as the continuous regional model, teaching fractions also makes use of the discrete set model. The set model uses discrete items that are identical in some way and identifies a subset of the items. For example, in a group of tiles, two are black and four are white; what fraction is black? The intent of the set model is to represent the fraction by the relationship between the number of items in a subset and the number of items in the whole set.

As with an additive use of the regional model, the discrete model of fractions may also contribute to the notion of a 'growing whole'. For example, in comparing one-third and one-sixth, a student can draw and shade one of three compared to one of six. However, a whole composed of six units is physically larger than a whole composed of three units. An important feature of

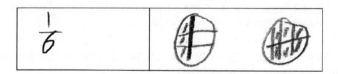

Figure 10.6   Representing a number of parts rather than the area of the parts

any model used to represent fractions to young students is being able to fix the size of the whole. A less commonly used model of fractions that requires quite a sophisticated appreciation of fractions is as a location on a number line.

Students can also interpret what may initially appear to be area models as discrete models. In Figure 10.6, it is clear that the student is attending to the number of parts when drawing subdivided shapes, rather than the relative area of the parts. In determining which is larger, $\frac{1}{3}$ or $\frac{1}{6}$, the diagram used to represent the reasoning behind the answer of $\frac{1}{6}$ shows circles with three and six parts marked for one-third and one-sixth respectively. This representation is clearly about the number of parts rather than the area of the parts. That is, subdivided regional models can be taken as discrete representations of fractions by some students.

From the student's point of view, a significant limitation of all of these models is that they do not by themselves provide ready access to the idea of fractions as relational numbers. As described earlier, regional models rely on a sound understanding of area, the set model depends upon recognizing both the whole set and the subset, and the number line is itself a sophisticated representation of the infinite set of real numbers.

The value of characterizing fractions as either quantity fractions or partitioned fractions is the emphasis such a categorization gives to introducing the fraction notation. The fraction notation relies upon a very sophisticated way of representing a relationship between two numbers as an indicated division. That is 3 ÷ 4 is $\frac{3}{4}$, representing both process and result. Moreover, 6 ÷ 8 is $\frac{6}{8}$ which also happens to be the same as $\frac{3}{4}$. Equivalent fractions draw upon the special importance assigned to the unit-less notion of one whole as a number. That is, $\frac{3}{4} = \frac{6}{8}$ because they are both quantity fractions whereas $\frac{3}{4}$ as a partitioned fraction could be greater than, less than or even not comparable to $\frac{6}{8}$ as a partitioned fraction.

One of the longstanding problems students have with fractions is giving meaning to the notation. To illustrate the difficulty that many students have with fraction notation, consider the answers students provide to the following problem.

$$\frac{4}{5} + \frac{11}{12} \quad \text{is about} \quad \text{(a) 1} \quad \text{(b) 2} \quad \text{(c) 15} \quad \text{(d) 17}$$

When 52,800 Year 7 students (12–13 years old) in Australia were asked this question, 58% chose an answer of 15 or 17. Although the sum, being equal to a little less than 2, is nowhere near 15 or 17, it is likely that these answers were chosen because the numbers in the fractions could readily be manipulated to produce them (i.e., adding the numerators results in 15 and adding the denominators results in 17). When the same question was asked to 50,880 Year 8 students, more than half also chose an answer of 15 or 17. This result is consistent with the third

National Assessment of Educational Progress (NAEP) in the USA where 55% of 13-year-olds chose similar answers, reflecting a lack of any sense of the size of fractions using standard fraction notation (Bezuk and Cramer, 1989).

The power of the notation for dual representation – fraction as a number and an indicated division – means that the creation of the equal whole remains invisible for many students. The notation system for fractions can be described as an opaque rather than transparent system. Whitehead referred to the opaque use of symbols in 1911 by stating that 'by relieving the brain of all unnecessary work, a good notation sets it free to concentrate on more advanced problems' (in Cajori, 1974: 332). However, the educational price of fractions employing an opaque symbol system has been that teaching has traditionally attended solely to actions on the inscriptions, rather than reasoning about the entities to which the inscriptions are assumed to refer.

The common fraction notation is very different from the decimal fraction notation. Decimal fractions describe a positional system of powers of ten, where the size of a number is interpreted as the sum of its parts. That is, 3.25 is taken to mean $3 + 2 \times 10^{-1} + 5 \times 10^{-2}$ or $3 + \frac{2}{10} + \frac{5}{100}$. The decimal system needs to be represented in teaching practice as a particular case of a more general concept of positional notation. This is why decimals are not addressed in this chapter on fractions. We need to decouple the curriculum topics of fractions and decimals in both curriculum design and delivery.

4. Fractions Beyond One Whole

To appreciate the multiplicative relationship between the part and the whole, students need opportunities to recreate the whole from a part, and to iteratively create unit fraction parts to exceed the whole, making it necessary to reform the unit whole. The contexts used in introducing improper fractions need to have clearly identifiable whole units. For example, students can be shown a fractional part of a liquorice strip, and asked to reproduce the length of the whole strip. Starting with a unit-fraction part such as one-fourth, it is reasonable to extend beyond the whole to produce say, five-fourths of the whole liquorice strip. When students exceed the whole with a number of unit-fraction parts and reorganize the parts to form the whole, they are coordinating units on three levels.

Figure 10.7 shows the use of units at three levels: the four-thirds, the one-whole and the thirds. Understanding improper fractions is a major advance in students' fraction thinking and their ability to coordinates units (Hackenberg, 2007; Tzur, 1999).

5. Equivalent Fractions

Equivalent fractions reflect both the power of the fraction notational system and a significant challenge for students. As Lamon (1999: 22) has suggested, the hardest part for some students is understanding that 'what looks like the same amount might actually be represented by different numbers'. Yet equivalent fractions start with partitioned fractions, that is, they are equivalent

This drawing represents a piece of chocolate.

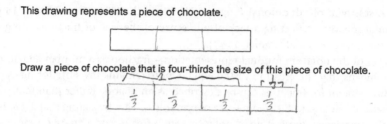

Draw a piece of chocolate that is four-thirds the size of this piece of chocolate.

What is the fraction name of each of the parts in your drawing?

Figure 10.7 Drawing four-thirds and showing coordination of units at three

Figure 10.8 People and pancakes drawing

partitions of something. Consequently, equivalent fractions can readily be introduced through sharing contexts. The equivalent fraction notation can be introduced from carefully planned problems that use the same context.

For example, using different table seating arrangements at a pancake restaurant can extend the context of sharing pancakes. Streefland (1991) used the pancake restaurant context to introduce 'table notations'. If eight people are seated at one table with six pancakes it could be drawn as in Figure 10.8. By introducing larger numbers of people, say 24, drawing all of the people becomes onerous and provides the motivation for introducing a simple notation. A table notation indicating the number of people and pancakes at the table (see Figure 10.9) suggests the two-number fraction notation $\frac{6}{8}$. If you were a member of a table of four with three pancakes, this could be recorded as $\frac{3}{4}$ and you would receive an equivalent proportion of pancakes.

Equivalent fractions can also be introduced through the use of 'equivalence tables'. Proportion tables like the one in Figure 10.9 can demonstrate the multiplicative nature of the relationship

Number of pancakes	?	6
Number at the table	4	8

Figure 10.9 People and pancakes table

and suggest the equivalent fraction notation. Extending this table will produce a range of equivalent fractions.

Making Sense of Fraction Research

A great deal of research has been carried out in the last 25 years on the learning of fractions. Some researchers have analysed different subconstructs or interpretations of fractions, such as part–whole, measure, ratio, operator and quotient (Behr et al., 1992; Carraher, 1996; Charalambous and Pitta-Pantazi, 2005; Kieren, 1976; Lamon, 2001). Thinking about these subconstructs assists in designing a wide range of fraction question types in a school curriculum.

Other research has emphasized the importance of real contexts and the informal knowledge that students bring to working with fractions (Mack, 1990, 1993, 1995, 2001; Streefland, 1991, 1993). More recently there has been a focus on describing mental schemes that have proven useful in supporting children's development of fraction-based reasoning (Hackenberg and Tillema, 2009; Norton, 2008; Olive, 1999; Steffe, 2002, 2003, 2004; Tzur, 2004). Central to these schemes is the way that students operate with units and coordinate units in giving meaning to fractional quantities (Hackenberg, 2007; Norton and Wilkins, 2009; Olive and Vomvoridi, 2006; Watanabe, 1995).

Across all of the research the challenge remains in understanding the methods students use to partition and how they apply these to their interpretation of fractions. Students who build up an additive part–whole representation through iterating parts may not use simultaneous partitioning nor have a (multiplicative) part–whole scheme.

Looking Back

Thinking quantitatively about fractions relies upon equal partitioning and the invariance of the whole. In representing a number less than one, the whole should be of a fixed size in order to allow comparison of fractions. The invariance of the whole is essential in comparing quantity fractions, that is, those that reference a universal unit. Although the equal whole is a critically important concept in understanding the multiplicative structure of fractions, it appears that the equal whole concept is difficult to acquire. Without the equal whole concept, ordering fractions as quantities appears to draw upon significantly different mental models of fractions compared to ordering fractions based on numeric rules.

Coming to understand fractions as quantities is also influenced by the different interpretations of the fraction notation. The fraction notation is a very powerful but subtle tool for handling proportional reasoning. Time and effort is required to develop students who can unleash the power of the notation. The use of $\frac{a}{b}$ to record a parts out of b parts needs be linked to transforming a divided by b into the mathematical object (number) $\frac{a}{b}$. For many students, abstract quantity fractions may currently be indistinguishable from partitioned fractions.

11

Connecting the Teaching and Learning of Fractions
Peter Gould

In Chapter 10 we outlined the prominent landmarks that help us to chart a path to guide learning to a robust understanding of fractions as quantities. These landmarks include the multiplicative nature of fractions, how units are coordinated at different levels and the links between models of fractions and the notation of quantity fractions. In this chapter, we add more detail to the map in the form of a pathway as well as advice on how to gain your bearings through assessment.

Learning Fractions

Children tend to work through a number of levels in coming to understand fractions as numbers. At the foundation of fraction knowledge is the process of equal partitioning. Next, the essential role of the fixed equal whole is established as students generalize operating with partitive fractions to create an abstract system of quantity fractions and the powerful algebraic notation system used with fractions. The following descriptions of the levels are designed to provide an overview of the journey towards understanding fractions as numbers. These levels are founded on research and are designed to be a practical guide to pedagogy rather than a purely theoretical description.

Level 0: Emergent Partitioning

Emergent partitioning involves students in breaking things into parts and allocating the pieces. No attention is given to the specific size of the pieces. At this level, when a student uses the term half it generally means a piece, which may or may not be one of two equal pieces.

Level 1: Halving

Halving to form two *equal* pieces is an early fractioning process (Pothier and Sawada, 1983; Steffe and Olive, 2010). The term *equal* is emphasized here to draw attention to the need to

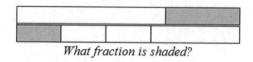

What fraction is shaded?

Figure 11.1   What fraction is shaded?

be aware of the **basis of determining equality**. At Level 1, finding **half way** is typically used to halve. That is, the basis of determining half of a rectangular piece of paper relies on length rather than area. In a similar way, repeated halving with respect to length can form quarters.

Level 2: Equal Partitions

Constructing thirds and fifths by partitioning a continuous quantity is difficult. Although some curriculum documents introduce fifths before thirds in an attempt to introduce decimal fractions quickly, partitioning to create thirds is clearly easier than partitioning to create fifths. Due to the difficulty of being able to simultaneously partition continuous quantities into an odd number of parts, the emphasis at Level 2 is not on the student being able to partition into fifths and thirds but rather on being able to **verify** that particular partitions represent fifths and thirds. Students can be provided with strips of paper partitioned as in Figure 11.1 and asked to determine the indicated partitions as fractions of the whole.

Students at Level 2 verify continuous (and discrete) linear arrangements have been partitioned into thirds or fifths by checking the equality and number of parts forming the whole. (This is sometimes referred to as the partitive unit fraction scheme for composite units (Norton, 2008).) Similarly, students could be given a short strip of paper (e.g. $\frac{1}{3}$ of a longer strip of paper) and asked what fraction of the longer un-partitioned strip they have. This form of learning opportunity provides a way of moving beyond a focus solely on partitioning to teaching strategies that support students' development of iterating operations.

Level 3: Re-forming the Whole

When iterating a fraction part such as one-third beyond the whole, the student re-forms the whole (see Figure 11.2). The whole is treated as a composite unit, simultaneously three-thirds and one whole. Some students consistently regard an improper fraction produced via iteration of a unit fraction as a new whole (Tzur, 1999). That is, they think of $\frac{1}{4}$ iterated five times as $\frac{5}{5}$ and each part is considered as being transformed into $\frac{1}{5}$. This belief could be attributed to students failing to re-form the iterated four-fourths into the equivalent unit-whole.

Even when successfully creating seven-fifths of a drawing of a chocolate bar, some students view the resulting pieces as not being fifths but rather sevenths – 'they turned into seven pieces instead of five pieces' (Hackenberg, 2007: 33). This reorganization of iterated fraction units,

1. This drawing represents a piece of chocolate.

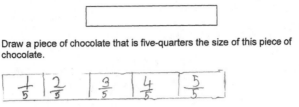

Draw a piece of chocolate that is five-quarters the size of this piece of chocolate.

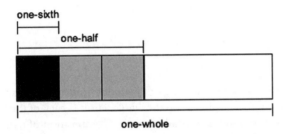

Figure 11.2   Five-quarters recast as five-fifths

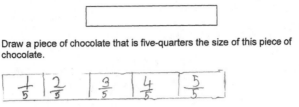

Figures 11.3   Coordinating units at three levels with proper fractions

recognizing when the whole has been formed, is necessary to make the transition from an additive iteration of units to a multiplicative association between parts of a uniform equal-whole.

Level 4: Fractions as Numbers

At Level 4 the student can coordinate composition of partitioning (see Figure 11.3). For example, given one-half and asked to create one-sixth of a whole, the student finds one-third of one-half. This requires coordinating composition of units at three levels to move between equivalent fraction forms.

Moving between equivalent fraction forms can also include improper fractions (Hackenberg, 2007). For example, conceiving of $\frac{4}{3}$ as an improper fraction means conceiving of it as a unit of 4 units, any of which can be iterated 3 times to produce another unit (the whole), a three-levels-of-units structure. One level is $\frac{4}{3}$ as a unit, another level is the whole and the final level of units is one-third. Dealing with equivalent proper fractions also requires operating across three levels of units. Consider also how units are used at different levels with composition of partitioning in the student's answer (Figure 11.4).

Sue and Michele share a two-finger Kit Kat. Just after Sue breaks her Kit Kat finger in half Alice comes along. How can Alice be given a fair share of the two Kit Kat fingers? Explain your answer.

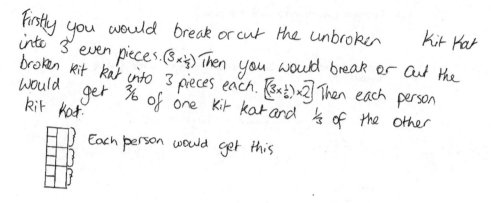

Firstly you would break or cut the unbroken   Kit Kat into 3 even pieces. $(3 \times \frac{1}{3})$ Then you would break or cut the broken kit kat into 3 pieces each. $[(3 \times \frac{1}{6}) \times 2]$ Then each person would get $\frac{3}{6}$ of one kit kat and $\frac{1}{3}$ of the other kit kat.

Each person would get this

Figure 11.4   Coordinating composition of partitioning and units at 3 levels

The explanation shows an understanding of the multiplicative relationship between the fractional value ($\frac{1}{3}$), the number of pieces and the whole. Further, each of the halves of the broken Kit Kat finger is divided into thirds to produce sixths (composition of partitioning). The coordination of units at three levels is evident in the drawings (halves, sixths and thirds of the equal wholes). The use of the fraction notation in justifying reasons suggests that the student is at least at Level 4, and may be at Level 5.

Level 5: Multiplicative Partitioning

At this level, the student uses fractions as numbers, i.e. $\frac{1}{3} > \frac{1}{4}$. For example, in determining the relative size of fractions such as 1/3 and 1/6, care is taken in representing the two fractions with uniform equal wholes – unlike the response in Figure 11.5. In this student's response, no attempt has been made to use equal wholes when comparing 1/3 and 1/6. It is also clear that for this student the fraction notation does not link to regional models of fractions.

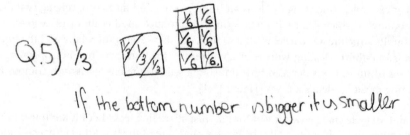

Q.5) ⅓

If the bottom number is bigger it is smaller

Figure 11.5   Comparing the size of 1/3 and 1/6 without referencing equal wholes

At this level the student is aware of the need for the fixed unit-whole to compare quantity fractions and appreciates the difference between partitioned fractions and fractions as unit-less numbers. Coordinating units linked with the idea of a universal equal whole, is also important in addressing the distinct problem of fractions having multiple representations of the one quantity ($\frac{1}{3} = \frac{2}{6} = \frac{3}{9}$) within the same representational system. The notational equivalence of fractions including improper fractions and mixed numbers is implicitly dependent on the existence of a universal one, a whole that is always the same size.

Although Level 5 follows Level 4, it is not meant to be absolutely hierarchical. That is, fraction notation, which represents fractions as numbers, can be introduced while students are working at an earlier level. The difference in fraction notation at Level 5 is that the fractions are numbers, independent of any model.

Introductory Assessment Tasks

In assessing students' understanding of fractions it is necessary to be mindful of a number of issues. Although teachers use regional models to introduce fractions, some students attend to the discrete, countable features of the area models. This can lead to the intended continuous 'parts of a whole' fraction analogue being construed as countable objects. Similarly, students in the early years cannot use the underpinning idea of area as a quantifiable attribute to interpret regional models if they do not understand how to determine the area of the various regions of the model. Care should also be taken when the fraction notation is introduced in problems instead of the fraction words. The standard fraction notation itself encourages a count interpretation of the regional 'parts of a whole' model.

The following Assessment Tasks can be used with individual students or with groups of students. The tasks have been designed using the principle that it is not sufficient for a student to know what a fraction such as a quarter is, but rather that a student also needs to know what a quarter is not. These introductory Assessment Tasks have been selected as some of the most time-efficient questions to determine students' foundational fraction understanding.

Interpreting Half and Quarters (Divided Length)

Ask the student to watch carefully as you fold a strip of paper in half, unfold, fold one-half in half, then unfold (see Figure 11.6).

Figure 11.6   Folded strip of paper

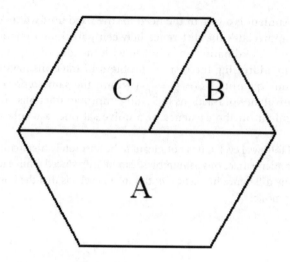

Figure 11.7   Region with patterns blocks

1. Point to one-half of the strip (A) and move your hand across it so that the student is clear as to which part you are referring to. *What fraction of the strip is this piece of paper?*
2. Point to the outside quarter of the strip (B) and move your hand across it so that the student is clear as to which part you are referring to. *What fraction is this piece?*
3. Point to the inside quarter (C) of the strip and move your hand across it so that the student is clear as to which part you are referring to. *What fraction is this piece?*

Interpreting Regional Models with Non-equal Parts

Place three pattern blocks together to form a hexagon as shown in Figure 11.7.

1. Point to the trapezoidal shape (A). *What fraction of the whole shape is this piece?*
2. Point to the equilateral triangle (B). *What fraction of the whole shape is this piece?*
3. Point to the rhombus (C). *What fraction of the whole shape is this piece?*

Fractional Lengths

Materials: Three strips of paper, one blue (200 x 15 mm), one yellow (150 x 15 mm) and one green (50 x 15 mm).

1. *What fraction of the length of the yellow strip of paper is the green strip of paper? How do you know?*
2. *What fraction of the length of the blue strip of paper is the green strip of paper? How do you know?*

3. *What fraction of the length of the blue strip of paper is the yellow strip of paper? How do you know?*
4. *Exactly how many blue strips is the same length as five green strips?*
5. *If the blue paper strip is half of a red strip, fold it to show what one-sixth of a red strip would look like.*

Fractions as Numbers

About how much is $\frac{7}{8} + \frac{7}{8}$?

The role of assessment for learning provides a bridge from assessment to teaching. Good teaching activities are often indistinguishable from effective Assessment Tasks as they provide opportunities to draw out the specific ways that students have developed for working with fractional quantities. The Instructional Activities at the end of the chapter also provide opportunities for detailed assessment of learning, located within a planned learning trajectory.

A Teaching Sequence

One of the major limitations of teaching fractions in many countries is the over-reliance on representations that assume a multiplicative part–whole relationship instead of using activities designed to foster that relationship. Shading or attaching notation to pre-partitioned diagrams is typical of assuming that students have already developed this relationship.

Partitioning Length

When introducing partitioned fractions, begin with a clear focus on partitioning length. The models used should be able to be described as 'long, thin ones'. Whether the models are uncut loaves of bread, lengths of string or liquorice strips, the attribute being operated on is length. If discrete objects are introduced, arrange them so that they are equally spaced in a line. This will make the transition from linear models to numerical magnitudes more natural. The focus on length readily produces halves and fourths for both discrete and continuous linear arrangements (Figures 11.8 and 11.9).

Following on from halving 'long, thin things' to produce halves and fourths, the other partitioned fractions can be identified and verified by students. The emphasis is not on the student

Figure 11.8   Halving a discrete linear arrangement

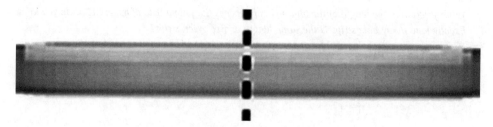

Figure 11.9 Halving an equivalent linear arrangement

being able to partition into fifths and thirds but rather being able to verify that particular partitions represent fifths and thirds. Students can be provided with strips of paper with one part marked and asked to determine the indicated part as a fraction of the whole. Similarly, students could be given a short strip of paper (e.g. one-third of a longer strip of paper) and asked what fraction of the longer un-partitioned strip they have. This form of learning opportunity provides a way of moving beyond a focus solely on partitioning to teaching strategies that support students' development of iterating operations. Non-unit fractions are introduced with the corresponding unit-fraction. Two-thirds is not more difficult for students than one-third and we clearly want students to appreciate that three-thirds is the whole.

Moving Beyond the Unit-whole

An important transition in the instructional sequence is from fractions as part of a collection or parts of objects, to fractions as numbers. To make this step, students need opportunities to create fractional parts of a unit-whole and then increase the number of these parts so that it exceeds the whole. This begins with partitioned fractions. The idea of the whole becomes clearer when it is exceeded, making it necessary to reform the unit-whole.

To establish the unit-whole as a fixed quantity, select models for partitioned fractions that have clear sub-dividable wholes, such as Kit Kat fingers. Using these in sharing contexts introduces equivalent partitioned fractions arising from subdividing equivalent unit-wholes (see the example under Level 4). These sharing contexts provide opportunities to move beyond the unit-whole to reorganize fractional units in a way that supports working with related units at three levels.

From Partitioned Fractions to Quantity Fractions

Thinking quantitatively about fractions relies upon equal partitioning and the invariance of the whole. The importance of identifying the whole can be introduced by using contexts where the unit-whole can come in different sizes. For example, pizzas come in different sizes, as do liquorice strips. Creating eighths of different sized lengths of string or strips of paper can be followed

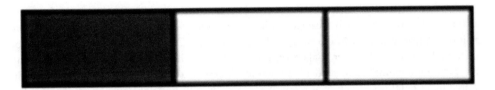

Figure 11.10   One-third of a bar

by a question such as: *Could three-eighths of a liquorice strip ever be less than two-eighths of a liquorice strip?* Understanding that the magnitude of the unit whole needs to be fixed and universal before comparisons of fractional parts is possible, underpins the move from partitioned fractions to quantity fractions.

Introducing Fraction Notation

The shift from partitioned fractions to quantity fractions is facilitated by the way that the fractions are named. Descriptions of partitioned fractions must carry the name of the unit-whole. Sharing a chocolate bar among three people results in each person receiving a piece of chocolate, as in Figure 11.10. Sharing the chocolate bar among three people does not result in the unit-less quantity.

An advantage of maintaining the name of the partitioned unit-whole while fraction notation is introduced is that it makes it relatively easy to see the fraction as operating on the unit. For example, if you know that the chocolate bar weighs 60g then $\frac{1}{3}$ of a bar will weigh 20g. That is, the partitioned fraction also operates on the weight.

Equivalent partitioned fractions are readily produced from sharing contexts. Sharing three chocolate bars among four people can result in students' recordings showing each receives one-half and one-fourth or each receives three-fourths. The equivalence of these ways of sharing suggests that:

$$\frac{1}{2}\text{ bar} + \frac{1}{4}\text{ bar} = \frac{1}{4}\text{ bar} + \frac{1}{4}\text{ bar} + \frac{1}{4}\text{ bar}.$$

That is,

$$\frac{1}{2}\text{ bar} = \frac{1}{4}\text{ bar} + \frac{1}{4}\text{ bar and }\frac{1}{4}\text{ bar} + \frac{1}{4}\text{ bar} = \frac{2}{4}\text{ bar}.$$

We can record that

$$\frac{1}{2}\text{ bar} = \frac{2}{4}\text{ bar}$$

and recognize that although these partitioned fractions are equivalent they are not the same. The first refers to a bar divided into two equal pieces and the second refers to a bar divided into four equal pieces.

The pedagogical value of characterizing fractions as either quantity fractions or partitioned fractions is the emphasis such a categorization gives to introducing the fraction notation. The fraction notation can be introduced as a shorthand way of recording the fraction names for partitioned fractions. However, 'naked fraction notation' is not needed until students operate with fractions as numbers, in particular, fraction × fraction. The power of the fraction notation for dual representation – fraction as a number and as an indicated division – has meant that the creation of the equal whole has remained invisible for many students. For many students, abstract quantity fractions may be indistinguishable from partitioned fractions.

Looking Back

There is always more than one possible pathway to a robust understanding of fractions as numbers. What is outlined in this chapter is a pathway to fraction understanding that is designed to assist more students to complete the journey. The teaching sequence starts with developing a multiplicative link between the part and the unit whole for partitioned fractions. Students verify the relationship between the part and the whole inherent in partitions, record their sharing of quantities and move to fraction notation through recognizing the importance of the equal whole. The unit-whole needed to define a fractional part becomes more apparent in students' thinking when the whole is exceeded. When this occurs, students need to coordinate units on a number of different levels. Equivalent fractions can then be introduced by using an equivalence table, as in Activity IA11.12. Finally, as there is more than one way to interpret the fraction notation, students need opportunities to come to recognize that the fraction notation records both a division and the result of a division.

INSTRUCTIONAL ACTIVITIES

The following examples of teaching activities relate to the described sequence for teaching fractions. However, the activities do not constitute a complete teaching programme, but rather suggest simple contexts that start with linear partitioning and progress through the levels involved in coming to understand fractions as numbers. Each activity emphasizes the need for students to justify their answers. It is important to seek to understand students' reasoning to avoid the risk of reinforcing correct answers obtained through faulty reasoning.

ACTIVITY IA11.1: Finding Half Way

Intended learning: To find halfway along an object by estimating a linear partition and verifying the closest answer.

Description: Attach a length of ribbon or paper tape to the wall. Tell your students that you are going to move a ruler (held vertically to act as a pointer) across in front of the ribbon and ask them to put up their hands when the pointer is half way across. If multiple answers are suggested, select and record the location of two or three of the answers together with names of the students who suggested them. Ask your students to tell you how we could determine who was closest to half way. Invite a student to demonstrate his or her method of determining half way and explain which answer was closer.

Photo 11.1   Finding half way

Variation: Select and record two answers and ask your students to line up behind whichever student they believe is closest to half way. Next ask your class if the two lines of students are equal. Does half of the class support one answer or is it more than half of the class?

ACTIVITY IA11.2: Line Up

Intended learning: To find halfway along a linear arrangement of discrete objects and to see that adding the same quantity to both ends doesn't change the halfway point.

Description: Invite a number of your students (say, three with young children or seven with older students) to line up at the front of the classroom and face the class. Ask your students if they can tell you which student is half way down the line, that is, who is in the middle of the line and how they know. Invite a student to demonstrate his or her method of determining who is in the middle of the line. Ask two more students to join the line, one on each end, and repeat the question of determining who is half way down the line. Invite a student to explain why the half way location doesn't change.

Variation: Have the two additional students face the opposite direction to the rest of the line of students. This will make it easier to focus on the change. First, add the two students to one end of the line and then compare this with having one go to each end.

Alternatively, have your students explain what happens when you have an even number of students in the line.

ACTIVITY IA11.3: Finding One-quarter of the Way

Description: Attach a length of ribbon or paper tape to the wall. Tell your students that you are going to move a ruler across in front of the ribbon and ask them to put up their hands when the ruler is one-quarter of the way across. If multiple answers are suggested, select and record the location of two or three of the answers. Ask your students to tell you how we could determine who was closest to one-quarter of the way.

Variation: After the location of one-quarter has been determined, ask where three-quarters of the length would be.

ACTIVITY IA11.4: What Fraction of the Length is That?

Intended learning: To distinguish a linear partition of length from a number of parts representation of a fraction.

Materials: A strip of paper not completely segmented into equal parts with one part shaded. Additional strips of paper for small group work.

Description: Show the class a strip of paper divided and shaded as in Figure 11.11. Ask your students to estimate what fraction of the strip is shaded and to record their estimates. You can provide some additional structure by asking them to select their answers from one-third, one-quarter, one-fifth or other. If your students are familiar with the fraction notation this could be used to record their answers. Ask your students if anyone knows of a way to check to see who is correct. If a student suggests measuring the pieces, affirm that you could do this, but ask if he or she could explain how it could be done without using a ruler.

Distribute strips of paper marked up as in Figure 11.12 to each pair of students. Ask your students to record what they agree is the fraction of each strip that is shaded.

Figure 11.11   Folder paper: *what fraction of the length is that?*

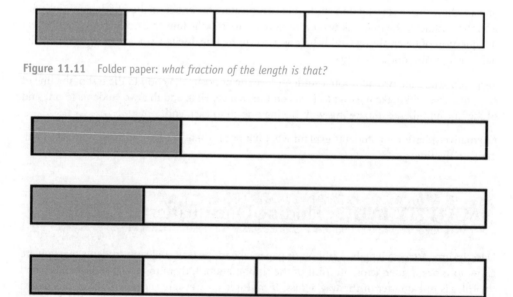

Figure 11.12   Three strips of paper

Figure 11.13 Strips of paper: variation

Figure 11.14 Strips of paper: more variations

Variation: Focus the lesson on eighths. Start the whole class activity with the strip shown in Figure 11.13. After the whole-class discussion, distribute the strips shown in Figure 11.14 and have your students record what they agree is the fraction of each strip that is shaded. You might ask students to show where one-half and one-fourth of the strip would be as a way to look at fraction equivalents.

ACTIVITY IA11.5: One-half, One-quarter and One-eighth

Intended learning: To learn to express the equivalence between quarters, eighths and half of the same unit of length.

Materials: A paper streamer approximately 90 cm long.

Description: Write the fractions one-half, one-quarter and one-eighth on the board. Hold up a paper streamer and ask your students which one of the fractions of the length of the streamer would be easiest to make and why. Follow up with, *How do you know that you have one-half (or one-quarter or one-eighth) of the length?* Fold the paper streamer in half and then fold one-half in half. Unfold the streamer and display it to the class. Point to each part in turn and ask, *What fraction of the streamer is this part? How do you know? If I fold one-quarter in half, what will I have?* Fold the quarter in half and, as before, point to each part in turn and ask, *What fraction of the streamer is this part? How do you know? How else could I describe two-eighths of the streamer?* Ask your students to draw the streamer and to show on the drawing how halves, quarters and eighths of the length of the streamer are related to each other.

ACTIVITY IA11.6: Three-eighths of the Way Across the Board

Intended learning: To learn to create eighths by composition of partitioning through repeated halving and to use the relationship between one-eighth and three-eighths, or one-quarter and one-half.

Materials: A whiteboard and marker pens or a blackboard and chalk, a piece of string longer than the width of the board and a pair of scissors.

Description: Invite three students to estimate where three-eighths of the width of the board would be, mark the point and put their initials next to their estimates. Students can be selected to obtain variation in the estimates. Ask your students to tell you how we could determine who was closest to three-eighths of the way across the board. Show the string and the pair of scissors and ask if anyone could use the string to show who is closest to three-eighths. Students must partition the string into eighths and justify their reasoning by iterating one-eighth three times.

ACTIVITY IA11.7: One-third of a Circle

Although the recommended method of introducing fractions starts with a focus on linear models, at some stage students will need to partition circular regions. The following activity is a simple yet effective way to allow students to partition a circular region into three equal parts.

Intended learning: To use drawings to record partitioning and distribution strategies.

Description: Ask your students to draw a circle on a sheet of paper using a plate or lid as a template and to imagine that it is the top view of a round cake. *I want you to work out where we would cut the cake to have three equal slices with none left over. Use pencils or popsticks to work out where the cuts would go before you draw them.*

Observe the sequence of approximations that students use in developing the idea of dividing a circle into three equal parts.

(a) 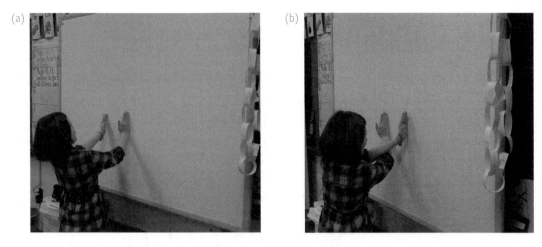 (b)

Photo 11.2 (a) and (b)   Time series of locating three-eighths of the length of the whiteboard

(a) 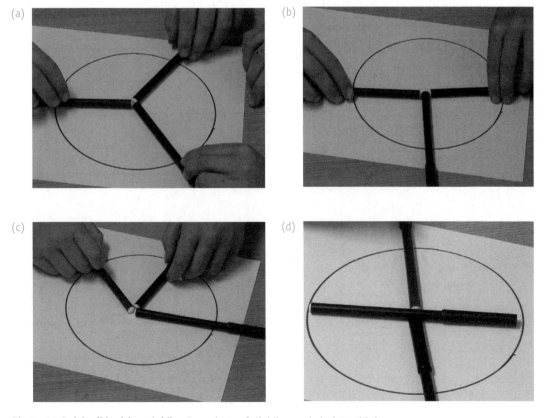 (b)

(c) (d)

Photo 11.3 (a), (b), (c) and (d)   Four shots of dividing a circle into thirds

ACTIVITY IA11.8: Recording Partitioning

Intended learning: To use drawings to record partitioning and distribution strategies.

Description: Ask the following questions involving sharing multiple continuous quantities. Figures 11.15–11.20 show student responses to each prompt.

I have 6 cups of milk. A recipe needs half of a cup of milk. How many times can I make the recipe before I run out of milk? Can you sketch your answer? (See Figure 11.15.)

Sketch what would happen if I have 6 cups of milk and a recipe needs three-quarters of a cup of milk. How many times can I make the recipe before I run out of milk? (See Figure 11.16.)

Figure 11.15 A response showing correct partitioning and developing notation

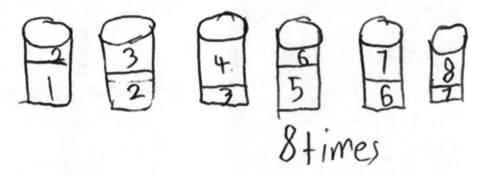

Figure 11.16 A response showing accumulated three-quarters

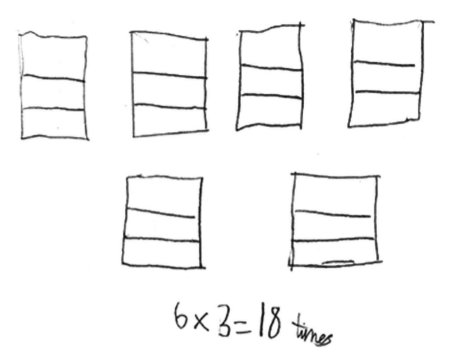

Figure 11.17   The multiplicative relationship between fractional parts and the whole

Sketch what would happen if I have 6 cups of milk and a recipe needs one-third of a cup of milk. How many times can I make the recipe before I run out of milk? (See Figure 11.17.)

How would you share 5 pancakes between 2 people? Can you sketch your answer? (See Figure 11.18.)

Sketch what would happen if you had to share 6 pancakes among 4 people. (See Figure 11.19 for a student response involving economical partitioning.)

Sketch what would happen if you had to share 9 pancakes among 12 people. (See Figure 11.20 for a student response involving partitioning in quarters.)

ACTIVITY IA11.9: Building Towers

Intended learning: To learn to recreate the whole from a fractional part (represented as discrete but linked units) and to go beyond the whole.

Materials: Linking cubes.

Description: Display a tower of nine connected cubes. *If this tower is one-and-a-half, can you make or sketch a tower of one?*

Figure 11.18   Introducing mixed numbers

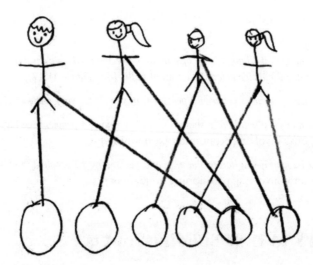

Figure 11.19   Economical partitioning

Display six connected cubes. *This tower is three-eighths of the whole tower. Can you sketch (or show me) what one-eighth of the whole tower would be? Can you sketch what one-half of the whole tower looks like?*

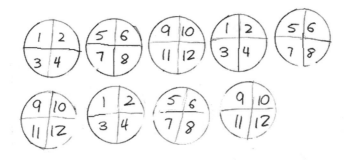

They each get 3.

Figure 11.20   Partitioning involving quarters

(a)

(b)

Photo 11.4 a & b   Building towers activity: reasoning about fractions with linking cubes

ACTIVITY IA11.10: Ooops!

Intended learning: To learn to recreate the whole from a fractional part and to go beyond the whole.

Materials: A paper streamer or a length of paper tape.

Description: *I am going to make a special length of paper.* Measure a length of paper and cut it. *Ooops! I have accidentally cut off three-quarters of the length. How can we work out how long the whole piece should be?* Using only the cut piece of paper, invite students to explain how long the whole piece should be. Ask students to explain where one-half of the whole length would be and then one and one-quarter of the whole length. Repeat the activity starting with accidentally cutting one-third and asking the students to show where four-thirds of the length would be.

Photo 11.5   Oops activity: reasoning about fractional length

ACTIVITY IA11.11: How Many Are At Your Table?

Intended learning: To learn to identify equivalent fractions arising from sharing problems as an introduction to equivalent fractions.

Materials: A supply of paper discs to represent pancakes.

Description: Have your students act out the following problems or represent them by drawing.

(a) If 12 children sit at a table that has 9 pancakes, how many pancakes does each child get?
(b) If 8 children sit at a table that has 6 pancakes, how many pancakes does each child get?
(c) If 4 children sit at a table that has 3 pancakes, how many pancakes does each child get?

What did you notice about the answers? Why does this happen?

(d) If 12 children sit at a table that has 21 pancakes, how many pancakes does each child get?
(e) If 8 children sit at a table that has 14 pancakes, how many pancakes does each child get?
(f) If 4 children sit at a table that has 7 pancakes, how many pancakes does each child get?

What did you notice about the answers?

(g) If 12 children sit at a table that has some pancakes, and each child gets 3/4 of a pancake, how many pancakes are at this table?

Number of pancakes	?	6							?
Number at the table	4	8							40

Figure 11.21   Pancake and people recording table

(h) If some children sit at a table that has 12 pancakes, and each child gets 3/4 of a pancake, how many children are at this table?

What did you notice about the answers? Why does this happen?

ACTIVITY IA11.12: Keeping Records at the Pancake Place

Intended learning: To introduce a notation to record equivalent fractions arising from sharing by table problems.

Materials: Prepared table columns to jointly construct a table (see Figure 11.21).

Description: Establish the context of serving pancakes to children seated at tables in a restaurant.

At a pancake restaurant 8 children are seated around a table with 6 pancakes. If there are two smaller tables each with 4 children how many pancakes should be placed at the tables so that they receive the same amount of pancake? If 40 more children arrive at the restaurant, how many pancakes are needed so that if they all sat at the one table they also would receive the same share?

Introduce the pancake table by adding the row headings to the board and having students complete the columns for 4, 8 and 40 at the table. Ask the students to think of other problems that belong on the table and to complete those values. *Does it matter which table group you join at the pancake restaurant described above?*

ACTIVITY IA11.13: Time for a Break

Intended learning: To learn to subdivide (partition) composite units.

Materials: An image of a four-finger Kit Kat or similar.

Description: Draw four connected rectangles on the board to represent a four-finger Kit Kat. Ask the following division question and have a student show his or her answer on the board.

Explain how you would share a four-finger Kit Kat among six people. How much of the Kit Kat would each person receive and how would you do this practically?

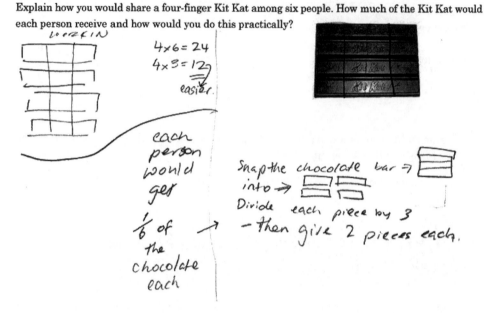

Figure 11.22   Kit Kat bar prompt

(a)   *If I have a four-finger Kit Kat and wish to give each of my friends half of a finger, how many friends can I share it with?*

(b)   *If I have a four-finger Kit Kat and wish to give each of my friends a quarter of a finger, how many friends can I share it with?*

Have your students work in pairs to solve the following problems. See Figure 11.22 for a student response.

(c)   *Explain how you would share four Kit Kat fingers among three people. How much of the Kit Kat would each person receive and how would you do this practically?*

(d)   *Explain how you would share four Kit Kat fingers among six people. How much would each person receive and how would you do this practically?*

Glossary

Abstract composite unit. A construct by which one can simultaneously regard an abstract number as both a composite and a unit. For example, ten is an abstract composite unit when it can be regarded as both ten ones and one ten. This can be distinguished from numerical composite which involves regarding an abstract number as a composite but not as a unit.

Addend. A number to be added. In 7 + 4 = 11, 7 and 4 are addends, and 11 is the sum.

Additive task. A generic label for tasks involving what adults would regard as addition. The label 'additive task' is used to emphasize that children will construe such tasks idiosyncratically, that is, differently from each other and from the way adults will construe them.

Algorithm. A step-wise procedure for carrying out a task. In arithmetic, a procedure for adding, subtracting, and so on. Also used to refer to the standard, written procedures for calculating with multi-digit numbers, for example, the division algorithm.

Alternative algorithm. See Semi-formal written strategy.

Arithmetic knowledge. A collective term for all the student knows about arithmetic (i.e. number and operations). The term 'knowledge' is sometimes juxtaposed with 'strategies' and in that case refers to knowledge not easily characterized as a strategy (for example, knowing the names of numerals).

Arithmetic rack. See Appendix.

Array. See Appendix.

Arrow cards. See Appendix.

Associative principle. The operation of addition is associative because, when any three numbers are added: 7 + 4 + 5, the order of performing the two addition operations does not affect the sum, for example, $(7 + 4) + 5 = 7 + (4 + 5)$. Multiplication is also associative whereas subtraction and division are not associative.

Automaticity. A capacity to quickly recall or figure out the answer to basic facts (e.g. 7 + 9, 4×8).

Automatization. The development of automaticity.

Backward number word sequence (BNWS). See Number word sequence.

Bare number tasks. Arithmetic tasks presented in the absence of a setting or context, for example, 47 + 35, 86×3.

Base ten. A characteristic of numeration systems and number naming systems whereby numbers are expressed in a form that involves grouping by tens, tens of tens, and larger powers of ten (1000; 10,000; etc.).

Base-ten dot materials. See Appendix.

Base-ten materials. A generic name for instructional settings consisting of materials organized into ones, tens, hundreds, and so on, such as bundling sticks and base-ten dot materials.

Base-ten thinking. Thinking of numbers in terms of ones, tens, hundreds, and so on, for example thinking of 257 as consisting of 200 + 50 + 7.

Basic facts. Combinations or number bonds of the form a + b = c (basic facts for addition) or a × b = c (basic facts for multiplication) where a and b are numbers in the range 0 to 10. Also, corresponding combinations involving subtraction or division.

Bundling sticks. See Appendix.

Centuple. A multiple of 100 (e.g. 100, 200, 300, 1300, 2500). This is distinguished from century which means a sequence of 100 numbers, for example from 267 to 366 or a period of 100 years.

Century. See Centuple.

Column computation. Arithmetical computation with multi-digit numbers that involves organizing numbers into columns, typically used before the formal algorithms are taught.

Combinations. An alternative name for number bonds or basic facts, for example, 5 + 3 = 8, 8 − 2 = 6, 7 × 9 = 63, 48 ÷ 8 = 6.

Combining. An arithmetical strategy involving combining (i.e. in a sense adding) two numbers whose sum is in the range one to 10, without counting, for example, 4 and 3, 7 and 2.

Commutative principle. The operation of addition is commutative because, for any two numbers, their sum is unchanged when the numbers are commuted, for example, 7 + 4 = 4 + 7. Multiplication is also commutative whereas subtraction and division are not commutative.

Compensation strategy. An arithmetical strategy that involves first changing one number to make an easier calculation and then compensating for the change, for example 17 + 38: calculate 17 + 40 and subtract 2.

Complementary addition. A strategy for subtracting based on adding up, for example, 82 − 77 is solved as 77 + ? = 80, 80 + ? = 82, answer 5.

Conceptual place value (CPV). An instructional topic focusing on developing students' facility to increment and decrement flexibly by ones, tens, hundreds, and so on. CPV is distinguished from conventional place value, that is, the conventional instructional topic that is intended to provide a basis for learning formal written algorithms.

Conventional place value. See Conceptual place value.

Coordinating units. Conceiving of a unit fraction and a whole simultaneously. This involves knowing how to iterate a unit fraction such as one-third to form a whole.

Counting by ones. A range of strategies used to solve arithmetical tasks. Some examples are, counting-on, counting-back and counting from one. Contrasted with non-counting (non-count-by-ones) strategies, that is, arithmetical strategies which do not involve counting by ones such as adding through ten, using a double, using a five-structure.

Decade. See Decuple.

Decrementing. See Incrementing.

Decimalizing. Developing base-ten thinking, that is, approaches to arithmetic that exploit the decimal (base-ten) numeration system, such as using 10 as a unit, and organizing calculations into 1s, 10s and 100s.

Decuple. A multiple of ten (e.g. 10, 20, 30, 180, 240). Distinguished from decade which means a sequence of 10 numbers, for example, from 27 to 36 or a period of 10 years.

Difference. See Minuend.

Digit. The digits are the ten basic symbols in the modern numeration system, that is '0', '1', … '9'.

Digit cards. See Appendix.

Distancing materials. An instructional technique involving progressively reducing the role of materials, for example, materials are unscreened, then flashed and screened, then screened without flashing and used only to check, and so on.

Distributive principle. The principle that multiplication distributes over addition and subtraction as does division, for example, $(7 - 5) \times 3 = (7 \times 3) - (5 \times 3)$.

Dividend. In a division equation such as $29 \div 4 = 7$ r 1, 29 is the dividend, 4 is the divisor, 7 is the quotient and 1 is the remainder.

Divisor. See Dividend.

Domain. Used to refer to a broad area of arithmetical learning such as, 'Number Words and Numerals', 'Conceptual Place Value'.

Dot tiles. See Appendix.

Doubles. The addition basic facts that involve adding a number to itself: $1 + 1$, $2 + 2$, … $10 + 10$.

Drop-down notation. An informal notation for recording a split strategy for multi-digit addition and subtraction.

Empty number line (ENL). See Appendix.

Equidistant parallel partitioning. Drawing a set of equidistant parallel lines when attempting to partition a region into fractions of a specified size (e.g. fifths).

Facile. Used in the sense of having good facility, that is, fluent or dexterous, for example, facile with a compensation strategy, or facile with the backward number word sequence.

Factor. If a number F, when multiplied by a whole number gives a number M, we call F a factor of M and M a multiple of F. For example, 3 is a factor of 27 and 27 is a multiple of 3, because $3 \times 9 = 27$.

Finger patterns. Arrangements of fingers used by students when calculating.

Five-wise pattern. A spatial pattern on a ten-frame for a number in the range 1 to 10. Five-wise patterns are made by filling first one row, then the second. For example, a five-wise pattern for 4 has a row of 4 and a row of 0, a five-wise pattern for 7 has a row of 5 and a row of 2. This is contrasted with pair-wise patterns which are made by progressively filling the columns. For example, a pair-wise pattern for 4 has two pairs, a pair-wise pattern for 7 has three pairs and one single dot. On an arithmetic rack, these patterns can be made for numbers in the range 1 to 20. As well, ten-wise patterns can be made by first filling one row of the rack.

Flashing. A technique which involves briefly displaying (typically for half a second) some part of an instructional setting. For example, a ten-frame with 8 red and 2 black dots is flashed.

Formal algorithm. A standard written procedure for calculating with multi-digit numbers that relies on the conventions of formal place value; for example, the column-based procedures for adding, subtracting, and so on, contrasted with an informal strategy, for example, solving 58 + 25 by adding 58 and 20, and then 78 and 5.

Formalizing. Developing an approach to arithmetic that involves more formal notation or more formal procedures. The term 'formal' is used to indicate adult-level, abstract mathematics.

Forward number word sequence (FNWS). See Number word sequence.

Generalizing. Reasoning that involves proceeding from a few cases to many cases.

Groupable base-ten materials. Base-ten materials such as bundling sticks that can be aggregated into tens and disaggregated. This is contrasted with base-ten materials already grouped into tens (or hundreds and tens, etc.) which are referred to as pre-grouped base-ten materials.

Higher decade addition. Typically used to refer to additions of a 2-digit number and a 1-digit number, for example 72 + 5, 47 + 6.

Higher decade subtraction. Typically used to refer to subtraction involving a 2-digit number and a 1-digit number, for example 37 − 4, 52 − 7.

Hurdle number. A number where students commonly have difficulty continuing a number sequence. For example, students may say '106, 107, 108, 109, 200': there is a hurdle at 110.

Incrementing. Increasing a number, typically by one or more ones, tens, hundreds or some combination of these. Similarly, decreasing a number in this way is called decrementing.

Inquiry mode. A mode of working where students typically are investigating mathematical topics that are new to them and trying to solve tasks that are genuine problems for them. Contrasted with rehearsal mode which is a mode of working that involves repeating something with which the student is acquainted, with the intention of increasing familiarity and ease, and perhaps working towards automatization.

Inquiry-based teaching. An approach to teaching that emphasizes the inquiry mode. Thus tasks are designed to be at the cutting-edge of students' current levels of knowledge.

Inverse relationship. Commencing with a number N, if another number, for example 6, is added to N and then subtracted from the sum obtained, then the result will be N. Thus addition and subtraction have an inverse relationship – each is the inverse of the other. Similarly, multiplication and division have an inverse relationship.

Jump strategy. A category of mental strategies for 2-digit addition and subtraction. Strategies in this category involve starting from one number and incrementing or decrementing that number by first tens and then ones (or first ones then tens). Is also used with 3-digit numbers.

Jump to the decuple. A variation of the jump strategy where the first step is to add up to the next decuple, for example, 37 + 25 as 37 + 3, 40 + 20, 60 + 2. Similarly for subtraction, for example, 73 − 35 as 73 − 3, 70 − 30, 40 − 2.

Linking cubes. Instructional materials consisting of interlocking plastic cubes.

Mathematization. See Progressive mathematization.

Mental computation. Typically refers to doing whole number arithmetic with multi-digit numbers, and without any writing. Contrasted with written computation that is computation that involves writing.

Minuend. The number from which another number is subtracted, for example in 12 − 3 = 9, 12 is the minuend, 3 is the subtrahend, that is the number subtracted, and 9 is the difference, that is the number obtained.

Missing addend task. An arithmetical task where one addend and the sum are given, for example, 9 + ? = 13.

Missing subtrahend task. An arithmetical task where the minuend and the difference are given, for example, 11 − ? = 8.

Multi-digit. Involving numbers with two or more digits.

Multi-lid screen. See Appendix – Numeral roll and multi-lid screen.

Multiple. See Factor.

Multiplicand. The number multiplied, for example in 12 × 8 = 96 (interpreted as 12 multiplied by 8), 12 is the multiplicand, 8 is the multiplier and 96 is the product.

Multiplier. See Multiplicand.

Non-canonical. The number 64 can be expressed in the form of 50 + 14. This form is referred to as a non-canonical (non-standard) form of 64, whereas 60 + 4 is the canonical form of 64. Knowledge of non-canonical forms is useful in addition, subtraction, and so on.

Non-counting strategy. See Counting by ones.

Non-regrouping task. See Regrouping task.

Notating. Purposeful writing in an arithmetical situation, for example, notating a jump strategy on an empty number line.

Number. A number is the idea or concept associated with, for example, how many items in a collection. We distinguish among the number 24 – that is, the concept – the spoken or heard number word 'twenty-four', the numeral '24' and also the read or written word 'twenty-four'. These distinctions are important in understanding students' numerical strategies.

Number word. Number words are names or words for numbers. In most cases the term 'number word' refers to the spoken and heard names for numbers rather than the read or written names.

Number word sequence (NWS). A regular sequence of number words, typically but not necessarily by ones, for example the NWS from 97 to 112, the NWS from 82 back to 75, the NWS by tens from 24, the NWS by threes to 30.

Numeral. Numerals are symbols for numbers, for example, '5', '27', '307'.

Numeral identification. Stating the name of a displayed numeral. The term is used similarly to the term 'letter identification' in early literacy. When assessing numeral identification, numerals are not displayed in numerical sequence.

Numeral cards. See Appendix.

Numeral roll. See Appendix.

Numeral track. See Appendix.

Over-jump strategy. A variation of a jump strategy that involves going beyond a given number and then adjusting, for example 53 – 19 as 53 – 20 and then 33 + 1.

Pair-wise pattern. See Five-wise pattern.

Part–whole construction of number. The ability to conceive simultaneously of a whole and two parts. For example conceiving of 10 and also of the parts 6 and 4. This is characteristic of students who have progressed beyond a reliance on counting-by-ones to add and subtract.

Partitioned fraction. A fraction regarded as being in a context or setting, for example, half an apple, two-fifths of a rectangle. This is contrasted with quantity fraction, that is, a fraction regarded as a number (rational number) in abstract mathematics.

Partitioning. An arithmetical strategy involving partitioning a number into two parts without counting, for example, when solving 8 + 5, 5 is partitioned into 2 and 3.

Partitions of a number. The ways a number can be expressed as a sum of two numbers, for example, the partitions of 6 are 1 and 5, 2 and 4, 3 and 3, 4 and 2, and 5 and 1.

Partitive division. A division equation such as 15 ÷ 3 is interpreted as distributing 15 items into three groups, that is, three partitions. This is contrasted with Quotitive division where 15 ÷ 3 is interpreted as distributing 15 items into groups of three, that is, groups with a quota of three.

Pedagogical engineering. The pedagogical process of designing, trialling and refining instructional procedures.

Period. A part of a numeral consisting of three decimal places. In the numeral 46,275,406, for example, 275 is the thousands period.

Pre-grouped materials. See Groupable base-ten materials.

Procedure. See Strategy.

Product. See Multiplicand.

Progressive mathematization. The development over time, of the mathematical sophistication of students' knowledge and reasoning, with respect to a specific topic, for example, addition.

Quantity fraction. See Partitioned fraction.

Quotient. See Dividend.

Quotitive division. See Partitive division.

Regional model. A shape with shaded regions drawn to illustrate a fraction, for example, shading a circle to illustrate one-sixth.

Regrouping task. In the case of addition of two 2-digit numbers, a task where the sum of the numbers in the ones column exceeds 9, for example, in 37 + 48, 7 + 8 exceeds 9. In the case of subtraction involving two 2-digit numbers, a task where, in the ones column, the subtrahend exceeds the minuend, for example in 95 − 48, 8 exceeds 5. This is similarly applied to addition and subtraction with numbers with three or more digits.

Rehearsal mode. See Inquiry mode.

Remainder. See Dividend.

Scaffolding. Actions on the part of the teacher to provide support for students to reason about or solve a task beyond what they could manage on their own.

Screening. A technique used in the presentation of instructional tasks which involves placing a small screen or cover over all or part of an instructional setting (for example, screening a collection of 6 bundles of sticks).

Semi-formal written strategy. A well-organized, standardized, written strategy – less formal than a formal written algorithm – for performing an arithmetical calculation.

Setting. Materials used as a standard context for posing arithmetical tasks, for example, Two-colour ten-frames, Numeral roll and multi-lid frame, Bundling sticks, Arrow cards. See Appendix for more examples.

Split strategy. A category of mental strategies for 2-digit addition and subtraction. Strategies in this category involve splitting the numbers into tens and ones and working separately with the tens and ones before recombining them. Split strategies can also be used with 3-digit and larger numbers.

Split-jump strategy. A hybrid strategy, for example, 47 + 25 as 40 + 20, 60 + 7, 67 + 5.

Strategy. A generic label for a method by which a student solves an arithmetical task, for example, an add through ten strategy: 8 + 6 as 8 + 2, and 10 + 4. The term procedure is used with similar meaning.

Structuring numbers. Coming to know numbers through organizing numbers in terms of networks of relationships, and applying that knowledge to computation. For example, thinking of 16 as $10 + 5 + 1$ or as double 8.

Subtrahend. See Minuend.

Sum. See Addend.

Symbolization. A process of symbolizing in the sense of developing and using symbols in a context of arithmetical reasoning.

Task. A generic label for problems or questions presented to a student.

Ten-frame. See Appendix.

Ten-wise pattern. See Five-wise pattern.

Transforming strategy. An arithmetical strategy that involves simultaneously changing two numbers to make an easier calculation, for example, $17 + 38$ is transformed to $15 + 40$, $83 - 17$ is transformed to $80 - 14$.

Unit. A thing that is countable and therefore is regarded as a single item. For example, when one counts how many 3s in 18: one 3, two 3s, three 3s ... six 3s; the 3s are regarded as units.

Unitizing. A conceptual procedure that involves regarding a number larger than one, as a unit, for example, three is regarded as a unit of three rather than three ones, or 10 is regarded as a unit of 10. Unitizing enables students to focus on the unitary rather than the composite aspect of the number.

Written computation. See Mental computation.

Appendix
Instructional Settings

Arithmetic rack. An instructional device consisting of two rows of ten beads  which can be moved like beads on an abacus. In each row the beads appear in two groups of five, demarcated by colour. The rack is used to support students' additive reasoning in the range 1 to 20. See Figure 4.2.

Array. A rectangular grid of dots used as a setting for multiplication, for example, a 6 × 4 array has six rows and four columns. See Figure 7.12.

Arrow cards. A set of 36 cards with a card for each of the following numerals: 1, 2, … 9; 10, 20, … 90 100, 200, … 900 1000, 2000, … 9000. The cards are used to build multi-digit numerals, and each card has an arrow on the right hand side to support students' orienting and locating the cards. See Figure 3.2.

Base-ten dot materials. Materials consisting of strips with 1 to 9 dots, strips with 10 dots and squares with 100 dots. Dots are grey or black in order to demarcate a 5 in the 6- to 9-dot strips, two 5s in the 10-dot strip and two 50s in the 100-dot square.

Bundling sticks. Wooden sticks used to show 10s and 1s. Rubber bands are used to make bundles of 10 and groups of ten 10s. See Figure 5.2

Digit cards. A set of cards used to build numerals. Each card displays a digit (i.e. 0, 1, 2 … 9). A set includes several cards for each digit, in order to account for numerals with repeating digits (e.g. 464, 3333).

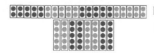 **Dot tiles.** An instructional setting for multiplication consisting of tiles with a given number of dots. Hence 2-tile, 3-tile and so on. See Figure 7.6.

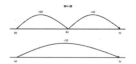 **Empty number line (ENL).** A setting consisting of a simple arc or line which is used by students and teachers to record and explain mental strategies for adding, subtracting, multiplying and dividing. See Figure 5.6.

Numeral cards. A set of cards with each card displaying a numeral.

Numeral roll. An instructional setting consisting of a long strip of paper containing a relatively long sequence of numerals, increasing from left to right, for example, from 1 to 120 or 80 to 220.

Numeral roll and window. A numeral roll threaded through a slotted card so that one numeral only is displayed.

 **Numeral roll and multi-lid screen.** A numeral roll and a screen with 10 or more lids enabling screening and unscreening of individual numerals See Figure 3.1.

Numeral track. An instructional setting consisting of a strip of cardboard containing a sequence of numerals and for each numeral, a hinged lid which can be used to screen or display the numeral.

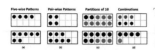 **Ten-frame.** An instructional setting consisting of a card with a 2 × 5 rectangular array used to support students' additive reasoning in the range 1 to 10. See Figure 4.1.

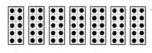 **Ten-frames – 10-dot cards.** Ten-frames with 10 dots of one colour. See Figure 6.7.

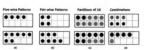 **Ten-frames – combinations.** A set of ten-frames with the different combinations of (a) 0 to 5 dots in the upper row, and (b) 0 to 5 dots in the lower row, typically with the rows in differing colours. A total of 36 cards. See Figure 4.1.

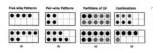 **Ten-frames – five-wise.** A set of 11 ten-frames showing the five-wise patterns for 0, 1, … 10. See Figure 4.1.

Ten-frames – pair-wise. A set of 11 ten-frames showing the pair-wise patterns for 0, 1, … 10. See Figure 4.1.

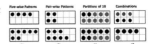

Ten-frames – partitions. A set of 11 ten-frames showing the partitions of 10 demarcated by colour (i.e. 10 & 0, 9 & 1, 8 & 2, … 0 & 10). Typically, a five-wise set and a pair-wise set. See Figure 4.1.

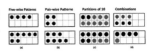

References

Anghileri, J. (1989) An investigation of young children's understanding of multiplication. *Educational Studies in Mathematics* 20: 367–385.

Anghileri, J. (2001) What are we trying to achieve in teaching standard calculating procedures? In M. Van den Heuvel-Panhuizen (ed.), *Proceedings of the 25th Annual Conference of the International Group for the Psychology of Mathematics Education* (Vol. 2, pp. 41–48). Utrecht, The Netherlands: PME.

Anghileri, J. (2006) *Teaching Number Sense* (2nd edn). London: Continuum.

Anghileri, J., Beishuizen, M. and Putten, C. (2002) From informal strategies to structured procedures: Mind the gap! *Educational Studies in Mathematics* 49(2): 149–170.

Armstrong, B.E. and Novillis Larson, C. (1995) Students' use of part–whole and direct comparison strategies for comparing partitioned rectangles. *Journal for Research in Mathematics Education* 26(1): 2–19.

Askew, M., Brown, M., Rhodes, V., Wiliam, D. and Johnson, D. (1997) *Effective Teachers of Numeracy: Report of a Study Carried out for the Teacher Training Agency*. London: King's College, University of London.

Ball, D.L. and Bass, H. (2000) Interweaving content and pedagogy in teaching and learning to teach: Knowing and using mathematics. In J. Boaler (ed.), *Multiple Perspectives on Mathematics Teaching and Learning*. Westport, CT: Ablex.

Battista, M.T., Clements, D.H., Arnoff, J., Battista, K. and Van Auken Borrow, C. (1998) Students' spatial structuring of 2D arrays of squares. *Journal for Research in Mathematics Education* 29(5): 503–532.

Behr, M.J., Harel, G., Post, T.R. and Lesh, R. (1992) Rational number, ratio and proportion. In D. Grouws (ed.), *Handbook of Research on Mathematics Teaching and Learning* (pp. 296–333). New York: Macmillan.

Beishuizen, M. (1993) Mental strategies and materials or models for addition and subtraction up to 100 in Dutch second grades. *Journal for Research in Mathematics Education* 24(4): 294–323.

Beishuizen, M. (1999) The empty number line as a new model. In I. Thompson (ed.), *Issues in Teaching Numeracy in Primary Schools* (pp. 157–168). Buckingham: Open University Press.

Beishuizen, M. (2001) Different approaches to mastering mental calculation strategies. In J. Anghileri (ed.), *Principles and Practices in Arithmetic Teaching* (pp. 119–130). Buckingham: Open University Press.

Beishuizen, M. and Anghileri, J. (1998) Which mental strategies in the early number curriculum? A comparison of British ideas and Dutch views. *British Educational Research Journal* 24(3): 519–538.

Beishuizen, M., Van Putten, C.M. and Van Mulken, F. (1997) Mental arithmetic and strategy use with indirect number problems up to one hundred. *Learning and Instruction* 7(1): 87–106.

Bezuk, N. and Cramer, K. (1989) Teaching about fractions: What, when, and how? In P. Trafton (ed.), *National Council of Teachers of Mathematics 1989 Yearbook: New Directions For Elementary School Mathematics* (pp. 156–167). Reston, VA: National Council of Teachers of Mathematics.

Blanton, M. and Kaput, J. (2003) Developing elementary teachers' 'Algebra eyes and ears'. *Teaching Children Mathematics* 10: 70–77.

Bobis, J. (1996) Visualisation and the development of number sense with kindergarten children. In J.T. Mulligan and M.C. Mitchelmore (eds), *Children's Number Learning* (pp. 17–33). Adelaide: Australian Association of Mathematics Teachers/Mathematics Education Research Group of Australasia.

Bobis, J. (2007) The empty number line: A useful tool or just another procedure? *Teaching Children Mathematics* 13(9): 410–413.

Cajori, F. (1974) *A History of Mathematical Notations* (Vol. 1). La Salle, IL: The Open Court Publishing Company.

Carpenter, T.P., Corbitt, M.K., Kepner, H.S., Lindquist, M.M. and Reys, R.E. (1981) *Results from the Second Mathematics Assessment of the National Assessment of Educational Progress.* Washington, DC: National Council of Teachers of Mathematics.

Carpenter, T.P., Franke, M.L., Jacobs, V.R., Fennema, E. and Empson, S.B. (1998) A longitudinal study of invention and understanding in children's multidigit addition and subtraction. *Journal for Research in Mathematics Education* 29(1): 3–20.

Carpenter, T.P., Franke, M.L. and Levi, L. (2003) *Thinking Mathematically: Integrating Arithmetic and Algebra in the Elementary School.* Portsmouth, NH: Heinnemann.

Carraher, D.W. (1996) Learning about fractions. In L.P. Steffe, P. Nesher, P. Cobb, G. A. Goldin and B. Greer (eds), *Theories of Mathematical Learning* (pp. 241–266). Mahwah, NJ: Lawrence Erlbaum.

Carruthers, E. and Worthington, M. (2006) *Children's Mathematics: Making Marks, Making Meaning.* London: Paul Chapman Publishing.

Cayton, G.A. and Brizuela, B.M. (2007) First graders' strategies for numerical notation, number reading and the number concept. In J.H. Woo, H.C. Lew, K.S. Park and D.Y. Seo (eds), *Proceedings of the 31st Conference of the International Group for the Psychology of Mathematics Education* (Vol. 2, pp. 81–88). Seoul: PME.

Charalambous, C.Y. and Pitta-Pantazi, D. (2005) Revisiting a theoretical model of fractions: Implications for teaching and research. In H.L. Chick and J.L. Vincent (eds), *Proceedings of the 29th Conference of the International Group for the Psychology of Mathematics Education* (Vol. 2, pp. 233–240). Melbourne: PME.

Clark, F.B. and Kamii, C. (1996) Identification of multiplicative thinking in children in grades 1–5. *Journal for Research in Mathematics Education* 27(1): 41–51.

Clarke, B., McDonough, A. and Sullivan, P. (2002) Measuring and describing learning: The early numeracy research project. In A. Cockburn and E. Nardi (eds), *Proceedings of the 26th Annual Conference of the International Group for the Psychology of Mathematics Education* (Vol. 1, pp. 181–185). Norwich, UK: PME.

Clarke, D., Lovitt, C. and Stephens, M. (1990) Reforming mathematics: Supporting teachers to reshape their practice. In S. Willis (ed.), *Being Numerate: What Counts?* (pp. 162–187). Melbourne: Australian Council for Educational Research.

Clarke, D.M. (1997) The changing role of the mathematics teacher. *Journal for Research in Mathematics Education* 28(3): 278–308.

Cobb, P. (1991) Reconstructing elementary school mathematics. *Focus on Learning Problems in Mathematics* 13(3): 3–33.

Cobb, P. (2000) Conducting teaching experiments in collaboration with teachers. In A. Kelly and R. Lesh (eds), *Handbook of Research and Design in Mathematical and Science Education* (pp. 307–333). Mahwah, NJ: Lawrence Erlbaum Associates.

Cobb, P. and Wheatley, G. (1988) Children's initial understandings of ten. *Focus on Learning Problems in Mathematics* 10(3): 1–26.

Cobb, P., Gravemeijer, K., Yackel, E., McClain, K. and Whitenack, J. (1997) Mathematizing and symbolizing: The emergence of chains of signification in one first-grade classroom. In D. Kirshner and J.A. Whitson (eds), *Situated Cognition Theory: Social, Semiotic, and Neurological Perspectives* (pp. 151–233). Mahwah, NJ: Lawrence Erlbaum.

Cobb, P., Confrey, J., diSessa, A., Lehrer, R. and Schauble, L. (2003) Design experiments in educational research. *Educational Researcher* 32(1): 9–13.

Confrey, J. (1994) Splitting, similarity, and rate of change: A new approach to multiplication and exponential functions. In J. Confrey and G. Harel (eds), *The Development of Multiplicative Reasoning in the Learning of Mathematics*. Albany, NY: State University of New York Press.

Davis, B. (1997) Listening for differences: An evolving conception of mathematics teaching. *Journal for Research in Mathematics Education* 28(3): 355.

Denvir, B. and Brown, M. (1986) Understanding of number concepts in low attaining 7–9 year olds: Part 1. Development of descriptive framework and diagnostic instrument. *Educational Studies in Mathematics* 17: 15–36.

Dowker, A.D. (2004) *Children with Difficulties in Mathematics: What Works?* London: DfES.

Ellemor-Collins, D. and Wright, R.J. (2007) Assessing pupil knowledge of the sequential structure of number. *Educational and Child Psychology* 24(2): 54–63.

Ellemor-Collins, D. and Wright, R.J. (2008) Assessing student thinking about arithmetic: Videotaped interviews. *Teaching Children Mathematics* 15(2): 106–111.

Ellemor-Collins, D. and Wright, R.J. (2009a) Developing conceptual place value: Instructional design for intensive intervention. In R. Hunter, B. Bicknell and T. Burgess (eds), *Crossing Divides: Proceedings of the 32nd Annual Conference of the Mathematics Education Research Group of Australasia* (Vol. 1, pp. 169–176). Palmerston North, NZ: MERGA.

Ellemor-Collins, D. and Wright, R.J. (2009b) Structuring numbers 1 to 20: Developing facile addition and subtraction. *Mathematics Education Research Journal* 21(2): 50–75.

Empson, S.B. and Jacobs, V.R. (2008) Learning to listen to children's mathematics. In D. Tirosh and T. Wood (eds), *Tools and Processes in Mathematics Teacher Education* (pp. 257–282). Rotterdam: Sense Publishers.

Falkner, K., Levi, L. and Carpenter, T. (1999) Children's understanding of equality: A foundation for algebra. *Teaching Children Mathematics* 6: 78–85.

Fosnot, C.T. and Dolk, M. (2001a) *Young Mathematics at Work: Constructing Multiplication and Division*. Portsmouth, NH: Heinemann.

Fosnot, C.T. and Dolk, M. (2001b) *Young Mathematics at Work: Constructing Number Sense, Addition, and Subtraction*. Portsmouth, NH: Heinemann.

Foxman, D. and Beishuizen, M. (2002) Mental calculation methods used by 11-year-olds in different attainment bands: A reanalysis of data from the 1987 APU survey in the UK. *Educational Studies in Mathematics* 51(1–2): 41–69.

Freudenthal, H. (1983) *Didactical Phenomenology of Mathematical Structures*. Dordrecht, The Netherlands: D. Reidel Publishing Company.

Freudenthal, H. (1991) *Revisiting Mathematics Education*. Dordrecht, The Netherlands: Kluwer Academic Publishers.

Fuson, K.C. (1992) Research on whole number addition and subtraction. In D.A. Grouws (ed.), *Handbook of Research on Mathematics Teaching and Learning* (pp. 243–275). New York: Macmillan.

Fuson, K.C., Richards, J. and Briars, D. (1982) The acquisition and elaboration of the number word sequence. In C.J. Brainerd (ed.), *Progress in Cognitive Development: Vol. 1 Children's Logical and Mathematical Cognition* (pp. 33–92). New York: Springer-Verlag.

Fuson, K.C., Wearne, D., Hiebert, J., Murray, H., Human, P., Olivier, A., et al. (1997) Children's conceptual structures for multidigit numbers and methods of multidigit addition and subtraction. *Journal for Research in Mathematics Education* 28: 130–162.

Gattegno, C. (1970) *What We Owe Children: The Subordination of Teaching to Learning*. London: Routledge and Kegan Paul.

Gattegno, C. (1988) *The Science of Education. Part 2B: The Awareness of Mathematization*. New York: Educational Solutions.

Ginsburg, H., Jacobs, S. and Lopez, L.S. (1998) *The Teacher's Guide to Flexible Interviewing in the Classroom: Learning What Children Know about Math*. Boston, MA: Allyn and Bacon.

Goldenberg, E.P., Shteingold, N. and Feurzeig, N. (2003) Mathematical habits of mind. In F.K. Lester (ed.), *Teaching Mathematics through Problem-solving: Prekindergarten–Grade 6*. Reston, VA: NCTM.

Gould, P. (2008) Children's quantitative sense of fractions. Unpublished PhD thesis, Macquarie University, Sydney.

Gravemeijer, K.P.E. (1991) An instruction-theoretical reflection on the use of manipulatives. In L. Streefland (ed.), *Realistic Mathematics Education in Primary School* (pp. 57–76). Utrecht: Freudenthal Institute.

Gravemeijer, K.P.E. (1994a) Educational development and developmental research in mathematics education. *Journal for Research in Mathematics Education* 25(5): 443–471.

Gravemeijer, K.P.E. (1994b) Instructional design as a learning process. In K.P.E. Gravemeijer (ed.), *Developing Realistic Mathematics Education* (pp. 17–54). Utrecht: Freudenthal Institute.

Gravemeijer, K.P.E. (1997) Mediating between concrete and abstract. In T. Nunes and P. Bryant (eds), *Learning and Teaching Mathematics: An International Perspective*. East Sussex: Psychology Press.

Gravemeijer, K.P.E. (2001) Fostering a dialectic relation between theory and practice. In J. Anghileri (ed.), *Principles and Practices in Arithmetic Teaching – Innovative Approaches for the Primary Classroom* (pp. 147–161). Buckingham: Open University Press.

Gravemeijer, K.P.E. (2004) Local instruction theories as means of support for teachers in reform mathematics education. *Mathematical Thinking and Learning* 6(2): 105–128.

Gravemeijer, K.P.E. and Stephan, M. (2002) Emergent models as an instructional design heuristic. In K.P.E. Gravemeijer, R. Lehrer, B. van Oers and L. Verschaffel (eds), *Symbolizing, Modeling, and Tool Use in Mathematics Education* (pp. 145–169). Dordrecht, The Netherlands: Kluwer.

Gravemeijer, K.P.E., Cobb, P., Bowers, J.S. and Whitenack, J. W. (2000) Symbolizing, modeling and instructional design. In P. Cobb, E. Yackel and K.J. McClain (eds), *Symbolizing and Communicating in Mathematics Classrooms: Perspectives on Discourse, Tools, and Instructional Design* (pp. 225–273). Hillsdale, NJ: Lawrence Erlbaum Associates, Inc.

Gray, E. (1991) An analysis of diverging approaches to simple arithmetic: Preference and its consequences. *Educational Studies in Mathematics* 22: 551–574.

Gray, E. and Tall, D. (1994) Duality, ambiguity, and flexibility: A 'proceptual' view of simple arithmetic. *Journal for Research in Mathematics Education* 25(2): 116–140.

Greeno, J.G. (1991) Number sense as situated knowing in a conceptual domain. *Journal for Research in Mathematics Education* 22: 170–218.

Hackenberg, A. (2007) Units coordination and the construction of improper fractions: A revision of the splitting hypothesis. *Journal of Mathematical Behavior* 26(1): 27–47.

Hackenberg, A. and Tillema, E.S. (2009) Students' whole number multiplicative concepts: A critical constructive resource for fraction composition schemes. *Journal of Mathematical Behavior*, 28: 1–18.

Hart, K. (1989a) Fractions: Equivalence and addition. In D.C. Johnson (ed.), *Children's Mathematical Frameworks 8–13: A Study of Classroom Teaching* (pp. 46–75). Windsor, Berks: Nfer-Nelson.

Hart, K. (1989b) There is little connection. In P. Ernest (ed.), *Mathematics Teaching: The State of the Art.* Lewes: The Falmer Press.

Heege, H. ter (1985) The acquisition of basic multiplication skills. *Educational Studies in Mathematics* 16: 375–388.

Heirdsfield, A. (2001) Integration, compensation and memory in mental addition and subtraction. In M. Van den Heuvel-Panhuizen (ed.), *Proceedings of the 25th Conference of the International Group for the Psychology of Mathematics Education* (Vol. 3, pp. 129–136). Utrecht, Netherlands: PME.

Hewitt, D. and Brown, E. (1998) On teaching early number through language. In A. Olivier and K. Newstead (eds), *Proceedings of the 22nd Conference of the International Group for the Psychology of Mathematics Education* (Vol. 3, pp. 41–48). Stellenbosh, South Africa: PME.

Isoda, M., Stephens, M., Ohara, Y. and Miyakawa, T. (eds) (2007) *Japanese Lesson Study in Mathematics: Its Impact, Diversity and Potential for Educational Improvement.* Singapore: World Scientific.

Jacobs, V.R., Ambrose, R., Clement, L. and Brown, D. (2006) Using teacher-produced videotapes of student interviews as discussion catalysts. *Teaching Children Mathematics* 12(6): 276–281.

Kamii, C. and Dominick, A. (1998) The harmful effects of algorithms in grades 1–4. In L.J. Marrow (ed.), *The Teaching and Learning of Algorithms in School Mathematics: 1998 Yearbook* (pp. 130–140). Reston, VA: National Council of Teachers of Mathematics.

Kaput, J. (2008) What is algebra? What is algebraic reasoning? In J. Kaput, D. Carraher and M. Blanton (eds), *Algebra in the Early Grades* (pp. 5–17). New York: Lawrence Erlbaum/ NCTM.

Kerslake, D. (1986) *Fractions: Children's Strategies and Errors: A Report of the Strategies and Errors in Secondary Mathematics Project.* London: NFER-Nelson.

Kieren, T.E. (1976) On the mathematical, cognitive and instructional foundations of rational numbers. In R.A. Lesh (ed.), *Number and Measurement: Papers from a Research Workshop* (pp. 101–144). Columbus, OH: ERIC/SMEAC.

Klein, A.S., Beishuizen, M. and Treffers, A. (1998) The empty number line in Dutch second grades: Realistic versus gradual program design. *Journal for Research in Mathematics Education* 29(4): 443–464.

Kouba, V.L. (1989) Children's solution strategies for equivalent set multiplication and division word problems. *Journal for Research in Mathematics Education* 20: 147–158.

Lambdin, D.V. (2003) Benefits of teaching through problem-solving. In F.K. Lester (ed.), *Teaching Mathematics through Problem-solving: Prekindergarten–Grade 6*. Reston, VA: NCTM.

Lamon, S.J. (1999) *Teaching Fractions and Ratios for Understanding*. Mahwah, N.J: Lawrence Erlbaum Associates.

Lamon, S.J. (2001) Presenting and representing from fractions to rational numbers. In A.A. Cuoco (ed.), *The Roles of Representation in School Mathematics* (pp. 146–165). Reston, VA: NCTM.

Lord, B. (1994) Teachers' professional development: Critical colleagueship and the role of professional communities. In N. Cobb (ed.), *The Future of Education: Perspectives on National Standards in Education* (pp. 175–204). New York: College Entrance Examination Board.

MacGregor, M. and Stacey, K. (1999) A flying start to algebra. *Teaching Children Mathematics* 6: 78–85.

Mack, N.K. (1990) Learning fractions with understanding: Building on informal knowledge. *Journal for Research in Mathematics Education* 21: 16–32.

Mack, N.K. (1993) Learning rational numbers with understanding: The case of informal knowledge. In T.P. Carpenter, E. Fennema and T.A. Romberg (eds), *Rational Numbers: An Integration of Research* (pp. 422–441). Hillsdale, NJ: Lawrence Erlbaum Associates.

Mack, N.K. (1995) Confounding whole-number and fraction concepts when building on informal knowledge. *Journal for Research in Mathematics Education* 26: 422–441.

Mack, N.K. (2001) Building on informal knowledge through instruction in a complex content domain: Partitioning, units, and understanding multiplication of fractions. *Journal for Research in Mathematics Education* 32(3): 267–295.

Mason, J. (1998) Enabling teachers to be real teachers: Necessary levels of awareness and structure of attention. *Journal of Mathematics Teacher Education* 1(3): 243–267.

Mason, J. (2002) *Researching Your Own Practice: The Discipline of Noticing*. London: RoutledgeFalmer.

Mason, J. (2008) Making use of children's powers to produce algebraic thinking. In J. Kaput, D. Carraher and M. Blanton (eds), *Algebra in the Early Grades* (pp. 57–94). New York: Lawrence Erlbaum/NCTM.

Mason, J. and Johnston-Wilder, S. (2006) *Designing and Using Mathematical Tasks*. St Albans: Tarquin Publications.

Mason, J., Drury, H. and Bills, L. (2007) Studies in the Zone of Proximal Awareness. In J. Watson and K. Beswick (eds), *Mathematics: Essential Research, Essential Practice (Proceedings of the 30th Annual Conference of the Mathematics Education Research Group of Australasia)* (Vol. 1, pp. 42–58). Adelaide: MERGA.

McIntosh, A.J., Reys, B.J. and Reys, R.E. (1992) A proposed framework for examining basic number sense. *For the Learning of Mathematics* 12: 2–8.

Menne, J. (2001) Jumping ahead: An innovative teaching program. In J. Anghileri (ed.), *Principles and Practices in Arithmetic Teaching–Innovative Approaches for the Primary Classroom* (pp. 95–106). Buckingham: Open University Press.

Merttens, R. (1999) Family numeracy. In I. Thompson (ed.), *Issues in Teaching Numeracy in Primary Schools* (pp. 78–90). Buckingham: Open University Press.

Montessori, M. (1912/1964) *The Montessori Method*. New York: Schocken Books.

Moss, J., Beatty, R., Barkin, S. and Shillolo, G. (2008) 'What is your theory? What is your rule?' Fourth graders build an understanding of functions through patterns and generalizing problems. In *Algebra and Algebraic Thinking in School Mathematics: 70th Yearbook of the National Council of Teachers of Mathematics* (pp. 155–168). Reston, VA: NCTM.

Mulligan, J.T. (1998) A research-based framework for assessing early multiplication and division. In C. Kanes, M. Goos and E. Warren (eds), *Proceedings of the 21st Annual Conference of the Mathematics Education Research Group of Australasia* (Vol. 2, pp. 404–411). Brisbane: Griffith University.

Mulligan, J. and Mitchelmore, M. (1997) Young children's intuitive models of multiplication and division. *Journal for Research in Mathematics Education* 28(3): 309–330.

Mulligan, J. and Mitchelmore, M. (2009) Awareness of pattern and structure in early mathematical development. *Mathematics Education Research Journal* 21(2): 33–49.

Munn, P. (1997) Writing and number. In I. Thompson (ed.), *Teaching and Learning Early Number*. Buckingham: Open University Press.

Munn, P. (2006) The teacher as learner. In R.J. Wright, G. Stanger, A.K. Stafford and J. Martland, *Teaching Number in the Classroom with 4–8 Year-olds* (pp. 177–192). London: Paul Chapman Publishing.

Ni, Y. and Zhou, Y.-D. (2005) Teaching and learning fraction and rational numbers: The origins and implications of whole number bias. *Educational Psychologist* 40(1): 27–52.

Norton, A. (2008) Josh's operational conjectures: Abductions of a splitting operation and the construction of new fractional schemes. *Journal for Research in Mathematics Education* 39(4): 401–430.

Norton, A. and Wilkins, J.L.M. (2009) A quantitative analysis of children's splitting operations and fraction schemes. *Journal of Mathematical Behavior* 28: 150–161.

Olive, J. (1999) From fractions to rational numbers of arithmetic: A reorganization hypothesis. *Mathematical Thinking and Learning* 1(4): 279–314.

Olive, J. (2001) Children's number sequences: An explanation of Steffe's constructs and an extrapolation to rational numbers of arithmetic. *The Mathematics Educator* 11(1): 4–9.

Olive, J. and Vomvoridi, E. (2006) Making sense of instruction on fractions when a student lacks necessary fractional schemes: The case of Tim. *Journal of Mathematical Behavior* 25: 18–45.

Pepper, K. and Hunting, R. (1998) Preschoolers' counting and sharing. *Journal for Research in Mathematics Education* 29: 164–183.

Pirie, S.E.B. and Kieren, T.E. (1994) Growth in mathematical understanding: How can we characterise it and how can we represent it? *Educational Studies in Mathematics* 26: 165–190.

Plunkett, S. (1979) Decomposition and all that rot. *Mathematics in Schools* 8(3): 2–5.

Pothier, Y. and Sawada, D. (1983) Partitioning: The emergence of rational number ideas in young children. *Journal for Research in Mathematics Education* 14(5): 307–317.

Resnick, L.B. (1983) A developmental theory of number understanding. In H.P. Ginsburg (ed.), *The Development of Mathematical Thinking* (pp. 109–151). New York: Academic Press.

Rivkin, S.G., Hanushek, E.A. and Kain, J.F. (2005) Teachers, schools, and academic achievement. *Econometrica* 73(2): 417–458.

Rousham, L. (2003) The empty number line: A model in search of a learning trajectory? In I. Thompson (ed.), *Enhancing Primary Mathematics Teaching* (pp. 29–39). Maidenhead: Open University Press.

Ruthven, K. (1998) The use of mental, written, and calculator strategies of numerical computation by upper primary pupils within a 'calculator aware' number curriculum. *British Educational Research Journal* 24(1): 21–42.

Schifter, D., Russell, S. and Bastable, V. (2009) Early algebra to reach the range of learners. *Teaching Children Mathematics* 16: 230–237.

Selter, C. (2001) Addition and subtraction of three-digit numbers: German elementary children's success, methods and strategies. *Educational Studies in Mathematics* 47(2): 145–173.

Sfard, A. (2000) Symbolizing mathematical reality into being – or how mathematical discourse and mathematical objects create each other. In P. Cobb, E. Yackel and K.J. McClain (eds), *Symbolizing and Communicating in Mathematics Classrooms: Perspectives on Discourse, Tools, and Instructional Design* (pp. 37–98). Hillsdale, NJ: Lawrence Erlbaum Associates, Inc.

Sherin, B. and Fuson, K.C. (2005) Multiplication strategies and the appropriation of computational resources. *Journal for Research in Mathematics Education* 36: 347–395.

Shulman, L.S. (1986) Those who understand: Knowledge growth in teaching. *Educational Researcher* 15(2): 4–14.

Siemon, D., Izard, J., Breed, M. and Virgona, J. (2006) The derivation of a learning assessment framework for multiplicative thinking. In J. Novotná, H. Moraová, M. Krátká and N. Stehlíková (eds), *Proceedings of the 30th Conference of the International Group for the Psychology of Mathematics Education* (Vol. 5, pp. 113–120). Prague: PME.

Skwarchuk, S. and Anglin, J.M. (2002) Children's acquisition of the English cardinal number words: A special case of vocabulary development. *Journal of Educational Psychology* 94(1): 107–125.

Steffe, L.P. (1988) Children's construction of number sequences and multiplying schemes. In J. Hiebert and M. Behr (eds), *Number Concepts and Operations in the Middle Grades* (pp. 119–141). Hillsdale, NJ: Erlbaum.

Steffe, L.P. (1992) Schemes of action and operation involving composite units. *Learning and Individual Differences* 4: 259–309.

Steffe, L.P. (1994) Children's multiplying schemes. In G. Harel and J. Confrey (eds), *The Development of Multiplicative Reasoning in the Learning of Mathematics* (pp. 3–39). Albany, NY: State University of New York Press.

Steffe, L.P. (2002) A new hypothesis concerning children's fractional knowledge. *Journal of Mathematical Behavior* 20: 267–307.

Steffe, L.P. (2003) Fractional commensurate, composition, and adding schemes: Learning trajectories of Jason and Laura: Grade 5. *Mathematical Behavior* 22(3): 237–295.

Steffe, L.P. (2004) On the construction of learning trajectories of children: The case of commensurate fractions. *Mathematical Thinking and Learning* 6(2): 129–162.

Steffe, L.P. and Cobb, P. (1988) *Construction of Arithmetic Meanings and Strategies*. New York: Springer-Verlag.

Steffe, L.P. and Olive, J. (2010) *Children's Fractional Knowledge*. New York: Springer.

Stephan, M.L. and Whitenack, J. (2003) Establishing classroom social and sociomathematical norms for problem-solving. In F.K. Lester (ed.), *Teaching Mathematics through Problem-solving: Prekindergarten–Grade 6*. Reston, VA: NCTM.

Stephan, M. L., Bowers, J.S., Cobb, P. and Gravemeijer, K.P.E. (eds) (2003) *Supporting Students' Development of Measurement Conceptions: Analyzing Students' Learning in Social Context*. Reston, VA: NCTM.

Streefland, L. (1991) *Fractions in Realistic Mathematics Education: A Paradigm of Developmental Research*. Dordrecht: Kluwer Academic.

Streefland, L. (1993) Fractions: A realistic approach. In T.P. Carpenter, E. Fennema and T.A. Romberg (eds), *Rational Numbers: An Integration of Research* (pp. 289–326). Hillsdale, NJ: Lawrence Erlbaum Associates.

Sullivan, P., Clarke, D.M., Cheeseman, J. and Mulligan, J. (2001) Moving beyond physical models in learning multiplicative reasoning. In M. Van den Heuvel-Panhuizen (ed.), *Proceedings of the 25th Annual Conference of the International Group for the Psychology of Mathematics Education* (Vol. 4, pp. 233–240). Utrecht: PME.

Tabor, P. (2008) An investigation of instruction in two-digit addition and subtraction using a classroom teaching experiment methodology, design research, and multilevel modeling. Unpublished PhD thesis, Southern Cross University, Lismore.

Thomas, J., Tabor, P. and Wright, R.J. (2010) First-graders' number knowledge. *Teaching Children Mathematics* 17(5): 298–308.

Thompson, I. (1997) Mental and written algorithms: Can the gap be bridged? In I. Thompson (ed.), *Teaching and Learning Early Number*. Buckingham: Open University Press.

Thompson, I. (1999) Written methods of calculation. In I. Thompson (ed.), *Issues in Teaching Numeracy in Primary Schools* (pp. 167–183). Buckingham: Open University Press.

Thompson, I. (2003) Place value: The English disease? In I. Thompson (ed.), *Enhancing Primary Mathematics Teaching* (pp. 181–190). Maidenhead: Open University Press.

Thompson, I. and Smith, F. (1999) *Mental Calculation Strategies for the Addition and Subtraction of 2-digit Numbers (Report for the Nuffield Foundation)*. Newcastle upon Tyne: University of Newcastle upon Tyne.

Thompson, I. and Bramald, R. (2002) *An Investigation of the Relationship between Young Children's Understanding of the Concept of Place Value and their Competence at Mental Addition (Report for the Nuffield Foundation)*. Newcastle upon Tyne: University of Newcastle upon Tyne.

Threlfall, J. (2002) Flexible mental calculation. *Educational Studies in Mathematics* 50(1): 29–47.

Tierney, C. and Nemirovsky, R. (1997) A foundation for algebraic reasoning in the early grades. *Teaching Children Mathematics* 3: 336–339.

Treffers, A. (1991) Didactical background of a mathematics program for primary education. In L. Streefland (ed.), *Realistic Mathematics Education in Primary School* (pp. 21–56). Utrecht: Freudenthal Institute.

Treffers, A. (2001) Grade 1 (and 2) – Calculation up to 20. In M. van den Heuvel-Panhuizen (ed.), *Children Learn Mathematics* (pp. 43–60). Utrecht: Freudenthal Institute, Utrecht University/SLO.

Treffers, A. and Beishuizen, M. (1999) Realistic mathematics education in the Netherlands. In I. Thompson (ed.), *Issues in Teaching Numeracy in Primary Schools* (pp. 27–38). Buckingham: Open University Press.

Treffers, A. and Buys, K. (2001) Grade 2 and 3 – Calculation up to 100. In M. van den Heuvel-Panhuizen (ed.), *Children Learn Mathematics* (pp. 61–88). Utrecht: Freudenthal Institute, Utrecht University/SLO.

Treffers, A., Nooteboom, A. and de Goeij, E. (2001) Column calculation and algorithms. In M. van den Heuvel-Panhuizen (ed.), *Children Learn Mathematics* (pp. 147–171). Utrecht: Freudenthal Institute, Utrecht University/SLO.

Tzur, R. (1999) An integrated study of children's construction of improper fractions and the teacher's role in promoting that learning. *Journal for Research in Mathematics Education* 30(4): 390–416.

Tzur, R. (2004) Teacher and students' joint production of a reversible fraction conception. *Journal of Mathematical Behavior* 23(1): 93–114.

van den Heuvel-Panhuizen, M. (ed.) (2001) *Children Learn Mathematics: A Learning-Teaching Trajectory with Intermediate Attainment Targets for Calculation with Whole Numbers in Primary School*. Utrecht: Freudenthal Institute, Utrecht University/SLO.

Warren, L. and Cooper, T. (2008) Patterns that support early algebraic thinking in the elementary school. In *Algebra and Algebraic Thinking in School Mathematics: 70th Yearbook of the National Council of Teachers of Mathematics* (pp. 113–126). Reston, VA: NCTM.

Watanabe, T. (1995) Coordination of units and understanding of simple fractions: Case studies. *Mathematics Education Research Journal* 7(2): 160–175.

Watson, A. and Sullivan, P. (2008) Teachers learning about tasks and lessons. In D. Tirosh and T. Wood (eds), *Tools and Processes in Mathematics Teacher Education*. Rotterdam: Sense Publishers.

Wigley, A. (1997) Approaching number through language. In I. Thompson (ed.), *Teaching and Learning Early Number* (pp. 113–122). Buckingham, UK: Open University Press.

Wright, R.J. (1992) Number topics in early childhood mathematics curricula: Historical background, dilemmas, and possible solutions. *Australian Journal of Education* 36(2): 125–142.

Wright, R.J. (1994) A study of the numerical development of 5-year-olds and 6-year-olds. *Educational Studies in Mathematics* 26: 25–44.

Wright, R.J. (1998) Children's beginning knowledge of numerals and its relationship to their knowledge of number words: An exploratory, observational study. In A. Olivier and K. Newstead (eds), *Proceedings of the 22nd Annual Conference of the International Group for the Psychology of Mathematics Education* (Vol. 4, pp. 201–208). Stellenbosh, South Africa: PME.

Wright, R.J. (2001) The arithmetical strategies of four 3rd-graders. In J. Bobis, B. Perry and M. Mitchelmore (eds), *Numeracy and Beyond* (*Proceedings of the 25th Annual Conference of the Mathematics Education Research Group of Australasia, Sydney*) (Vol. 2, pp. 547–554). Sydney: MERGA.

Wright, R.J. (2002) Assessing young children's arithmetical strategies and knowledge: Providing learning opportunities for teachers. *Australian Journal of Early Childhood* 27(3): 31(36).

Wright, R.J., Martland, J. and Stafford, A.K. (2006a) *Early Numeracy: Assessment for Teaching and Intervention* (2nd edn). London: Sage.

Wright, R.J., Martland, J., Stafford, A.K. and Stanger, G. (2006b) *Teaching Number: Advancing Children's Skills and Strategies* (2nd edn). London: Sage.

Wright, R.J., Stanger, G., Stafford, A.K. and Martland, J. (2006c) *Teaching Number in the Classroom with 4–8 Year-olds*. London: Sage.

Wright, R.J., Ellemor-Collins, D. and Lewis, G. (2007) Developing pedagogical tools for intervention: Approach, methodology, and an experimental framework. In J. Watson and K. Beswick (eds), *Proceedings of the 30th Annual Conference of the Mathematics Education Research Group of Australasia, Hobart* (Vol. 2, pp. 843–852). Hobart: MERGA.

Yackel, E. (1997) A foundation for algebraic reasoning in the early grades. *Teaching Children Mathematics* 3: 276–280.

Yackel, E. (2001) Perspectives on arithmetic from classroom-based research in the United States of America. In J. Anghileri (ed.), *Principles and Practices in Arithmetic Teaching – Innovative Approaches for the Primary Classroom* (pp. 15–31). Buckingham: Open University Press.

Yackel, E. (2003) Listening to children: Informing us and guiding our instruction. In F.K. Lester (ed.), *Teaching Mathematics through Problem-solving: Prekindergarten–Grade 6*. Reston, VA: NCTM.

Yoshida, H. and Kuriyama, K. (1995) Linking meaning of symbols of fractions to problem situations. *Japanese Psychological Research* 37: 229–239.

Yoshida, K. (2004) Understanding how the concept of fractions develops: A Vygotskian perspective. Paper presented at the 28th Conference of the International Group for the Psychology of Mathematics Education, Bergen, Norway.

Yoshida, M. (2008) Exploring ideas for a mathematics teacher educator's contribution to lesson study: Towards improving teachers' mathematical content and pedagogical knowledge. In D. Tirosh and T. Wood (eds), *Tools and Processes in Mathematics Teacher Education*. Rotterdam: Sense Publishers.

Young-Loveridge, J. (2002) Early childhood numeracy: Building an understanding of part–whole relationships. *Australian Journal of Early Childhood*, 27(4): 36–42.

Index

Note: Whole numbers are represented as numerals at the beginning of the index rather than as spelt out number words filing within the alphabetic sequence (e.g. '10' rather than 'ten'). Fractions are spelt out and filed within the alphabetic sequence (e.g. 'fifths'). The letter 'b' following a page number refers to a box; the letter 'f' refers to a figure; the letter 'p' refers to a photo; the letter 't' refers to a table.